Praise for Gary M.

"A masterful work nearly as great as the mighty Dipper himself."
—*The Nashville Tennessean*

"More than any athlete since Babe Ruth, Wilt Chamberlain transcended his sport, and author Gary Pomerantz shows that beautifully in *Wilt, 1962*, the story of Chamberlain's 100-point game."
—*San Francisco Chronicle*

"Pomerantz unfolds a meticulous and engaging narrative that illustrates how a combination of obsequious teammates, forgiving rims, and more than a little showmanship (picked up playing a year for the Globetrotters) converged to make a historic evening—and a slam dunk of a read."
—*Entertainment Weekly*

"Gary Pomerantz's decision to get at the man and his times through the prism of his 100-point night against the New York Knicks on March 2, 1962, was a wise one. . . . The joy of *Wilt, 1962* is in the background details. . . . By the conclusion of the book, the reader feels as if he had been among the 4,000 or so lucky souls in the arena on a seemingly unforgettable night that had somehow been forgotten."
—*Sports Illustrated*

"Gary Pomerantz's *Wilt, 1962* is beautifully written, well reported, and compelling. But what's so special about this book, what causes it to linger, is the atmosphere that Pomerantz has captured through his words, so bittersweet and haunting. You love Wilt Chamberlain. You feel the aura of his isolation as he towered above the rest of us in life, and you wish more than ever he was still around because of his very individuality."
—Buzz Bissinger, author of *Friday Night Lights*

"A book that turns the box score into a tapestry of sweaty faces, squeaking sneakers, and roaring emotions. . . . From one man, one game, and 100 points, Pomerantz expands his narrative in every direction. His grasp of even the most arcane detail helps to create a vibrant sociological and historical context for Chamberlain. . . . The narrative follows, loosely, the four-quarter structure of the game, and even though we know the outcome, Pomerantz deliciously describes the drama leading up to that 100th point."

—*New York Times Book Review*

"Genius is in the details, and Gary Pomerantz's *Wilt, 1962* proves that."

—John Feinstein, author of *A Season on the Brink* and *A Good Walk Spoiled*

"Deeply researched, beautifully written . . . Pomerantz uses Chamberlain's historic game against the New York Knicks to illuminate forgotten worlds and obscure figures while detailing a sport—and a nation—on the cusp of dramatic change. *Wilt, 1962* hinges on hindsight, the magic power that enables writers to see how things are and also what they are becoming. . . . A marvelous book."

—*The Raleigh News & Observer*

"Gary Pomerantz has distilled Chamberlain's essence as well as anyone has in print. The book is ostensibly about the night Wilt scored 100 points in a game, which Pomerantz documents with a terrific reporting job full of details and anecdotes. But his book, at heart, is a love poem to Chamberlain's massive impact on his sport's culture."

—*San Jose Mercury News*

"An enthralling chronicle. Wilt Chamberlain scored 100 on a strange and wonderful night in Hershey. *Wilt, 1962* explores that night in sumptuous detail. . . . There aren't many sports books as flat-out fascinating as this one."

—*The Charlotte Observer*

"*Wilt, 1962* not only retells the story of that game, but captures the complexity of Wilt Chamberlain with a riveting narrative and novelistic flair. The result is a uniquely Philadelphia work, told with an insight and poignancy nearly unparalleled in the nonfiction sports book genre."

—*Philadelphia Weekly*

"Thanks to Mr. Pomerantz's keen imagination and the 250-plus interviews he conducted, there's not a page of the book that doesn't crackle with perfectly chosen details."

—*New York Observer*

"Meticulously researched and superbly crafted, *Wilt, 1962* revisits and vividly re-creates a seminal but overlooked moment in American sports history. On that transformative evening in Hershey, Pennsylvania, Wilt Chamberlain scored 100 points and staked a black man's claim to the city game. In Gary Pomerantz's deft possession-by-possession retelling, Chamberlain soars again. The gangly, uncompromising seven-footer who always seemed too big for the uniform he inhabited thunders back to life."

—Jane Leavy, author of *Sandy Koufax: A Lefty's Legacy*

"Chamberlain was a uniquely dominating force, as Pomerantz makes eloquently clear. . . . *Wilt, 1962* draws one's attention to an uneasy but unsurprising fact: Athletes who strive for the impossible are driven by demons that ordinary folks cannot comprehend. Such feats exact a terrible price in solitude and compulsions. Pomerantz offers exquisitely painful details of his subject's isolation and the toll it took over the course of his career."

—*The Washington Post*

"Pomerantz paints a compelling portrait of Chamberlain, a stunningly gifted athlete with larger-than-life appetites and expectations who, in some sense, seemed unknowable. Pomerantz gives us as much of him as we may ever know."

—*The Philadelphia Inquirer*

"In this age of instant everything, few people have any idea who Wilt Chamberlain really was, and what he meant to sports. Gary Pomerantz shows us. In *Wilt, 1962* he puts us courtside for one of the greatest unexamined moments in sports history, the night Wilt scored 100 points. In a sweet return to his sportswriting roots, Pomerantz gives us Wilt in his realm, his rise to prominence and dominance, set against the backdrop of the NBA's coming of age. It's all irresistible."

—Michael Wilbon, cohost of ESPN's *Pardon the Interruption*

"Meticulous research (250 interviews) is welded to absorbing prose that merges basketball, biography, and history to capture a tipping point in the National Basketball Association's evolution. . . . While the astonishing achievement has always seemed a footnote to NBA history, Pomerantz has given it the defining chronicle it deserves."

—*Rocky Mountain News*

"*Wilt, 1962* scores 100 and more. . . . A gloriously crafted, remarkably researched portrait of Wilt, his times, and his country, the book offers us the detail of the man and that most momentous of games, the night he scored 100 points. Pomerantz is obsessed with detail and blessed with a lyrical touch, a blend that carries us to the moment, even when the moment was 43 years ago. . . . And yet the night is only a vehicle to expand upon Chamberlain, upon the growth of pro basketball, about the racial climate in America, about characters and issues some have forgotten and others never knew. Like Chamberlain himself, the book is special."

—*The Oakland Tribune*

"A sports book worth talking about, and a moving portrait of a great athlete and his era."

—*Kirkus Reviews* (starred review)

"Pomerantz takes us back to the Hershey Arena, to that one magical night, removing the layer of mystique that always had been wrapped around a game played in a chocolate-covered minor-league town, in a half-filled arena with no videotape ever made. . . . In this meticulously researched book . . . Pomerantz does a masterful job, weaving the narrative of the Philadelphia Warriors–New York Knicks game into the larger context of who Wilt was—and how he fit into both the pro basketball world and the larger American society."

—*The Buffalo News*

WILT, 1962

The Night of 100 Points and the Dawn of a New Era

GARY M. POMERANTZ

THREE RIVERS PRESS
NEW YORK

Copyright © 2005 by Gary M. Pomerantz

Images of trading cards used on endpapers courtesy
of Fleer Trading Cards.

Originally published in hardcover in the United States
by Crown Publishers, an imprint of the Crown Publishing Group,
a division of Random House, Inc., in 2005.

Library of Congress Cataloging-in-Publication Data
Pomerantz, Gary M.
Wilt, 1962 : the night of 100 points and the dawn of a
new era / Gary M. Pomerantz.
Includes bibliographical references.
1. Basketball—United States—History. 2. Chamberlain,
Wilt, 1936–1999. I. Title.
GV885.7.P66   2005
796.323'0973—dc22   2004025391

ISBN-13: 978-1-4000-5161-8
ISBN-10: 1-4000-5161-4

Printed in the United States of America

Design by Leonard Henderson

1 3 5 7 9 10 8 6 4 2

First Paperback Edition

For Dad,
the Dipper in my night sky,
guiding me still

CONTENTS

PART TWO

THE FOURTH QUARTER

PART THREE

AFTERMATH

The WIGWAM

35 ¢

PHILADELPHIA
WARRIORS

WILT CHAMBERLAIN

PHILADELPHIA WARRIORS
vs
NEW YORK KNICKS

PHILA. EAGLES
vs
BALTIMORE COLTS

Friday, March 2, 1962

HERSHEY ARENA
HERSHEY, PA.

The Rosters

PHILADELPHIA WARRIORS

Paul Arizin *(33 years old, 6-4, 200, Villanova)*
South Philly's own "Pitchin' Paul" has scored more than 16,000 points in the pro game, passing Cousy this season and ranking behind only Schayes among the NBA's all-time top scorers.

Tom Meschery *(23 years old, 6-6, 215, St. Mary's, CA)*
The Manchurian-born rookie, who speaks Russian and French with fluency, has quickly emerged as a sharp shooter and bullish rebounder.

Wilt Chamberlain *(25 years old, 7-1, 260, Kansas)*
The Big Dipper has rewritten the record books with fifty points and twenty-five rebounds per night. The former Globetrotter ranks as the greatest rebounder in league annals and his specialty is dunking.

Guy Rodgers *(26 years old, 6-0, 185, Temple)*
The flashy dynamo in his fourth pro season dribbles and passes like a magician and as a feeder ranks behind only Oscar Robertson.

Al Attles *(25 years old, 6-1, 180, North Carolina A & T)*
Emerging from obscurity, he has used his speed and rugged defense to earn the nickname of the Destroyer.

Tom Gola *(29 years old, 6-6, 205, LaSalle)*
After three years as an All-American at nearby LaSalle College, he is playing his sixth NBA season as the versatile Warriors captain and all-around Mr. Consistency.

York Larese *(23 years old, 6-4, 185, North Carolina)*
A record-breaking shooter of free throws at the University of North Carolina, he played for Coach Frank McGuire with the Tar Heels.

Joe Ruklick *(23 years old, 6-9, 220, Northwestern)*
A top scorer in the Big Ten, he has served as Chamberlain's understudy for three seasons, developing a nice hook shot and popularity with Philly fans, who have formed a fan club for him.

Ed Conlin *(29 years old, 6-6, 200, Fordham)*
The seven-year veteran had earlier stints with Syracuse and Detroit. He can play either front or back court and has an accurate outside set shot.

Ted Luckenbill *(22 years old, 6-6, 205, Houston)*
The hardworking rookie lefty, "Lucky" was the second best scorer in the history of the University of Houston.

Frank Radovich *(23 years old, 6-8, 235, Indiana)*
The burly frontline player, tough under the hoop, was obtained in the trade with St. Louis for Joe Graboski.

NEW YORK KNICKS

Willie Naulls *(27 years old, 6-6, 225, UCLA)*
The smooth all-star scorer and team captain, who as a collegian led UCLA to the Pacific Coast Conference crown, spurred the Knicks last season with a 23.4 scoring average and has been even better this season.

Johnny Green *(28 years old, 6-5, 200, Michigan State)*
Jumpin' Johnny often outleaps taller foes and in his best pro game produced twenty-seven points and twenty-five rebounds against Wilt Chamberlain.

Darrall Imhoff *(23 years old, 6-10, 220, California)*
A good defensive man and rebounder in his sophomore NBA season, he won a collegiate title with the University of California and a gold medal at the 1960 Olympics in Rome.

Richie Guerin *(29 years old, 6-4, 210, Iona)*
The Leatherneck, a fan favorite at Madison Square Garden, is enjoying his finest all-star season, scoring twenty-nine markers per game. He once scored a Knicks' team-record fifty-seven points in a game.

Al Butler *(23 years old, 6-2, 175, Niagara)*
The multitalented guard joined the Knicks in December on purchase from Boston and hopes to reproduce the scoring magic of his sensational career at Niagara University.

Cleveland Buckner *(23 years old, 6-8, 210, Jackson State)*
A rookie named to the All-NAIA team for two seasons while playing in Mississippi, he can play the pivot and the outside with his deft jump-shooting touch and strong ball-handling skills.

Phil Jordon *(28 years old, 6-10, 205, Whitworth)*
Traded back to New York from Cincinnati in the middle of last season, he matched a career high with thirty-three points versus Philly earlier this season. He first developed his shots playing AAU ball with the Buchan Bakers of Seattle.

Donnie Butcher *(26 years old, 6-3, 200, Pikeville)*
The fifteenth of sixteen children, with five older brothers once serving in World War II, the onetime shooting star of the All-Kentucky Athletic Conference plays a rugged game.

Sam Stith *(24 years old, 6-2, 185, St. Bonaventure)*
He rejoins Coach Eddie Donovan, his mentor in college. He and younger brother Tom Stith combined to average fifty-one markers a game for the Bonnies one season.

Whitey Martin *(22 years old, 6-2, 185, St. Bonaventure)*
A playmaker and defensive whiz for Donovan with the Bonnies, he has quick hands and an accurate two-hand set shot.

Dave Budd *(23 years old, 6-6, 210, Wake Forest)*
The former Atlantic Coast Conference standout showed promise as a rookie last year, his .432 shooting percentage rating second best on the Knicks.

THE STATS

Wilt Chamberlain's 100-Point Game

March 2, 1962, in Hershey, Pennsylvania

Philadelphia Warriors 169, New York Knicks 147

NEW YORK	26	42	38	41	147	
PHILADELPHIA	42	37	46	44	169	

Attendance: 4,124 / Referees: Willie Smith, Pete D'Ambrosio

NEW YORK	Minutes	FG (M-A)	FT (M-A)	R	A	F	Points
Willie Naulls	43	9-22	13-15	7	2	5	31
Johnny Green	21	3-7	0-0	7	1	5	6
Darrall Imhoff	20	3-7	1-1	6	0	6	7
Richie Guerin	46	13-29	13-17	8	6	5	39
Al Butler	32	4-13	0-0	7	3	1	8
Cleveland Buckner	33	16-26	1-1	8	0	4	33
Dave Budd	27	6-8	1-1	10	1	1	13
Donnie Butcher	18	3-6	4-6	3	4	5	10
Team Totals	240	57-118	33-41	56	17	32	**147**

PHILADELPHIA	Minutes	FG (M-A)	FT (M-A)	R	A	F	Points
Paul Arizin	31	7-18	2-2	5	4	0	16
Tom Meschery	40	7-12	2-2	7	3	4	16
Wilt Chamberlain	48	36-63	28-32	25	2	2	100
Guy Rodgers	48	1-4	9-12	7	20	5	11
Al Attles	34	8-8	1-1	5	6	4	17
Ed Conlin	14	0-4	0-0	4	1	1	0
Joe Ruklick	8	0-1	0-2	2	1	2	0
Ted Luckenbill	3	0-0	0-0	1	0	2	0
York Larese	14	4-5	1-1	1	2	5	9
Team Totals	240	63-115	43-52	57	39	25	**169**

WILT CHAMBERLAIN	Minutes	FG (M-A)	FT (M-A)	R	A	F	Points
First Quarter	12	7-14	9-9	10	0	0	23
Second Quarter	12	7-12	4-5	4	1	1	18
Third Quarter	12	10-16	8-8	6	1	0	28
Fourth Quarter	12	12-21	7-10	5	0	1	31
Totals	48	36-63	28-32	25	2	2	**100**

PREFACE

A T THE MOMENT OF HIS GREAT GLORY, a minute twenty-five to play, the kids in Hershey screaming, "Give it to Wilt! Give it to Wilt!" we see Wilt Chamberlain running the floor, a force of nature gathering power with each stride, and recognize him for what he is: unprecedented.

He came with a body and an ego perfectly sculpted for dominating his game. The ego was essential: For a player to score one hundred points in an NBA game, he must not only want to do it, he must, on a deeper level, need to do it—to take an opponent, an entire sport, and bend it to his will—to show that it could be done and only by him. In *one hundred* there was hubris but also a symbolic magic. In our culture the number connotes a century, a ripe old age, a perfect score on a test. Scoring one hundred points meant infinitely more than scoring, say, ninety-seven. One hundred was a monument.

Writers and players and coaches prophesied such a night for the young Wilt Chamberlain. He was a one-man revolution. He entered what was still largely a white man's game, took it above the rim, and made it his. The game's traditionalists, seeing the future, blanched. He was, at the core, an individualist, the ultimate alpha male. He loved his sport, he loved his women, and he loved himself. He was averaging fifty points per game during that 1961–62 season, and as his scoring numbers grew so did the prophecy. Pity the average NBA center of the day: Several inches smaller, not nearly as agile or strong or well conditioned, they became, against Chamberlain, desperate underdogs, some even sassing him by calling him "Globetrotter." Chamberlain luxuriated in the prophecy and admitted coyly that if he kept his cool, made his shots, then, yes, one hundred points was possible.

His body was a spectacle unto itself, like "a first sight of the New York skyline," according to one writer. Perfectly proportioned, seen from up close or afar, Chamberlain presented a physical majesty. He topped out at seven-foot-one and one-sixteenth and weighed 260 pounds, his upper body tightly coiled, not yet pumped up by the weightlifter's mass of later years. His broad back sloped downward gently to a dancer's thirty-one-inch waist. "The most perfect instrument ever made by God to play basketball," the veteran Dolph Schayes would say. So long were Chamberlain's legs, he wore kneepads high on his shins, where opposing knees were apt to strike. He pulled his socks up high, in part to hide scars from thousands of mosquito bites he suffered as a kid on visits to a farm his uncle worked in Virginia near the Rappahannock; he used rubber bands to hold those socks in place and, in a quirky habit dating to boyhood, still wore a spare rubber band on each wrist.

His father stood a touch over five-foot-eight and his mother just over five-foot-nine. He heard stories about a great-grandfather six-foot-ten or seven-foot-two but he half-wondered if the man existed. To call him Wilt the Stilt meant you were not his friend. He hated that name. It reminded him of a big crane standing in a pool of water. He preferred the Big Dipper. His family and all of west Philly called him Dippy either because of his "dip shot" dunk or because he dipped beneath doorways or because Philadelphia had its share of guys named Dippy—there was Dippy Carosi, Dippy Chamberlain, Dippy this, Dippy that. Nicknames were the rage in Philly then, with asphalt stars known as Tee, Misty, The Bird, and Hal "King" Lear. It's the same city that in the early Fifties sized up the Asian eyes of a high school basketball star, Ray Scott, and called him Chink—Chink Scott.

In spring 1962, professional sports in America, like the nation itself, stood at the river's edge, the waters beginning to rise and churn. The Fifties had seen Connie Mack, the "Tall Tactician," born during the Civil War, managing the Philadelphia A's in the Shibe Park dugout for the last time wearing his three-piece suit, necktie, detachable collar, and derby or straw skimmer. The Fifties had seen the NBA in its bumbling adolescence, the stepchild of the college game, virtually unloved and unwatched, with crowds so small (the joke went) the public address announcers introduced the players and then the fans. In those early years, it was a rough game played by military veterans and other assorted rogues rebounding with their elbows out, so rough some NBA dressing rooms kept boxes in which players deposited their false teeth before they went out to play. Players smoked cigarettes (even at halftime) and washed their own uniforms in hotel room sinks (or sometimes didn't). The game was that raw and run on a shoestring. One night, a young general manager, Marty Blake, lugged onto a train to Chicago two heavy boxes called "twenty-four-second clocks," mechanical devices used to time the length of each possession in a game. Blake served as p.a. announcer and official scorer for an exhibition doubleheader that night between the Minneapolis Lakers and Philadelphia Warriors. When someone forgot to bring basketballs, Blake scrounged around and found two for pregame warm-ups, one for the Lakers, one for the Warriors. As the game neared conclusion, Blake received bad news: The Harlem Globetrotters' plane could not land due to bad weather. This was a big problem. The Globetrotters were supposed to play the second game of the doubleheader. They were the main event. Blake called a timeout to stall. No use. He called a cab, two men grabbed the twenty-four-second clocks, and when the game ended, Blake stood by the arena's side door and announced, "Ladies and gentlemen, because of inclement weather, the Globetrotters' plane can't land. The second game has been cancelled." Blake broke through the side door to leave before the riot.

Into this carnival that passed for professional basketball, into the NBA's search for itself, strode Wilt Chamberlain. For the Warriors owner, a nickel-and-dime Barnum named Eddie Gottlieb, here, at last, was a must-see main act. In the old days in Philly, Gotty had scheduled and promoted any teams wearing spikes or sneakers—up to 500 semipro baseball games a week, the 2nd Ward Republican Club, the All-American Thespian League featuring baseball teams like the House of David and the Zulu Jungle Giants. It wasn't just that Wilt Chamberlain was a scoring champion. Gotty had had plenty of those: Joe Fulks, Neil Johnston, and Paul Arizin had each twice led the league. More than scoring, the Dipper added aesthetic value with his athletic grace and beauty. He moved with a dancer's elegance but at a higher plane. Gotty paid him $75,000 for this season, three times the amount he had paid for the entire franchise ten years earlier. He knew it would be a lovely relationship, an Old World Jew and a Philadelphia Negro, showmen both. The Dipper would score, stun, awe, win. People would talk. They'd pay to see him. They'd tell friends. Their friends would come, too. Gotty would win titles, help grow the young pro league. He would make a killing.

You had to stare at the Dipper, even if you were Red Auerbach. The Boston Celtics coach, a son of a Brooklyn dry cleaner, had seen Mikan and coached Russell, but even he, the great Auerbach, couldn't help himself the first time he saw Chamberlain, then in high school. Auerbach just stood and watched the Dipper walk. *Incredible*, he thought.

And so with a minute twenty-five to play on a winter night in a nowhere town made famous not by basketball but by chocolate, there unfolded a spectacle, a mesmerizing show of power, cigarette smoke, and a little Borscht Belt kitsch—the p.a. announcer Dave Zinkoff handing out free salamis and cigars.

Here came the Philadelphia Warriors guard York Larese, son of an immigrant tinsmith from northern Italy, leading the fast break. Larese took the ball to the middle, a teammate angling on either side of him, three Warriors moving toward the New York Knickerbockers basket, perfectly choreographed.

But from behind, covering ninety-four feet in twelve strides, Chamberlain was coming, and Larese felt the force. The local kids had left their seats in the Hershey Sports Arena by now, and they pressed close to the court and shouted, "Give it to Wilt! Give it to Wilt!"

From the Warriors bench, Coach Frank McGuire, a dandy from the Irish side of Greenwich Village, called out those same words. The tinsmith's son cradled the ball in his right hand and drove toward the basket, Knicks converging on him from all sides. At the last moment, Larese lifted the ball high—a lob pass to Chamberlain.

Larese's momentum carried him beneath the basket and beyond the baseline and, as he drifted from the play, he looked back, and what he saw was unforgettable . . . beautiful and monstrous, exquisite and terrifying, a hugeness unlike anything he'd ever seen on a basketball court, rising up, up, up, Chamberlain, long and lean, leaping with both arms extended above his head, revealing the "PHILA 13" across his white jersey, catching the ball twelve-and-a-half or thirteen feet above the hardwood floor—two-and-a-half or three feet above the flimsy rim—and in one motion, slamming it through the basket with a ferocity that branded itself in Larese's memory.

The ball bounced high off the floor, and the Zink called out on the public address system, "That's nine-tee eigghhhttt!"

INTRODUCTION

WILT CHAMBERLAIN DIED ON A MOUNTAINTOP, alone, in bed, beneath a retractable ceiling that allowed him to see the stars. The gardener found his body, which is how it often works in Hollywood. The Dipper lived alone, a life he chose. His gardener had arrived and called out to him but heard no response. He often did handyman work around the house and knew the house rarely was locked. He went inside and called out again; still no answer. Then he walked upstairs, into the master bedroom.

In a panic, the gardener's first call went to Chamberlain's attorney. Sy Goldberg had first met Chamberlain before that remarkable 1961–62 season. He'd set himself up in the San Fernando Valley in a Granada Hills storefront, orange groves all around, and hung out his shingle: SEYMOUR GOLDBERG, LAWYER. He accepted anything that walked through his door in those days: divorces, bankruptcies, wills, car accidents. It was a different era, a simpler time, hardly any money in it. Goldberg received a call seeking his counsel. Chamberlain, the young basketball star in Philadelphia, was building "Villa Chamberlain," a forty-unit apartment complex in downtown Los Angeles, near the Sports Arena. He intended to move his parents there to manage the complex and to get them out of the Philadelphia cold. But the money budgeted for construction was fully spent, mechanics' liens for unpaid bills had been filed, and workers were picketing. It made for bad press. Ike Richman, Chamberlain's Philadelphia attorney and business manager, was looking for legal help in L.A. "Sure," Goldberg said, "I handle everything."

That's how their friendship began. It deepened over the decades, with Goldberg serving as Chamberlain's financial advisor, lawyer, and confidant. The Dipper had long surrounded himself with Jewish attorneys, accountants, and advisors. Goldberg believed this was due, in part, to the Dipper's mother having worked years before as a domestic for Jewish families in Philadelphia with whom she shared warm relations. In 1958, Philadelphia Warriors owner Eddie Gottlieb and Harlem Globetrotters owner Abe Saperstein competed for rights to sign Chamberlain, who later confessed, "It was the first time I'd ever gotten between two Jews." Once Chamberlain showed up at Goldberg's house for the Passover Seder. Everyone was dressed casually, except Wilt, who wore a fine suit and proudly placed a yarmulke on his head. He insisted they read every word of the Haggadah. He wanted to hear the account of the Israelites' deliverance from slavery.

And this was how their friendship of nearly four decades ended: on October 12, 1999, Goldberg, ashen-faced, escorted into Chamberlain's bedroom by the Los Angeles Police Department.

The Dipper looked peaceful in bed, his head on a pillow, not a sign of strain in his face.

Goldberg told the LAPD what he knew. Wilt had not been feeling well. He'd had dental surgery recently, and it had caused him pain that he had described as his worst ever. He'd lost weight over the past few months, fifty pounds, maybe more. His hips caused him trouble, too. *How old?* Yes, he was sixty-three. *Any issues with his heart?* Well . . . over the years, yes.

Dazed, Goldberg heard an LAPD detective ask, "Can you tell if anything here is missing?"

He walked the detectives through the rooms. Chamberlain's house was a Hollywood celebrity in its own right. It was a period piece locked in the early 1970s, purple shag carpeting everywhere, a house described by one architectural critic as "a curiosity with moments of genius," an admiring critique that aptly summarized Wilt himself. *Ursa Major,* he called it, named for the constellation that included the Big Dipper. Built on a World War II Nike missile site, the house featured a series of interlocking equilateral triangles, an idea borrowed from Frank Lloyd Wright. Its five-story pitched roof resembled, from certain angles, Darth Vader's helmet. Made from 200 tons of stone and enough redwoods to build seventeen traditional houses, surrounded by a moat, Ursa Major had been filled with eccentricities: a fifty-five-foot tall stone fireplace, an indoor pool, a triangular front door, a bed-spread made from the stitched fur of 17,000 Arctic wolves' noses, a circular dining room table accompanied by a symbolic thirteen chairs (he wore jersey No. 13), and, in the master bedroom, only a few feet from the eight-foot by nine-foot bed, a gold-laced marble tub Cleopatra might have ad-mired. Downstairs contained another eccentricity, the "X-rated room," with mirrors and pink/peach upholstered foam sectionals surrounding a circular waterbed. Triangles abounded: Even above the oversized master bed, the thirteen-foot mirrored retractable ceiling allowed a triangular view of the heavens. He lived among celebrities. Farrah Fawcett once was a neighbor. The comedian Albert Brooks was down the street. Ronald and Nancy Rea-gan lived in Bel Air. The panoramic view from behind Ursa Major was lovely: the Stone River reservoir, the buildings of Century City, Westwood's Wilshire district, and beyond, the Pacific. On a clear day, which was not often, Chamberlain could see Catalina Island.

Sy Goldberg knew where Chamberlain hid his valuables. His diamond ring, his medallion. He found them in their usual places. This was clearly not a robbery. There was no sign of foul play.

He got word to Wilt's sister, Barbara Lewis, who rushed to the house. Calls were coming. Jerry West asked, *Is it true?* Bill Russell reached Goldberg on a cell phone. Goldberg heard a catch in Russell's voice when the Celtics legend said he'd heard that Wilt was dead and he needed to confirm it. *Is it true?* Russell sounded devastated.

Two dozen media members camped in Chamberlain's driveway, wait-ing for a statement. Word was sent out to the patrolman working the front gate: Tell them to wait.

Lynda Huey stood at the front gate, too. For nearly thirty years, Huey had been in and out of the Dipper's life, initially and for many years as a lover. She'd become like a nurse to him in more recent years, an aquatic therapist by profession helping him recover from elbow and hip surgeries. On Saturday night, three days before, Huey had spent a few hours with Chamberlain, his sister Barbara, and brother-in-law Elzie Lewis at Ursa Major, sharing chicken and dumplings and watching a movie on television. She saw the Dipper that night pause at the top of his stairway to catch his breath, but had no inkling the problem might be his heart. Stooped slightly, with a pained expression, he looked desperately uncomfortable, so different from their first meeting in 1971.

Huey had insinuated herself into his world then, a five-foot-three blonde, eleven years his junior, a track and field athlete in her own right who at San Jose State University during the Sixties had become captivated by black athletes and what she saw as the excitement and drama of their lives. From afar, she believed that she *belonged* in Wilt Chamberlain's world. At a friend's invitation, she caught a late-night plane from New York to L.A. to play in a beach volleyball tournament with him the next day. They played on the same team and lost horribly in the tournament but in between games flirted and challenged each other. Huey had a bravado of her own. "Hey, San Jose!" the Dipper called to her. She called him "old man." He treated her poorly during the match.

Afterward, beach chair in hand, Huey had walked up Temescal Canyon Boulevard, still angry at how he'd blamed her for their defeat. Yet there was the Dipper, in his Bentley convertible, inching along beside her, and trying to sweet-talk her into his car: "Come on, baby! Come on, come on, come on!" Seeking to burn off her anger with a workout at a nearby high school track, Huey found him waiting, lying on the grass, near the football goalposts. "Want to see a *pretty* runner?" the Dipper said, grinning. His language, bor- rowed from Muhammad Ali, was narcissistic, immodest, and sexualized. Huey told him she'd already seen the Olympian Tommie Smith: "I'm going to be comparing you to the *prettiest.*" The Dipper ran down the field, and Huey saw it instantly: fluidity, grace, a gazellelike motion. Gorgeous. Suddenly she wasn't angry with him anymore. He took her to Bel Air to see where his new home soon would rise. He was living in a trailer on the grounds. They slept together in his trailer that night, as both knew they would. Then Huey left town for a week, believing it the only way to keep the Dipper interested.

Their relationship never was conventional. It began as a conquest game played by sexual adventurers. The Dipper and Huey were of like mind, in the chase, collecting lovers. As a lover, the Dipper was "a lot of fun, just silly, playful and like a kid," Huey would say, "just romping around all day." But Huey learned the Dipper didn't treat his lovers well. He could quickly turn cold and mean. "You almost had to drop out of being a sexual partner if you wanted to be his friend," she would say. At times, Huey and Chamberlain wouldn't talk for months, even years. But then they would come together again, in the last years as friends. He was alternately big-hearted, generous, defensive, smart, perceptive, analytical, gruff. She asked him once, "Don't you think sometimes that since your image is so powerful in people's minds you might fall victim to it and begin to live that image for them?" The Dipper admitted to the possibility. Lynda Huey came to believe that "Wilt chose being a legend rather than having a life." Now, before Huey was admitted into the house, media members standing at the front gate recognized her as a long-term companion of Chamberlain's and interviewed her about his remarkable life.

Suddenly, Goldberg heard a buzzing sound overhead—helicopters, which is also how it often works in Hollywood. The press shot aerial views of Ursa Major from high over Mulholland Drive. Word of Chamberlain's death spread quickly. It was reported on CNN. News flashes broke across television screens in the Dipper's native Philadelphia, where the mayor soon ordered all flags lowered to half-mast. That day at Big Nate's Barbecue in San Francisco, Nate Thurmond stared at the poster on his restaurant's wall that showed the NBA's fifty greatest players of all time, named in 1996, Thurmond among them. A realization stung him. It was frightening to believe that the mighty Chamberlain had died, for if the Dipper had died it meant every NBA player of his generation was vulnerable. Theirs was the first generation of black superstars, the generation that had lifted the NBA from obscurity into a national phenomenon. The Dipper was at the center of that breakthrough, the ultimate individualist and the most skillful, compelling, and enigmatic character of all. "Almost by himself, he made the league a curiosity, made it interesting," Oscar Robertson would say. Without the league's defining black superstars of that generation, Robertson believes the league might have lost its small television contract, then withered and died. He pointed to the 1961–62 season. "People heard about Wilt scoring a hundred, averaging fifty a night, and they wanted to see the guy do it . . . I believe Wilt Chamberlain single-handedly saved the league." Over the decades, the Dipper had taken such fine care of his body that he'd seemed, if anyone could be, immortal. Thurmond also realized that Chamberlain's death was only the second among the fifty players on that poster: the first, dead of heart failure at forty while playing a pickup game in 1988, was "Pistol" Pete Maravich.

The LAPD controlled the press conference that afternoon in the Dipper's driveway outside the front gate. Two of Chamberlain's brothers, Wilbert and Oliver, and his sister Barbara, stood beside Sy Goldberg, who fought tears. The LAPD said only that Chamberlain had been found in bed at 12:30 P.M. and was declared dead by paramedics at 12:41 P.M. No foul play was suspected. Sy Goldberg stared into the cameras and said, "We think it may have been a heart attack."

The next morning obituary writers described the frame of the Dipper's life but missed the engine that drove it: his nearly obsessive need to prove, in ways large and small, his own greatness.

The Washington Post termed him "a Herculean figure on the basketball court whose massive dimensions, intimidating personality and unprecedented point production helped him become a sports icon and cultural legend." *The New York Times* said his "size, strength and intimidation made him probably the most dominant player in basketball history." "If Wilt Chamberlain can die, anyone can," *The Philadelphia Inquirer* editorialized. "He loved himself and the life he was living, and it was hard not to catch the gusto. In his undeniable excellence and egotism, Wilt Chamberlain was America itself, inspiring worship, ambivalence and downright awe." These obituaries recounted his rise to prominence beginning at Overbrook High School in Philadelphia followed by his years at the University of Kansas and how he left behind a two-season 42-8 record, including a traumatic triple overtime defeat to the University of North Carolina in the 1957 NCAA title game, a defeat Chamberlain believed had been blamed on him. They recounted his tours with the Harlem Globetrotters, his seven NBA scoring titles, two league championships, and his battles (mostly lost) with Bill Russell's Celtics. They recounted his dalliance with Richard Nixon's 1968 presidential campaign, his remarkable physical fitness regimen through middle age, his support for women's athletics, his firmly held, if self-pitying, belief that "Nobody roots for Goliath," his appearance in the Arnold Schwarzenegger movie *Conan the Destroyer,* his decades of playing volleyball on the beaches of Southern California, how he'd never married, how he'd once almost boxed Muhammad Ali, his incessant talk about making a comeback in the NBA at the age of forty or fifty, and his mythmaker's claim to have made love to 20,000 women.

More than insatiable, though, Chamberlain's need to prove his great-ness was a connective tissue in his life. His good friend in Harlem, Cal Ram-sey, who played briefly with the Knicks in 1959–60, had recognized this in the early Sixties by the way the Dipper cheated at cards (by sneaking glances at Ramsey's hand) and by criticizing the way Ramsey hung up his pants in a hotel room once ("Damn," Ramsey said, after the Dipper had demonstrated how to neatly fold the crease, "you're the best pants hanger-upper in the world, too!") and by the stories Chamberlain told about himself, nearly al-ways positioning himself in the role of manly hero. Once, alone in the country, the Dipper said he was attacked by a mountain lion that had leaped from rocks. "I killed him with my bare hands," the Dipper related, and as Ramsey raised a brow in doubt, Chamberlain pulled back his shirt to reveal several long scars on his shoulder, which Ramsey had to admit looked like claw marks.

The Dipper's death brought new attention to his signature performance, the hundred-point night against the New York Knicks on March 2, 1962, in Hershey, Pennsylvania, a performance that lives in the pantheon of sports history, both famous and famously obscure. Chamberlain's line score that night—thirty-six field goals in sixty-three shots and twenty-eight of thirty-two free throws—seems too fantastic to be believed, a basketball equivalent of the steel-driving folk hero John Henry, a hammer in his hand, outpound-ing the steam drill.

Four decades later, only four National Basketball Association *teams* aver-aged one hundred points a game.

In the history of professional team sports in America, there is no statis-tical equal of the Dipper's hundred-point game, no other individual accom-plishment in a single game so remarkable and outsized. Such a declarative statement is possible because of the way basketball is played. Chamberlain that night handled the ball more than 125 times, including his sixty-three shots from the floor, thirty-two free throws, and twenty-five rebounds. Ex-tended over forty-eight minutes of play, the Dipper's performance became a marathon of excellence that not only broke the existing scoring record in regulation (which was, of course, his own record), it exceeded it by twenty-seven points—and that year only six other NBA players averaged 27 points *a game.* Baseball allows for moments of greatness, but not for sustained effort that builds mountainous numbers in a single game; certainly, no batter will hit ten home runs one night, no pitcher will have forty strikeouts. Football aficionados celebrated a Gale Sayers game in December of 1965 when, in a 61-20 Chicago Bears victory over San Francisco on a quagmire at Wrigley Field, he rushed for four touchdowns, caught a touchdown pass, and returned a punt eighty-five yards for another touchdown—six touchdowns on 336 all-purpose yards. But Sayers touched the ball only sixteen times that day, and as brilliant a performance as his was—Bears owner George Halas, who founded the pro game a half century before, called it the greatest individual effort he ever saw—it had none of the unimaginable aspects of Chamberlain's. Indeed, Sayers's all-purpose yardage total has been exceeded several times, and other players have scored six touchdowns in a game.

In professional basketball, great scorers have come and gone—Kareem Abdul-Jabbar, Karl Malone, Elgin Baylor, Julius Erving, Larry Bird, Michael Jordan, Shaquille O'Neal, Allen Iverson—but in the forty-three years since the hundred-point game no player has approached the Dipper or, for that matter, even reached seventy-five points. Wilt Chamberlain's hundred-point night stands like a statistical Everest over the landscape of American sports.

It's impossible to know in sports when or where the unforgettable moment will happen. That's the beauty of it. It can be a place or a time. It can be a personality or a startling achievement.

We remember Babe Ruth's "called shot" in the 1932 World Series in Chicago because of the sheer force of the Babe's personality—not to mention the bluster and arrogance of the act—and because, in the darkness of the Depression, America needed heroes. Never mind that we still can't be certain if the Babe really pointed to the center field bleachers in Wrigley Field to show the hecklers in the Cubs dugout where he intended to hit his home run.

We remember Jesse Owens's performance in the 1936 Berlin Olympics because of its social and political significance. Owens, an African-American sprinter and jumper, won four gold medals to challenge the racial notions of the Aryan supremacist watching that day from a box seat—Adolf Hitler.

Beyond its Chocolate Town charm, Chamberlain's hundred-point game carried deeper import. Shot like a flare into the sky, it signaled that the pro game had changed in both the way it would be played and the men who would play it. It would be a game with a higher metabolism performed now at a greater speed, from in close and above the rim, by players who were no longer bound by gravity. The Dipper proved irrefutably that you could be a remarkable athlete even if you were seven feet tall or taller. Athletes had long been taught to be quiet and humble. Not the Dipper. He was fast becoming the most striking symbol of basketball's new age of self-expression and egotism—a development slightly ahead of the overall popular culture—and his hundred-point game gave him an imprimatur to continue being, boldly and unashamedly, the Dipper.

His hundred-point game was also a hyperbolic announcement of the ascendancy of the black superstar in professional basketball. A wave of black athletes had been achieving superstardom in other professional sports for more than a decade: Jackie Robinson had cleared the baseball path for Willie Mays, Henry Aaron, and others. Jim Brown was annihilating pro football's top defenses, while the young heavyweight Cassius Clay, with his father proclaiming, "He's the next Joe Louis!" set his sights, eight months hence, on Archie Moore and then later *the big ugly bear*, Sonny Liston. In 1958–59, the year before the Dipper had broken into the league, Elgin Baylor rated as the only black player among the NBA's top ten scorers; now, in 1961–62, there were five scoring leaders who were black, and by the later Sixties there would be seven. The hundred-point game was a revolutionary act—if not by intention then by effect—that announced the NBA as a white man's enclave no more. Against the Knickerbockers in Hershey, the Dipper symbolically blew to smithereens the NBA owners' arbitrary quota that limited the number of black players, a tacit understanding that was systemic in America (the joke among NBA writers was, "You can start only one black player at home, two on the road, and three if you need to win").

At the time of his hundred-point game, Chamberlain was twenty-five years old, still in the process of *becoming*, though already at the height of his considerable athletic powers. His standing reach was nine feet, seven inches, his arm span eighty-nine inches. He'd run the 440 in forty-nine seconds, leaped nearly twenty-three feet in the broad jump, and put the shot more than fifty-three feet. He could clean and jerk 375 pounds and dead-lift 625 pounds. If athleticism may be defined exclusively as a combination of size, strength, speed, and agility, then the young Wilt Chamberlain, at seven-foot-one, 260 pounds, might have been the twentieth century's greatest pure athlete. He would transform his sport, and its geometry, more than anyone ever did: He led the movement that took a horizontal game and made it vertical.

Already, he was a celebrated individualist, a bachelor with enormous cravings, an intergalactic nickname, and all the trappings of new money. He had a fancy car, a racehorse (Spooky Cadet), apartments on both coasts, and a famous Harlem nightclub—where Malcolm X had served as a teenaged waiter—that now bore the name Big Wilt's Smalls Paradise. The Warriors' owner, Eddie Gottlieb, worked hard to keep Chamberlain happy. As part of their agreement, Gotty rented the Dipper a gorgeous three-bedroom apartment at the Hopkinson House, a prestigious new high-rise. It overlooked Independence Hall, where the Founding Fathers ratified America's defining documents, and was near the nation's first Executive Mansion where George and Martha Washington lived during the 1790s (with eight Negro slaves). There, the Dipper roomed with Vince Miller, whom he had known since third grade, his deepest and most enduring boyhood friendship. Miller was his teammate at Overbrook High and even before at Shoemaker Junior High where they wore red-white-and-blue socks pulled up nearly to the knees. That's when he began using rubber bands to keep them in place. The Dipper wore spare rubber bands on his wrists throughout his NBA career to remind him of those early friendships, the ones that preceded the arrival of the groupies and sycophants.

In 1962, only its sixteenth season, the NBA struggled to compete with the more established college game, which had troubles of its own. Basketball had been damaged by the betting and point-shaving scandals in the colleges during the early Fifties; now, a decade later, a new college gambling scandal struck, twice the size of the first, involving at least fifty players from twenty-seven schools in nearly two dozen states. The NBA's failure to capture the American imagination showed in sparse crowds and small television ratings. The Warriors even played one game that season against the expansion Chicago Packers in a high school gymnasium in Indiana. NBA games could be physical, even violent. Fights broke out on the court. Penny-ante gamblers still worked the crowd in some NBA arenas. With only one team west of St. Louis, the NBA hardly seemed *national.* When the Lakers moved to Los Angeles in 1960 they found themselves virtual foreigners in a Pacific Coast League baseball town. The team dispatched players in sound trucks to Beverly Hills, Hollywood, and south central Los Angeles to give clinics and read from scripts: *"Hello, I'm Tommy Hawkins of the Los Angeles Lakers. We're going to be at the Sports Arena for the next ten days. First up: the New York Knicks on Friday. Please come out to see us."* The Lakers' attendance wasn't helped when the U.S. Army called for Private Elgin Baylor. Stationed in Fort Lewis in Washington, Baylor missed nearly half the 1961–62 season, doing his best to obtain passes to play games on weekends. The NBA, in its rudimentary development and reach, was in 1962 roughly the equal of baseball at the dawn of the live-ball era in the early 1920s, an old era fading and a new one rising with exciting possibilities.

Occasionally NBA games were played in outlying towns like Hershey in an attempt to attract new fans. The Knicks and Warriors rosters on March 2 were a snapshot of American manhood at midcentury, filled with first-generation Americans carrying their fathers' Old World names (Meschery, Larese, Radovich) and former U.S. Marines (Arizin, Guerin, Green). Their childhoods had been shaped by the Depression and World War II when their fathers worked as cops, for the railroads, in coal mines, and as common laborers. The father of one of the Dipper's teammates in Hershey fought with the White Russians against the Bolsheviks after the October 1917 revolution.

Chamberlain's hundred-point game was played in a drafty old gym in Pennsylvania Dutch country, up the street from Milton Hershey's famous chocolate factory, spreading its sweet fumes.

No television cameras were there.

Neither was the New York press.

Only two photographers showed up; one left in the first quarter, the other took just a few pictures.

Only 4,124 people attended, leaving nearly 4,000 seats empty. Chamberlain's hundred-point game played out under the media radar and lives largely in the memory of those who played in it or watched it.

On the bus ride home through the Amish lands late that night, Chamberlain's teammates spotted a farmer driving his horse-drawn buggy by a lantern's light. Chamberlain never saw that. He was in a new Cadillac, no bus for him, cruising back to his nightclub in Harlem. Showered and tired but exhilarated from his night's work, he still had time to celebrate. Big Wilt's Smalls Paradise didn't turn off its lantern lights until four in the morning.

•   •   •

Wilt Chamberlain would be cremated, per his family's wishes. For the memorial service in Los Angeles, Sy Goldberg sought a way to bring the Dipper and his memory into the church, to feel his presence. He would choose from among dozens of pictures of Chamberlain. He wanted the images to be symbolic of a full and memorable life—Wilt Chamberlain as he was. Goldberg canvassed his file of eight-by-ten glossies and finally selected two. He would blow them up to poster size, three feet by four feet, and place them on easels on the church dais, large enough for mourners in the back row to see. The first was of Chamberlain in his purple-and-gold Los Angeles Lakers uniform, circa 1972. Staring at the second, Goldberg smiled. The image satisfied him. *The pinnacle of Wilt's career,* he thought. The way he ought to be remembered. It showed a younger Chamberlain, sitting in a locker room, smiling and sweat-soaked, holding a piece of paper that read "100." It was taken in Hershey, Pennsylvania, on March 2, 1962.

PART ONE

Building Toward 100

MARCH 1962

CHAPTER 1

The Dipper in Harlem

THERE IS A PHOTOGRAPH OF THE DIPPER with James Baldwin on a Harlem street corner, the big man in a slim suit and snap-brim fedora, tilting his frame toward the writer, seemingly half his size. If not classically handsome, Chamberlain's face was arresting: a long, narrow brow over almond eyes lit by youth and restless ambition, high cheekbones, and a cool jazzman's trimmed mustache. Then, when he really wanted something (or someone), there came a starry smile and his deep baritone transformed to the smooth, soft patter of the FM radio deejay. It was Baldwin who in 1961, back in America after years of self-imposed exile in Europe, wrote words that defined his life's direction, words that Chamberlain may have heard. Baldwin wrote, "I had said that I was going to be a writer, God, Satan, and Mississippi notwithstanding, and that color did not matter, and that I was going to be free. And, here I was, left with only myself to deal with. It was entirely up to me."

Chamberlain, too, would create himself, would refuse to be defined by size or color or his sport. In 1962, the Dipper drove a white Cadillac convertible, but only until he could take delivery of a nobleman's car, a Bentley, custom-made in England at a cost of nearly $30,000 (including tax and shipping), roughly six times the average yearly salary for an American worker. Wealthy after his one season with the Globetrotters and three with the Warriors, he used his big money as a tool of self-creation. After buying his parents a house in west Philadelphia, he lavished upon himself twenty fine suits, thirteen pairs of stylish shoes, the Cadillac, and a chic, pricey, Oriental-motif apartment on Central Park West. It was a far cry from 401 Salford Street, where Chamberlain had been raised. With nine children, William and Olivia Chamberlain, a handyman and a domestic, at times had two, three, or four kids in each bedroom; at five-thirty each morning they felt the trolleys rumble past their rented row house in ethnic, working-class west Philly.

The young Dipper came of age noticing little discrimination, though once, when he was about four, on a bus in Virginia bound for Philadelphia, his mother wouldn't allow him to sit near the front. "No, mama, this seat right here is open," the young Dipper protested, even as she tried to steer him toward the rear of the segregated bus. It prompted the white bus driver to intervene, "No, sonny, you go back there with your mother like a good little boy," and he did, though uncertain as to why.

So valuable was Chamberlain's name now, so incandescent his persona, that a historic Harlem nightclub, Smalls Paradise, let him buy in as part-owner and put his name first on the marquee in exchange for his presence. He loved Harlem, the neon, the ladies, James Brown, Etta James, Redd Foxx, a lush life with jazz the soundtrack. And when Wilton Norman Chamberlain moved through Big Wilt's Smalls Paradise, there attached to him an aura suggesting he owned not only this place, but all of Harlem, perhaps all of New York. His presence in the club was signaled by the white Cadillac parked out front by one of the nightclub boys on the corner of 135th Street, while Chamberlain strode around the club's dark interior greeting his guests, draping an arm around Tom "Satch" Sanders of the Boston Celtics, squeezing a shoulder, "Good to see you, Satch. Sit down, relax, and enjoy yourself." Reminiscing years later, the Dipper would recall this as the greatest time in his life.

At Big Wilt's Smalls Paradise, the bandleader King Curtis worked deep into the night, and the denizens turned up wearing sharkskin suits and memorable monikers: Big Pete, Little Pete, an intellectual straight shooter known as Knowledge, and of course, Charlie Polk, Wilt's right-hand man, always at his side, Robin to his Batman. His name, called out so often, rolled off the Dipper's tongue: *Chollypolk*. Small and thin as straw, Polk was, as one Harlem nightclub regular would say, "one of those types of guys who if he latched on to you, he didn't let go." Whatever the Dipper wanted—his shirts picked up at the cleaners, his friend's wife picked up at the bus stop and taken shopping—Chollypolk got it done. When a beautiful woman at Smalls caught the Dipper's eye, Chollypolk became his emissary, quietly letting the woman know of his boss's interest and gauging her availability. He loved being on stage at the club, and though he couldn't sing or dance and he stuttered slightly, he was a riotous emcee. If you put a microphone in his hand, Chollypolk might never let go of it, and Redd Foxx would sit beside the stage, waiting, waiting to begin his gig.

Foxx, a bawdy redheaded comic, was a Harlem favorite. "Lincoln got his head on all the pennies. Roosevelt got his head on all the dimes," Foxx would say. "I just want to get my *hands* on some." In his first New York nightclub date in a decade, Foxx, a rising national star (to all but the censors), appeared at Smalls Paradise in December 1961. In smoky clubs, perspiring beneath the spotlight, Foxx would deliver his raunchy routines, unafraid of the social taboos of sex and race. In one, using his trademark off-color double entendres, he told of how everyone in his hometown had bought a jackass. "Even the little bitty kids, they had a ass of their own," Foxx would say. "Preacher's wife had the biggest ass in town. I know because I rode her big ass all the time." And, Foxx said, her husband, the preacher, "didn't have such a bad ass himself," though when a fire broke out in the church's back pew, "Reverend took a long running jump out the window to land on his ass. But somebody had stolen Ol' Reverend's ass and he wasn't there. Reverend fell down into a deep hole in the ground and that's where they found him." Foxx gave a comic's pause. "Just goes to show you, don't it? Some folks don't know their ass from a hole in the ground."

Smalls Paradise was a legend that dated back to the Harlem Renaissance of the Twenties when its waiters danced or roller-skated across the room with service trays held high; the club was known then as the Hottest Spot in Harlem. Chamberlain had long wanted his own nightclub, an environment that had always drawn him as a stage for his fabulousness—why, even when he was just sixteen, his rival at West Philadelphia High, Ray Scott, had spotted him at a dance at the O.V. Catto Elks Lodge in Philadelphia and noticed how the Dipper flourished in such a setting, managing what all of the other boys couldn't, a laid-back, Miles Davis, be-bop cool. Chamberlain well knew the precedents of black athletes owning such places in New York. Back in the Twenties, Club Deluxe in Harlem briefly was owned by the prizefighter Jack Johnson, a controversial figure excoriated by the white press in the early part of the century for having twice married white women and later imprisoned for transporting a woman across state lines in violation of the Mann Act. Now Joe Louis and Ray Robinson lent their names and money to The Brown Bomber and Sugar Ray's. It wasn't so much the fast life that attracted the Dipper to buy a piece of Smalls in the spring of 1961. He rarely drank or smoked and he exercised every day, pushing his own physical limits. (Before one weekend trip to Atlantic City, his friend Cal Ramsey tried to pick up Chamberlain's suitcase but found it too heavy. Ramsey looked inside and discovered why—the Dipper's barbells.) What attracted Chamberlain to Smalls Paradise was the chance to explore new avenues of his own celebrity.

In calm moments, the Abyssinian Baptist Church crowd came for early Sunday dinners. But on most other nights, the nightclub was, like its part owner, full of the energy and exuberance of youth. "The Twist" by Philadelphia's Chubby Checker was yet the rage, and the Tuesday night Twist contests packed the downstairs Wilmac Room. Limousines and taxis carrying big-money whites triple-parked out front. "Meeting again at Smalls Paradise as their fathers did before them, a brand-new generation of monied fun-seeking whites is flocking happily to Harlem," *Ebony* magazine noted. "And Wilt Chamberlain's cash registers are running as hot as the gyrations on the floor." It was a see-and-be-seen crowd, sophisticated, elite, and integrated. Smiling for pictures for *Ebony* magazine on a Tuesday Twist night were comic Jack Carter, famed saxophonist Cannonball Adderly with actress Olga James, a Rockefeller, an Astor, Edward Smalls (the former owner who sold the club in 1955), the Greek ambassador to the United Nations, singer Lloyd Price, and of course, the Dipper himself.

His nightclub impressed other African-American players in the NBA, not only for its high style and glitz but because it suggested Chamberlain's business acumen. They considered Big Wilt's Smalls Paradise a must-stop along the Strip in Harlem along with Jocks and the Red Rooster. The Knicks' Willie Naulls and Johnny Green were regulars at Smalls. The Celtics'

K.C. Jones, in with Bill Russell once, met James Brown, and was overwhelmed by the magnitude of the Godfather of Soul's ego.

Here, in Harlem, was the Wilt Chamberlain few white Americans knew: easing comfortably through what W.E.B. Du Bois once had called "the Black World Beyond the Veil." Here was the Apollo Theater and Showman's Lounge, the Big Apple bar, The Harlem Moon, Lickity Split, and Roy Campanella's liquor store. The neighborhood was thirty years past its heyday; no longer the hub of black intellectual and cultural life, Harlem had become riddled with crime, dope, and storefront vacancies, an urban despair and bleakness suffused with racial tension and frustration. Still, the Strip retained some of its old-time flair. In the neon flash and bustle, crowds moved from one nightclub to the next. At the Red Rooster, where Willie Mays had held sway during the early 1950s, you could still find Congressman Adam Clayton Powell surrounded by admirers. A club hopper could see comic Nipsey Russell at the Baby Grand on 125th Street, stop by Sugar Ray's on 126th, and then walk six blocks over to Count Basie's club. Next door to Count Basie's on 132nd was Shalimar by Randolph, a nightclub that featured a late-night beauty salon. When Knicks first-year guard Sam Stith, a Harlem resident, came out to the Strip in 1962, he dressed to the nines and no one crowded him. A few years before, Stith had taken his girlfriend to Shalimar by Randolph at 11:00 one night to get her hair done. She finished at 3:00 A.M. While he waited, Stith saw a hustler, all primped up, enter and shout, "Suits!" The hustler looked at the Knicks guard. "What size?" he asked. Stith replied, "Forty-two." The hustler put the same question to another man sitting nearby, then said, "I'll be back in an hour." Stith looked at his watch: 1:00 A.M. An hour passed, back came the hustler, suits in hand. Stith didn't buy; the other guy did. Another hour later, Stith and his girlfriend headed to Wells Restaurant for the famous chicken and waffles, a perfect way to end the night, or start the morning.

In this animated environment, Big Wilt's Smalls Paradise remained a bright light. So hot was the revelry at Smalls on Twist nights, local columnist Jesse H. Walker asked, "Will this thing never end?" In Harlem, Jackie Robinson co-hosted a cocktail party for New York's Republican governor Nelson Rockefeller; Malcolm X, in his dark suit and shined black shoes, made his rounds through the streets surrounding the Nation of Islam's Mosque Seven in Harlem (and periodically ridiculed the nonviolent movement, including sit-ins, saying, "Anybody can sit. An old woman can sit. A coward can sit. . . . It takes a man to stand."); and Wilt Chamberlain moved through his own celebrated orbit. If Philadelphia was his workplace, Harlem was his living room. He gravitated to a black world shared with whites, not an exclusive world or an excluding one. Each night in the NBA, the Dipper played for white team owners and predominantly white crowds, but here, at Big Wilt's Smalls Paradise, surrounded by icons of black life in the lingering glow of Harlem glamour, whites came to him—to his place.

The March 2 game in Hershey meant little to Chamberlain . . . except another Friday night away from Harlem. He had spent Thursday night, and the wee hours of Friday morning, doing what the Dipper often did, enjoying the spoils of his celebrity. He dropped off his date at her home in Queens at 6:00 A.M. and only then set his sights on Hershey. He would travel the 170 miles to Chocolate Town on his own.

Wilt Chamberlain had one incentive in Hershey. On another scoring rampage, he was closing in on 4,000 points for the 1961–62 season; no other NBA player had ever scored even 3,000 points. On the previous Sunday, the Dipper had torn into the Knicks for sixty-seven points. Two days later, in St. Louis, he scored sixty-five in a victory over Bob Pettit's Hawks. On Wednesday, he had annihilated the great rookie big man, Walt Bellamy, and the expansion Chicago Packers, scoring sixty-one on Bells and blocking twelve of his shots. In that game, the Dipper also made thirteen of his seventeen free throws, typically the Achilles heel of his game. Chamberlain, who loved statistics (especially his own), needed 237 more points over the remaining five games to reach the once-unthinkable 4,000.

On top of his statistical rampage, he was revolutionizing his sport stylistically much as Babe Ruth had revolutionized his in the 1920s. What the garrulous Ruth did with the home run, Chamberlain was doing with the Dipper Dunk. Slam dunks still were relatively rare. It's not that NBA players were incapable of stuffing the ball through the basket; they simply didn't do it. Basketball traditionalists believed dunks suggested poor sportsmanship or showboating. As the NBA's second tallest player (Syracuse's Swede Halbrook stood seven-foot-three), Chamberlain was beginning to break with tradition by dunking with some regularity. Even so, he remained more of a finesse player around the basket, with finger-rolls and put-backs. He dunked with real force only when the spirit, or perhaps an opponent's well-placed elbow, moved him.

As Ruth, with his fifty-four home runs in 1920, had lifted baseball from the dead-ball era, so Chamberlain was lifting pro basketball into a new realm of scoring possibilities. At Madison Square Garden, the Dipper once proved like the gluttonous Ruth in another way, sending a ballboy to get him two hot dogs, and then eating them, while in uniform, on the bench, just before the game started. And like the Babe, the Dipper kept his eye on pretty women in the crowds. A married man, Ruth could be loud and coarse, once telling his teammates, "You should have seen this dame I was with last night. What a body. Not a blemish on it." The bachelor Chamberlain was more careful about his liaisons in winter 1962. "The blonde sitting underneath the basket," he whispered to a Warriors official sitting at the scorer's table during a game. The Dipper raised a brow and whispered, "Get her number for me."

CHAPTER 2

The Shooting Gallery

AFTER ANOTHER HARLEM NIGHT DEVOTED to wakeful pursuits that left minutes rather than hours for sleep, the Dipper made his way down to Hershey alone and unaware, as all were, that however splendid the night of March 1, 1962, had been, this night would be even grander.

"What are you doing?" he said to Ken Berman.

The Warriors' twenty-four-second clock operator, a third-generation Philadelphia jeweler, Berman had become Chamberlain's friend when the Dipper pulled hidden valuables from a sweat sock. He showed the jeweler a ten-carat diamond and ordered up a ring that Berman made. Now, in the Hershey Sports Arena's penny arcade, near a hot dog stand, Berman was shooting bears.

As tiny tin bears moved mechanically across the game's far end, players used a rifle to shoot 'em down. "I'll have you a match," Chamberlain said.

Faster than he could feed the machine its required nickels, the Dipper became a kid again. Playful, competitive, he shot every bear he saw and regaled fans gathered to watch.

Pro football's Eagles and Colts, arriving to play a preliminary basketball game that always proved popular with fans, saw Chamberlain in the arcade and heard him howling in delight. Two African-American running backs on the Eagles, Clarence Peaks and Tim Brown, knew the Dipper as onetime neighbors in west Philly. Brown had attended the same parties as the Dipper, dated a few of the same women. Peaks had been awed once when Chamberlain walked into his garage and lifted 350 pounds of weights as if it were nothing. Now, the two Eagles exchanged greetings with him. Gino Marchetti, the Baltimore Colts all-pro defensive end, came by, too. When the Eagles wide receiver Tommy McDonald shook Chamberlain's hand once after a practice, he had been amazed, horrified even, that his hand had disappeared entirely in the Dipper's massive mitt. Not so with the six-foot-five Marchetti. He wanted to ask the Dipper the same question he'd been asked too many times over the years, "How's the weather up there?" But he resisted that temptation. When he spotted the Dipper in Hershey, Marchetti told him that he had attended the University of San Francisco where he watched Bill Russell and K.C. Jones play. He chatted amiably with Chamberlain, while thinking *Russell never seemed this big,* and then left for the dressing room to suit up for the prelim. Though these prelims were meant to be relaxed, they rarely turned out that way. The NFL players usually earned about $50 for these games—Marchetti would spend about forty-five on beer afterwards—but they played to win. Outside shooting was preferred, especially by the Eagles' Sonny Jurgensen and Tim Brown, since driving to the basket might prompt a 280-pound lineman to get in their way. En route to the locker room, Marchetti had a passing thought about Chamberlain: *God, he would make a good tight end!*

As the Dipper kept racking up big numbers in the arcade, here came *The Philadelphia Daily News* sportswriter Jack Kiser, walking with a slight limp, a cigarette between his lips, and the sound of east Tennessee in his voice. Small, edgy, and combative, Kiser was the pugnacious Warriors beat reporter for the tabloid newspaper, a journalistic barnacle clinging to the hull of the leviathan Chamberlain. Kiser was always digging, always looking for a story. The best story was always Chamberlain; the Dipper was a beat unto himself. To best cover that beat, the hustler Kiser ingratiated himself to Wilt. Kiser heard a security man, sitting nearby, say, "Few people ever score four thousand on this here machine. I don't think I've ever seen anybody score over six-five." At that point, Chamberlain reached 7,700, and the guard said, "Impossible."

The Knickerbockers' bus pulled in from Harrisburg. Passing through the arcade, forward Dave Budd and center Darrall Imhoff heard the Chamberlain commotion, heard the Dipper yowling, "Man, look at this," heard him announce exactly how many free games he'd won, saw the big man animated by a kid's game, his greatness certified by knocking over tiny tin bears with a popgun. Imhoff thought, *That's Wilt,* and kept on walking.

The Knicks' players felt a small chill inside the big arena, a reminder of its original icy purpose. Upon its grand opening decades earlier, a time when the locals still proudly called their hockey team the Hershey B'ars, *The New York Herald-Tribune* opined, "The visitors saw what looked, from a distance, like a dirigible hangar, but once inside they were convinced that it deserved the title of 'finest hockey rink' which its builders claim for it." Like Wilt Chamberlain, the Hershey Sports Arena was born in 1936 and became a landmark for its time. Its monolithic barrel shell roof was a product of a technology brought over from Europe by the architect Anton Tedesko. Warming the newly poured concrete in winter had required a burst of Pennsylvania Dutch ingenuity—manure carted in from the farmlands did the trick. A hulking structure, designed to make a small town big league, it was foremost a hockey arena. Hanging beside the metal scoreboard now were the American and Canadian flags, and next to the COMING ATTRACTIONS sign, three maroon-and-white banners honoring the Hershey Bears as Calder Cup Champions in 1947, 1958, and 1959. It was a cold, cavernous place, cement on cement, a dirigible hangar still.

New York's rookie guard, Donnie Butcher, looked at the Hershey arena for the first time and cringed. *It isn't Madison Square Garden.* A Kentucky coal miner's son, the fifteenth of sixteen children, Butcher appreciated the NBA as the good life. When Knicks scout Red Holzman had shown up at his home in Paintsville, Kentucky, over Thanksgiving in an attempt to sign him, he had flashed thousands of dollars in a briefcase full of one hundred dollar bills. Those bills all looked good to this coal miner's son. But the Hershey Sports Arena did not. To Butcher, it reminded him of a coal mining camp, dingy, dirty, and gray.

Inside the arena, Bill Campbell set up his WCAU Radio equipment. Campbell was the defining voice of Philadelphia sports, working play-by-play for the Eagles and Warriors. It had been a long climb. He'd been in radio since 1941, initially a kid disc jockey at the Steel Pier and Million Dollar Pier in Atlantic City where the big bands of Glenn Miller and Tommy Dorsey played. (He'd even dated Miss Atlantic City that summer.) For a small man, Campbell had a big voice, deep, full, and so smooth one listener was convinced he gargled before each broadcast with Turtle Wax. His nightly sports show on WCAU in Philadelphia began with a rousing song of victory at sea and ended with the broadcaster intoning, "This is Bill Campbell, good night, good sports." Campbell wasn't happy about having to work this game in Hershey. But he had made the long drive, and now he set up his microphone on a table. He would work alone. Once the game started, he would lean forward slightly as he spoke into his microphone. He thought it would be hard to get excited about this game. Only five games remained in the regular season, and the Warriors, with a 46-29 record, remained in second place, eleven games back of Auerbach's first-place Celtics. The Knicks, in last place already, could not fall any lower. By the day after tomorrow, Campbell figured, no one would even remember the game was played.

As the game's legend would grow, so would the size of the crowd. Had they all been there, all those who in later years told the Dipper they saw him score the hundred points, they'd have been stacked atop one another a dozen high, for the Hershey Sports Arena had seats for little more than 8,000 souls.

Alas, half of those seats were empty on March 2. Gottlieb's enthusiastic crowd count was 4,124, a number that was, politely put, imprecise. Philadelphia sportswriters knew that Gotty famously fudged his crowd totals. Just because Gotty was round didn't mean his estimates were, and so 4,124 it was. The people of Hershey, out for a night on the town, dressed for the occasion. A panorama of the crowd revealed men in ties and overcoats, ladies in dresses, including a few (keeping up with the trends) in bouffant hairdos, and a slew of clean-scrubbed boys with crew cuts.

So many others later wished they'd been there to see the Dipper. They wished they'd seen the great man glistening in the arena's dim lights. They wished they'd had the foresight to be in the smoky building, to be part of the Pennsylvania Dutch army forming up behind Chamberlain the night of his march into history. But who knew?

Earl Whitmore had no plans to be in Hershey that night. Then, shopping on the town square in nearby Palmyra, he and his wife saw a General Electric refrigerator with a freezer compartment. Because the price, $549, seemed a sticking point for the two chocolate factory workers, the salesman made a proposition: "You're a sportsman, Mr. Whitmore, right? There's a game at the sports arena Friday night and here's two tickets—if you buy the refrigerator." So, with the incentive of two prime tickets that would have cost three dollars apiece at the gate, the Whitmores bought the refrigerator for $549. Come game night, Mrs. Whitmore stayed home with her new appliance. Her husband took a friend to see the Dipper.

Paul Vathis had already seen history through a camera lens. An Associated Press photographer from nearby Harrisburg, Vathis brought his ten-year-old son to the game as a birthday present. The previous spring, just after the Bay of Pigs fiasco, Vathis had been at the presidential retreat Camp David during a meeting of John Kennedy and his predecessor, Dwight Eisenhower. As these men representing America's future and past began to walk down a stone path, JFK's press secretary, Pierre Salinger, told the gathered photographers, "Okay, boys, that's it. Lids on." But Vathis, kneeling by the path, held his place, lens cap off, and overheard JFK say to Ike, "I've never been here before. Where do we go?" He heard Ike, who'd created the camp and named it after his grandson, reply, "I know a place up this path where we can go." Vathis clicked off one more shot, from behind, the two men pensive, heads bowed, Ike holding his hat in his hands behind his back. Salinger heard Vathis's shutter and shouted, "I told you, 'No more pictures!' " Fair enough, Vathis thought. He had a beauty already. On this night in Hershey, Vathis left his camera in the trunk of his car.

Bruised by his work, Hec Lalande, a hockey player for the Hershey Bears, came to the arena for a whirlpool treatment and rubdown. The Canadian brought along a friend, Bill Pavone, a young bartender at Martini's, a bar where Lalande lived in a back-room apartment. People in the bar said he and Pavone were look-alike twins. Nothing else to do, the buddies stayed for the game. The NBA players didn't much impress Lalande. "They can't even skate," he said.

The editorial page editor of *The Harrisburg Patriot* showed up in the Hershey Sports Arena crowd, too. Bern Sharfman had been raised in New York City, where his father had manufactured ladies' underwear and often play-

fully crowed, "I'm in ladies' panties. I *pull down* twenty thousand a year."
Sharfman inherited his father's humor and became a comedy writer for a
time (it was Buffalo Bob Smith, host of the *Howdy Doody Show,* who first
suggested shortening his name from "Bernard" to "Bern") before he turned
to newspapers. Since moving to Harrisburg in 1954 from New York, Sharfman had come to Hershey infrequently, and he had his reasons. He found
the people of Hershey very insular. He believed that Jews, such as himself,
and blacks were not really welcome there. Friends in the area told Sharfman
in 1954 "that the two places you didn't try to live—if you were a Jew or
black—was the West Shore of Harrisburg or Hershey."

A twenty-three-year-old worker at Bethlehem Steel named Ted Russ
brought two weightlifter friends from the Harrisburg YMCA. They were
big, all three guys, each more than 240 pounds with Popeye biceps. The
steelworker had met Chamberlain once at the High Hat Club in Harrisburg.
He talked to the Dipper that night and found him friendly, much different
than when he'd seen from the grandstands the perpetually scowling Bill
Russell.

In the second row, directly across from the Warriors bench, sat a man in
a fine-looking suit. That was the reason he sat in the second row—his fine-
looking suit. He'd come from Harrisburg with a milkman and a bartender.
They bought three cheap tickets, a dollar and a quarter apiece, nosebleed
section, Peanut Heaven. The guy in the fine suit, unhappy with those seats,
talked to a manager in the ticket office. "Look," he said, "I've got two salesmen with me. I'm trying to make an impression. Can you help me out?"
Presto! Three seats, second row. Never mind that the salesman was not a
salesman at all. James Hayney was just out of the Navy, where he'd been a
sonar man on a destroyer, and now was a twenty-two-year-old student at
Harrisburg Junior College. He was tall, too, and when a kid in the crowd approached to ask, eyes hopeful, "Are you a basketball player?" he replied,
"Why, sure!" He signed an autograph—"Jim Hayney"—and then a few
more kids came to him. He signed their programs, too.

Then there was the remarkable case of the Italian brothers, two men in
their midforties, Ermo and Evo, regulars at Hershey hockey games every
Wednesday and Saturday. Hockey, Evo knew. Basketball, no. Baseball, Evo
had been to one of the great American games, once seen the New York Yankees and that had been six years before, during the 1956 World Series. His

boss had asked that morning, "Evo, how'd you like to see the Yankees this afternoon?" Evo said sure. They flew on the small company airplane—Evo had never been on a little airplane before, either—and landed at a small New Jersey airfield called Teterboro. Arthur Godfrey's plane was parked one spot over. A limousine took them to the game. Inevitably, as a man seeing his first baseball game, Evo declared it boring. Nothing happened until the Yankees catcher Yogi Berra jumped into the pitcher's arms. How odd! Evo heard someone say Don Larsen had just pitched a perfect game, whatever that was. So, like everyone else, he cheered. But he never went to another baseball game. Now he would give basketball one try.

Before you could hitch yourself to history for a ride that would last a lifetime, you had to be near enough to reach up and grab hold. Kerry Ryman, a fourteen-year-old chocolate factory worker's kid, stole in to the arena that night. *Hooking in,* he called it. Same as sneaking in. Ryman and his scamp buddies, carrying monikers such as Sandman, Bugs, and Spammer, could have scared up enough quarters for tickets, but what's the thrill in that?

Decades later Ryman and his rascal friends couldn't be certain which method they'd used to sneak into the Hershey arena on this night, so often had they done it. They might have slid through a window of an out-of-the-way lower-level dressing room. Or perhaps they trod softly through the un-patrolled room where the Zamboni ice-smoothing machine was parked. Failing in those stratagems, they might've pooled enough coins to buy a single ticket at $1.25. Then, when an usher's attention was diverted, the boy with the ticket would have propped open a door on the backside of the arena to let everyone in. They would have scattered to all points of the compass, perhaps temporarily to the men's room; there they would have shut the stall doors and, to keep sneakered feet out of sight, clambered atop the toilets. As insurance against removal from the arena, they kept an eye to the floor for dropped ticket stubs they could claim as their own on the off-chance of apprehension by one of Hershey's part-time constables, quasi-police officers in chocolate brown uniforms.

The constables knew the boys' routines. The boys knew the constables' routines. The boys generally kept a step ahead, scouting for unoccupied seats they would fill. When the arena lights dimmed for the national anthem, the boys made their moves. They jumped a railing and, at "rockets' red glare," were in their initial chosen seats. Of course, by game's end, they usually had worked their way down to the front rows.

What is certain is that on this night Kerry Ryman, the Sandman, Bugs, Spammer, and others, hooked in. Safely inside the arena, they calculated their next moves at the very moment Wilt Chamberlain came out onto the floor.

CHAPTER 3

First Quarter

REFEREE WILLIE SMITH BOUNCED the leather ball at midcourt, echoes reverberating in the big arena from the temporary hardwood floor. It was a Gotty type of floor, cheap and functional. Created in 1936 for roller skating, it clicked together in sections over an ice rink, tongue in groove, to be unclicked by morning for the Rochester Amerks–Hershey Bears minor league hockey game. As the starting fives took their positions for the opening tip, nothing in the players' fatigued movements or expressions suggested this night might be memorable. With the Dipper, the Warriors started guards Guy Rodgers and Al Attles and forwards Paul Arizin and Tom Meschery. Since September, the Warriors had played ninety games (including exhibitions), the Knicks eighty-seven. Muscles, knees, and lower backs ached. The two teams knew each other well, too well, this being their eleventh meeting of the season (Philadelphia led six games to four). Just this week, the Warriors had played the Knicks at Convention Hall on Sunday and shared a doubleheader in Chicago on Tuesday. They would play in Hershey on this night and again in Madison Square Garden on Sunday. They'd seen each other more often than they had seen their wives. The Warriors had all but memorized the tendencies of the Knicks starters, guards Richie Guerin and Al Butler, forwards Johnny Green and Willie Naulls and the young center, Darrall Imhoff. Players on both teams had little to prove, or so it seemed. According to *The New York Herald-Tribune*'s betting line, the Warriors in Hershey were eleven-point favorites.

Now, Smith tossed the ball in the air, and Wilt Chamberlain and the Knicks' Darrall Imhoff rose to meet it, the Dipper winning the opening tip, as he usually did, tapping the ball to Rodgers. The Dipper moved down the court in long, loping strides, his movements athletic, elegant, even with a sore lower back. He arrived, just as Imhoff expected, at the usual spot, down low, on the left side. Rodgers swung a pass to Paul Arizin in the corner. Arizin's low-line jumper would one day carry him into the Hall of Fame. This time, though, he missed. The Dipper rebounded and dunked for the game's first points, even before some fans had made it to their seats.

Back in pro basketball's Paleozoic age, even before there was Chamberlain, there was George Mikan. On a cold day in late November 1950, in a Northwestern Railroad club car, among officials of an NBA team bound for Minneapolis, a conspiracy was hatched. The intent was to stop Mikan, at six-foot-ten the most dominant big man in the pro game. The unintended result nearly toppled the NBA. Ultimately, the conspiracy caused a change in the pro game that would make possible the Dipper's night in Hershey twelve years later. It began in the club car with Fort Wayne Pistons Coach Murray Mendenhall laying out his plan for his general manager, Carl Bennett, saying, "We've never beaten Minneapolis in Minneapolis. Let's just sit on the ball tonight. Let's just hold it and maybe if we're lucky we can beat them in the last minute." Mendenhall knew his Pistons had struggled to penetrate the Lakers zone defense. He knew his team could not match up with Mikan or with Lakers forwards Vern Mikkelsen and Jim Pollard, especially at the Minneapolis Auditorium, where the two-time defending league champion Lakers had won twenty-nine consecutive games. At the hotel, during the Pistons pregame meal, Mendenhall offered his strategy to his players: They would stall. His players were game to try it.

That night 7,000 fans showed up to see Mikan score his usual twenty-eight points. Instead they saw Mendenhall's guards holding the ball. A standoff ensued. The Pistons held the ball for three minutes at a time and longer without shooting, waiting for the Lakers to come out of their zone defense with Mikan in the middle. Minneapolis players stared back, waiting. Fans booed loudly and stomped their feet like a thundering herd. They hurled objects toward the Pistons bench: oranges, crushed paper cups, a shoe. After the first quarter, Fort Wayne led 8-7. Worse than boring, this was shameless. Pennies and game programs flew onto the court. By halftime, the Lakers had edged ahead, 13-11. Catcalls rained down from the rafters. After three quarters, Mikan's Lakers maintained a one-point lead, 17-16. "PLAY THE GAME!!!!" fans shouted. Minneapolis Coach John Kundla repeatedly told his players not to worry about the Pistons: "Let them do what they want." No matter, Kundla believed his team would win. The booing grew louder, ear splitting. The foot stomping rolled through the old auditorium. On the court, Lakers guard Slater Martin asked Ft. Wayne's Boag Johnson, "Why are you doing this?" Holding the ball, Johnson replied, "Well, you're playing a zone." On and on it went. Trailing 18-17 with only nine seconds to play, the Pistons passed to center Larry Foust, whose second shot of the game, over Mikan's outstretched arms, went in for the game-winner: Fort Wayne, 19-18. Only four points were scored in the entire fourth quarter.

At game's end, Fort Wayne players raced jubilantly to the locker room but not before a pregnant woman pulled out an umbrella and used it to strike Pistons guard Johnny Oldham in the back of the head. Another fan hit him with a wet towel; Oldham turned and coldcocked that fan. In the locker room, Pistons players slapped backs and laughed. They waited thirty minutes longer than usual before leaving, to keep out of the crowd's sight. Mikan had been nullified by the strategy. He took eleven shots and scored fifteen of his team's eighteen points. The Pistons attempted thirteen shots, roughly one every four minutes. Disbelieving Lakers fans at home inundated local newspapers and radio stations with calls to confirm the lowest scoring game in league history. *The Minneapolis Tribune* headline the next morning blared: "Lakers Defeated 19-18; That's Correct, 19-18;" *The St. Paul Dispatch* called it "slow motion that would shame the movies." "[The Pistons] gave pro basketball a great big black eye," Kundla said in the locker room. "Many more games like that and we can shut up shop."

NBA President Maurice Podoloff agreed. He thought 19-18 a sham, a mockery. "I want to find out to what extent league rules were violated and, if they were, to take proper action," Podoloff said. "In our game, with the numbers of stars we have, we of necessity run up big scores." Podoloff called Mendenhall and Kundla to New York for a meeting. The problem didn't go away. Later in the season, Indianapolis defeated Rochester, 75-73, in a six-overtime NBA game: Stalling by both teams produced two scoreless overtime periods. So shameless did the stalling become, in one of those five-minute sessions, neither team even attempted a shot.

The larger issue, of course, was the league's struggle for credibility; the NBA could hardly afford to lose its few fans. Team owners aspired for a faster-paced game with both teams scoring one hundred points. That's what fans wanted. In the 1950–51 season, each NBA team averaged slightly more than eighty points per game. But the issue wasn't about points: It was about flow, excitement, gate receipts, *money*. Team owners, including Gotty, wanted the game to pick up speed. Their concerns about Mikan's domination—or domination by any big man in the future, for they knew there would be more—led to the widening of the lane from six feet to twelve feet the following year, forcing Mikan to move further from the basket. With the pro game on the brink of extinction, 19-18 was held up as a danger sign and spurred an even more dramatic rule change, one that liberated the game, saving it from Mendenhall's strategy, saving it from itself—teams must shoot within twenty-four seconds of gaining possession. No longer could such stalls happen; teams would be compelled to shoot before a twenty-four-second clock clicked to zero or give up possession of the ball. The idea belonged to Syracuse owner Danny Biasone. He had noticed that each team averaged about sixty shots per game and so he did the math: 120 total shots divided by 48 minutes (or 2,880 seconds) equals 24 seconds per shot. After foot-dragging and haggling among team owners, the rule was instituted for the 1954 season.

Immediately, scoring by NBA teams rose to ninety-three points per game, and within a few years attendance had jumped to 4,800 per game, an increase of more than 40 percent. Fans wanted scoring and the NBA provided it. A half-century later, Fort Wayne's Johnny Oldham vaguely recalled that on the night of the 19-18 debacle, seated in the front row of the Minneapolis Auditorium were the Three Stooges. There was no record that anyone else saw them. Still laughing about it into the twenty-first century, Oldham decided that if the Three Stooges did not come to the 19-18 game they should have.

Where Mikan stood like a statue amid falling pennies and oranges as two teams scored a scandalously low thirty-seven points, now in 1962 it was predicted that Wilt Chamberlain, on a glorious night when the planets aligned, would score one hundred points by himself in a game. His coach said it would happen. So did Jack Kiser, the chain-smoking Philly newshound. It was predicted even by the Lakers' Elgin Baylor, an elegant scoring stylist about whom once it was said "he has more moves than a clock," the same Baylor whose record seventy-one point game against the Knicks in 1960 prompted team owner Bob Short to buy his team silver cufflinks that read "71." That's how dramatically the shot clock, the influx of new talent, and the Dipper's own unique skill set had changed the NBA: It was as if a corral door opened and the horses were loosed.

The NBA game became wide-open, fast-paced, shots fired in rapid succession, defense (and shooting percentages) be damned. By the end of the Dipper's first season in 1959, NBA teams averaged 115 points per game, and by his third season, nearly 119 points. Superior offensive talents ascended in the NBA, and many, including Baylor, Robertson, and the Dipper, were black. Of course, playing against Baylor always stirred the Dipper to competitive heights. Sitting on the Convention Hall stage and watching the first game of a doubleheader on December 8, 1961, Chamberlain saw Baylor walking past with his travel bag. "Hey, big man," the Dipper called to him, "you hear the news? I'm covering you one-on-one tonight. Just me and you. I'm going to take you outside and kill you with my jump shot." Baylor smiled and replied, "I'm nervous enough before a game. Don't shake me up, buddy." The Dipper said, "You better be nervous. You're my pigeon tonight." In triple-overtime that night, the Dipper scored seventy-eight points to shatter Baylor's record. Nevertheless, his Warriors lost, 151-147, with the *pigeon* Baylor scoring sixty-three points of his own. After the Lakers' two centers fouled out, Coach Fred Schaus deployed forward Howie Jolliff, only six-foot-seven, and a box zone against Chamberlain, to little avail. The Dipper scored twenty-five points during the three five-minute overtime periods. In all, during the sixty-three-minute game, he made half of his sixty-two shots—the most shots anyone ever had taken in an NBA game—but only sixteen of thirty-one free throws. Had he made a few more baskets and a few more free throws he would have reached ninety points. Of course, his critics would happily note that even with seventy-eight points the Dipper had lost the game. Afterwards, Coach Frank McGuire praised his center. "I think he played a great game," he said. "And I think he would have scored a hundred if he wasn't playing against a four-man defense. But I'll make this prediction: One of these days Wilt is going to score a hundred. Even against a five-man defense."

Chamberlain later told *The Philadelphia Evening Bulletin* sports columnist Sandy Grady that a hundred-point night was possible. "Someday I could do it if I were relaxed, cool, and had a terrific night when all the shots are dropping." "Hey, don't worry about it," Baylor told Lakers broadcaster Chick Hearn about his former scoring record, while taking a long drag on a cigarette. "The Big Fella is going to get one hundred one night real soon."

Now, in Hershey, Knicks guard Richie Guerin dribbled the ball near the top of the circle, searching for a small space through which to knife into the lane. That was Richie Guerin's style—always on the attack. In Hershey, Guerin would find a way inside. Through attitude alone, the all-star Guerin commanded attention at every moment. Not so with his teammate, forward Willie Naulls. Naulls was quieter, smoother. He moved now to the outside, virtually unseen. So smooth was Willie Naulls's game, so accurate his shot, he could score twenty points before breaking his first sweat. Guerin and Naulls carried the Knicks nightly. Earlier in the week, Guerin had scored fifty points and Naulls thirty-three to lead the Knicks past the Warriors in Philly. That afternoon Guerin had driven into the lane repeatedly, slashing in from odd angles. If the Dipper had moved in his way, Guerin passed to Naulls in the corner or to his center underneath. He kept probing, daring, and attacking. Guerin argued a call by a rookie referee with such vehemence that day you could hear him in Convention Hall's $1.25 cheap seats. That was Richie Guerin. One way or another, his voice would be heard.

Anyone who would score one hundred points in a game must have superior scoring talent and the inclination to use it as a bludgeon. At the same time, the opposition must be vulnerable where the scorer is strongest. But first, his teammates must give him the ball. At the center of the last is the scorer's relationship with his coach and teammates; they must want him to succeed and must be willing to help him. On this night in Hershey, as on all nights, Guy Rodgers was eminently willing, and able, to be the Dipper's accomplice. Passing was what Rodgers did best, sleight of hand, behind the back, over the shoulder, running the fast break with Attles and the Dipper or operating more deliberately in a half-court offense with Arizin, Tom Meschery, and the Dipper. Rodgers's passing skill, ofttimes breathtaking, had accounted for more than 1,700 assists over the past three seasons, the lion's share to the Dipper. Barely six feet tall, stubby in build, Rodgers was the shortest starting player in the NBA. He often practiced his dribbling and passing repertoire alone in the gym, using a chair. He imagined the chair as Bill Russell and dribbled at it, feinting one way and passing high the other way, to an imagined Dipper. He knew the Dipper's great strengths and how to take advantage of them. Rodgers was careening through an uneven season, moments of brilliance followed inexplicably by poor play. The Warriors' official scorer, Dave Richter, checking Rodgers into games, often said, "Good luck, 'Shake Hips,' " and the nickname seemed apt given the way Rodgers moved on the court, accelerating and decelerating, swiveling and whirling. But Rodgers had what his college teammate Hal Lear called *rabbit ears*. Any catcall from the crowd, Guy Rodgers heard it. The heckling preyed on his substantial self-doubt. Rodgers's playmaker role on the team was understood: Get the ball to Wilt—thread the needle, bounce it, or lob it high, whatever it took. Sometimes, McGuire thought Rodgers dribbled too much. To make the point, McGuire once snuck a deflated basketball into practice. "Okay, Guy," he said, "play with that one awhile." Rodgers would average eight assists per game for the season, better than Cousy, second in the league to Oscar Robertson's eleven. On this night, his passing would be masterful. Guy Rodgers would serve as Chamberlain's supply line to one hundred.

Let us now examine the Dipper in the flow of the Warriors half-court offense. Nearly always he sought to position himself in the most advantageous position: down low, on the left side, for he was right-handed. He stood inches beyond the lane, where he couldn't be penalized for violating the rule that forbids players to loiter in the area beneath the basket for as long as three seconds. In his favorite position, the Dipper loomed dangerously only six feet from the center of the basket. So tall and elastic was he, with one mammoth and unimpeded lunge toward the middle, he could reach the hoop and drop the ball through it. More often, though, he would take a large step backward, away from the basket, for his favorite fall-away bank shot from twelve to fifteen feet. When forced by opposing defenses to the right side of the basket, the Dipper fancied a different finesse shot: a finger-roll in which he stepped toward the basket, raising his arm toward it, opening his palm to the sky as if releasing a dove, and letting the ball roll delicately off his fingertips.

Now in Hershey, at his preferred spot, down low, six feet to the left of the basket, Chamberlain stood with the ball in his enormous hands, Darrall Imhoff pressed against his spine. New York gave its young center defensive help. The Knicks guards, Butler and Guerin, flashed in front of the Dipper. Forwards Green and Naulls sagged into the middle, just in case. Holding the ball high over his head, Chamberlain leaned back with his upper torso. Reduced to a recoiled position, Imhoff felt as if a tree were about to fall on him. Imhoff thrust his right forearm into Chamberlain's upper back, the point of his elbow delivering a message between the Dipper's shoulder blades. Imhoff also placed his right foot between Chamberlain's spread legs, and his left foot just to the outside of Chamberlain's left foot, to keep him from turning into the middle, toward the basket. But Chamberlain kept acting as if Imhoff wasn't even there. The Dipper made his first five shots. The Warriors broke to a 19-3 lead with Chamberlain scoring thirteen points. McGuire, in his fine suit, handkerchief folded neatly in his breast pocket, looked pleased. "Attaboy, Wiltie!" he said.

The game's pace was up-tempo, like a flash flood, Rodgers and Guerin controlling the flow, whenever possible fast breaking, or in the parlance of the game, *running-and-gunning*. Precious little defense was played on either side, not unusual in late-season NBA games. Both teams seemed in a hurry to finish the game, and the regular season. Referees Willie Smith and Pete D'Ambrosio kept watch. Typically neither worked as lead official, that being the privileged domain of Sid Borgia, Mendy Rudolph, Norm Drucker, Jim Duffy, Joe Gushue, Richie Powers, and Earl Strom. Because the NBA paid its officials stingily, all of them held other jobs. NBA referees worked seventy games a year or more, and so with just nine teams, they knew the players well. They would see them one night in Boston, the next in New York, and sometimes they even traveled on the same plane or train. They faced rough crowds. In Syracuse a fan smacked Gushue in the head with a newspaper as he walked off the court. "Did you see that?" Gushue asked a police officer. "The way you called the game," the cop said, "no one saw anything."

Smith and D'Ambrosio worked this contest because both lived nearby, saving the league travel expenses. Smith, earning $120 for this game, lived in Reading and D'Ambrosio, earning $90, in Philadelphia. D'Ambrosio soon would leave for Florida where he worked as a spring training umpire for major league baseball. Smith, on the other hand, worked only basketball. Players knew him as "Woozie" Smith and sometimes shared drinks with him at bars. To his fellow referees, Smith seemed somewhat of a neat freak: never a hair out of place, his clothes always folded neatly on hangers. He even brought his own brown paper to stand on in locker rooms, to keep his feet dry. A stubby five-foot-eight, Woozie Smith liked a sense of order in his basketball games, too.

The Dipper was in the flow of the game early, aggressively seeking the ball. Imhoff silently wished a stronger lead official was working this game, perhaps Strom or Rudolph or Powers. The Dipper backed into Imhoff again, pushing him out of position. Woozie Smith whistled Imhoff for his third foul against Chamberlain. Imhoff thought, *This is ridiculous. Why am I not allowed in here?* The Knicks' young center, in a dither, snapped at the referee, "Well, why don't you just give the guy a hundred now and we'll all go home!"

Saint Gola, as Warriors teammates playfully called their captain, Tom Gola, had been aware of Wilt Chamberlain from nearly the beginning. He'd seen the Dipper's star aborning back in Philly when they were both just kids, and now, as professionals, they were teammates. Resting his sprained lower back now at home, Gola, with a beer in hand and hoping to be ready for the start of the playoffs two weeks hence, listened to Bill Campbell's call on WCAU.

Many Philadelphians viewed Tom Gola as an embodiment of basketball perfection or nearly so; he was a local hero, their own Jack Armstrong, cut from the same celebrated cloth as the 1950 Phillies Whiz Kids, the greatest homegrown star in Philadelphia college basketball history. Gola was a one-time Olney altar boy and three-time all-American who, as NCAA player of the year, led La Salle to the 1954 NCAA title. Gola knew his value and as a rookie in 1955 told Gottlieb he wanted $17,500 a year. "No way," Gotty said, and offered $11,500. Finally, Gotty said, "You're a local kid so we'll have a night for you, and you'll get enough in gifts to get your seventeen thousand five hundred dollars." Gotty convinced local merchants to donate to Gola a few fine suits and a custom Dodge Royal Lancer. Everyone was happy, even Gotty, especially when his Warriors won the NBA title in Gola's rookie season.

The son of a Philadelphia cop, Izzy Gola, who left the police force after a shootout to work as a liquor store clerk, Tom Gola was a natural as Warriors team captain. He played hard, played hurt, and played for the team. His teammates respected him, his toughness, and essential integrity. Gola was the consummate team player: a six-foot-six forward asked to play guard and doing so without a gripe. He had played with league scoring champions such as Arizin and Neil Johnston and now Chamberlain. "Wilt was Philadelphia, I was Philadelphia," Gola would say. They shared the same city, but little else. "He had his agenda and I had mine."

They had played in a summer league game many summers before, Gola already at La Salle, the Dipper only a ninth grader. Gola thought him gangly then; the Dipper's coordination was not yet fully in place. "He wasn't a player." But the young Chamberlain left his mark on him that day, literally, with an accidental elbow that put a small dent in the bridge of Gola's nose. Gola had not seen the Dipper in more than six years when, in fall 1959, he arrived as a rookie at the Warriors training camp in Hershey. What Gola saw made him gasp. He noticed that Chamberlain had grown massive, especially in his shoulders and arms. *He's huge,* Gola thought, *absolutely huge.* The Dipper would so completely take over the Warriors offense that the Lakers Rod Hundley once saw Gola, before a game, throwing a ball absent-mindedly against the wall of the locker room. "What are you doing?" Hundley asked. Gola said, "Practicing our offense—throw the ball to Wilt and then stand there." Tom Gola had his own game, his own pride, but he submitted to Coach Frank McGuire's wishes. In Hershey, Gola heard the first quarter end, the Warriors leading, 42-26. The Dipper had made half of his fourteen shots and all nine free throws for twenty-three points. Already Chamberlain was thinking about a record—for most free throws (twenty-four) made in an NBA game. Back in Philadelphia, Gola was thinking about a second beer. He walked to a neighbor's house. There he would have his beer and listen to the rest of the game on radio.

CHAPTER 4

The Rise of the Dipper

OUT OF THE CRAMPED OVERBROOK HIGH School gym in west Philadelphia, Wilt Chamberlain's urban legend grew. His coach, Cecil Mosenson, only twenty-two years old, had left the back of his father's delivery truck filled with bagels and rye bread to coach his alma mater. Mosenson's parents were Rumanian Jews who wanted only for their son "to be a good boy." Fiery and competitive as a Temple University player, Mosenson, as Overbrook's new coach, quickly faced power struggles with Dippy Chamberlain. The young Dipper once ran onto the court for pregame warm-ups wearing a scarf, a beret, and dark sunglasses; he even shot a few layups in that getup. "Get out of here and take that off!" Mosenson screamed. Chamberlain assented, but once the game started, he refused to shoot. Mosenson benched him, saying, "If you're not going to shoot, you're not going to play." Without him, Overbrook struggled. "All right," Mosenson said minutes later from the bench, "are you ready to play?" No answer. In went Chamberlain. He still would not shoot. Out came Chamberlain. As a tight game reached its final minutes, Overbrook fans wondered what was happening with Dippy (*Is he sick? Hurt? Why does Dippy look so angry?*). Mosenson returned him to the game. Chamberlain took over, shooting and scoring at will, and Overbrook won. In the locker room afterwards, Mosenson fumed at his star: "You're not going to pull that crap on me ever again!" Mosenson thought, *He's testing me.*

Chamberlain's local legend had started with whispers: "There's this big kid named Wilt going to the 'Brook." Of course, in the early Fifties, *big* usually meant six-foot-five. The Dipper towered over his opponents at Overbrook, few of them taller than six-foot-four, and averaged more than forty-five points per game as a senior. Whenever his teammates encountered trouble on offense, they knew to blindly heave the ball toward the basket, certain Dippy somehow would grab it.

His performances generated barbershop conversations and sensational headlines in Philadelphia. Broadcaster Bill Campbell and NBA referee Pete D'Ambrosio felt compelled to see the Dipper play at Overbrook and came away impressed. One summer, Hal Lear, star guard at Temple University, received a call from a white friend in northeast Philly, hoping to arrange a game. "I want you to come up here and play us. I'm going to have Tommy [Gola] with me." So Lear replied, "Okay, well, I'm going to have a decent team, too." Lear said he would bring Guy Rodgers, his Temple teammate, and Overbrook's Dippy Chamberlain. Word of the game spread across town. When Chamberlain stepped from a car at A and Champlost in north Philadelphia for the game, Lear saw people gathered in the streets, awestruck, pointing at the Dipper and saying, "Woooooh!" Lear watched front doors thrown open and neighbors pouring into the gym to see if the legend of the young Philadelphia giant was true.

At Overbrook, meanwhile, the girls were swept up by the Chamberlain phenomenon. "How big is Wilt?" they asked Dave Shapiro, the only white player in Overbrook's starting lineup. "Six-eleven," Shapiro said. "No, you see him in the locker room," the girls said, suggestively. "How *big* is he?" The Dipper's fame at Overbrook once saved Shapiro from a tense racial confrontation in the school's hallway. A group of eight black classmates stood in front of Shapiro and another Jewish classmate, holding the classmate's sneakers. "Give him back his sneaks—he needs them for gym," Shapiro ordered. They refused and baited Shapiro: "And what are you going to do about it?" A showdown at hand, one of the black students recognized Shapiro as a basketball player. "Hey, wait a minute. This guy plays with Dippy," he said, stepping forward. He handed over the sneakers and apologized. "We're sorry, man. We didn't mean anything by it. Don't tell Dippy, okay?"

Overbrook lost just once in 1954–55, Chamberlain's senior year, a pre-season game in Johnstown, Pennsylvania, that ended with a referee's controversial call. Overbrook players returned to their locker room that night enraged. They dented lockers with their fists. Shapiro saw the Dipper pull from his satchel a BB gun the size of a pistol and shoot the wire-glass window in the locker room, chipping off pieces of glass. In preparation for a game against Chamberlain, the West Catholic High School coach stood one of his players atop a chair during practice and asked him to swat at shots with a broom. Meanwhile, Joe Goldenberg, star guard of West Philadelphia High, scouted an Overbrook game, and when his coach asked, "Where does Chamberlain shoot from?" Goldenberg answered honestly: "Mainly from above the rim." When Overbrook and West Philadelphia High played, a fight broke out on the court. Fans stood, many preparing to join the fight, but only until the Dipper, after separating the combatants, raised his arms at center court and motioned for fans to sit down. Miraculously, they did. Cecil Mosenson had never seen anything like it. Dippy Chamberlain was like a messiah.

The Dipper learned the nuances of basketball—and nightclubs—when he left Philadelphia for the University of Kansas and entered a segregated society in Lawrence, Kansas. He honed his game against double- and triple-teaming, drew huge crowds and, occasionally, racial taunts. Just as the NBA had legislated rule changes to diminish the dominance of six-foot-ten Lakers center George Mikan with his perceived unfair height advantage, the NCAA altered some of its game rules to slow the Dipper, including offensive goaltending (players now were forbidden to guide a teammate's shot into the hoop) and free-throw shooting. Kansas Coach Forrest "Phog" Allen had bragged that the freshman Chamberlain would become the first player to make every free throw; the Dipper, with a running start, would leap from behind the free-throw line and dunk his foul shots. The NCAA reacted to Allen's boasting by mandating a player's feet must be behind the free-throw line when the ball is released.

At Kansas, the Dipper's focus was not on the classroom. Discus thrower Al Oerter, winner of gold medals for four consecutive Olympics from 1956

to 1968, shared a business class with Chamberlain at KU. He always noticed
when Chamberlain was there, which by Oerter's estimate was "one out of
ten [classes]." Oerter looked up from his final examination and saw a small
white student signing his name on the exam as "Wilt Chamberlain." Oerter
whispered to the student, "Somehow you don't look like Wilt." Oerter
trained with Chamberlain during Kansas's outdoor track and field season;
they shared side-by-side lockers. The Dipper's strength and massive skeletal
structure impressed Oerter. Chamberlain wanted to become a decathlete,
no doubt to prove his strength and endurance in the most physically de-
manding of Olympic events. The Kansas track coach asked Oerter to in-
struct the Dipper how to throw the discus. Because of his height,
Chamberlain struggled with the throwing motion, though his raw power
amazed Oerter. He also saw that when Chamberlain placed his hand on a
sixteen-pound shot, his fingers wrapped around it and touched his palm.
These would become problems for the Dipper if he hoped to become a
world-class decathlete. (The pole vault event especially worried Chamberlain: "I'd get way up there, then find myself with a lot of legs.") After a
workout in spring 1957, Oerter saw the roly-poly Abe Saperstein appear in
the locker room beneath the KU stadium. He heard Saperstein offer Chamberlain one-third ownership of the Globetrotters if he signed with the team
at that moment. Eavesdropping, Oerter heard the Dipper say he wasn't interested, at least not yet.

　　Chamberlain found his escape from Jim Crow segregation in Lawrence
by driving to the vibrant African-American community in Kansas City, a city
known in the 1930s as the Paris of the Plains. There, Maurice King, his lone
black teammate at KU and a native of Kansas City, showed him the nightclubs along 18th and Vine, a street corner immortalized in song by Joe
Turner as being where "The boys jump and swing until broad daylight." For
the Dipper, Kansas City was a revelation. With King, he heard jazz jam sessions at nightclubs such as the Blue Room and El Capitan, played summer
basketball games down the street at the Negro YMCA, and met former
Kansas City Monarchs of the Negro baseball leagues Buck O'Neil, Satchel
Paige, and Wilbur "Bullet" Rogan. He also met the colorful former Globetrotter Goose Tatum. King once had seen Tatum being chauffeured by his
wife down 18th Street—well, actually he saw only Tatum's bare feet sticking out the back of his convertible. As a kid, Chamberlain had idolized

Tatum and relished the chance to know him. Tatum had a deft hook shot and, after converting one, was known to ask his opponent, "How'd you like that, young white boy?" He let the Dipper drive his car a few times, and together they made a trip to Detroit, Tatum's hometown.

At KU, Chamberlain briefly hosted his own radio show, "Flippin' with the Dipper," where he spun his favorite records, mostly jazz and the blues. (Years earlier, KU basketball star Clyde Lovellette had a show at the same radio station and played country music and was accompanied by Lester, his mythical hound dog.) King remembers that the Dipper's arrival challenged segregated practices at the movie theater and lunch counters in Lawrence. Before, King and his Kappa Alpha Psi fraternity brothers had been forced to sit in a section of the theater reserved for blacks. But when the Dipper joined the fraternity, "Nobody ever asked us to leave or refused us service," King would say. "They really wanted to cater to Wilt." Once, as Chamberlain drove along the new turnpike en route to Kansas City, a police car's flashing blue lights appeared behind his souped-up red and white Oldsmobile convertible. Sitting next to the Dipper, King tensed but only until the police officer, realizing it was Wilt Chamberlain's car, turned off his lights and drove away. Chamberlain would say often over the ensuing years, "I single-handedly integrated Kansas," and counted it among his proudest achievements. In truth, his was an integration of one. Because of his celebrity Chamberlain was granted honorary "white" status in Lawrence, but his actions did not diminish racial segregation there in any lasting way.

Saperstein got his man in 1958. Kansas Coach Dick Harp was working in his yard when the Dipper drove up. Chamberlain's car was already packed. He told Harp he had accepted an offer from Saperstein. He thanked Harp and left for Saperstein's one-year contract that, with guarantees, would pay him $65,000; this at a time when the average NBA player's salary was less than $10,000. With the Globetrotters, Chamberlain entered a world of slapstick entertainment, a basketball minstrel show. He made that choice for a simple reason—money. As racial strife in the South intensified, the Globetrotters performed yuk-it-up comedy that white crowds, particularly in the South, found comforting and unthreatening. With the Trotters, the Dipper joined teammates nicknamed Gipper and Ripper. He became a seven-foot-one guard and played so many games in his unwashed sweaty uniform that he wore Band-Aids over his nipples to keep the skin from rubbing raw. He reveled in the camaraderie with teammates. On bus trips, he was known to open two cans of salmon, two loaves of bread, and two cartons of milk and pass them around. He tried to blend in on the court with the more established Globetrotters stars but only until Saperstein showed up in the locker room at halftime to make a plea to his big-money gate attraction: "You gotta shoot more, Wilt. You gotta score." He traveled to Milan and Moscow and Germany and Switzerland, drawing attention from foreigners who had never seen a man so tall and impressing them by lifting the backs of cars to announce his strength. He chased women of all different races and nations along the way. That's what the Globetrotters did, Chamberlain quickly learned, first and foremost. *The greatest girl hounds I've ever seen.* The Globetrotters called their comedy acts "reams." If a Globetrotter spotted a pretty woman in the crowd, he'd write his name, hotel, and room number on a slip of paper, hide it in his mouth or in his jockstrap, and connive a ream to approach the pretty woman whereupon he would secretly hand her the note—"dropping the bomb," they called it. The Dipper began to see himself as an entertainer. Playing in Germany on a plywood floor laid atop a dusty soccer field, Chamberlain watched five-foot-seven Louis "Red" Klotz steal the ball from him and chortle, "You're in my country now, Wilt." But moments later Klotz fell to the floor, dust swirling all around him, and suddenly he felt a big shoe on his back. Klotz looked up and saw Wilt towering over him and saying, "Now you're in my country, Red."

"I need you for a couple hours tonight," Ike Richman told his son, in May 1959. Richman hated to drive, but his boy, Mike, still in high school, had obtained his driver's license—a ready-made chauffeur. "Drive me to 4700 North Broad Street," Richman said. As they pulled away from their home in the Melrose Park area of Philadelphia, Ike Richman said, cryptically, "When we get there make a U-turn and pull over." His son didn't ask any questions, not even, "Why, Dad?" Ike Richman was that kind of father, that kind of man. You didn't ask him questions—you answered his. Richman was Eddie Gottlieb's attorney and friend. He was smart, definitive, and combustible. His son drove him to 4700 North Broad Street in Philadelphia, a commercial district in transition. He made a U-turn and pulled over. They waited. Soon a white Cadillac convertible pulled up. Ike Richman got out of his car and told his son, "Wait here. I'll be back." The son couldn't tell who was driving the Cadillac as his father opened the front door and got inside. The Cadillac drove off. In the darkness, the son waited for more than an hour. The Cadillac returned, Ike Richman got out and waved to the man inside as he drove off. He got back into his own car. "Let's go home," Ike Richman said. They drove home in silence until finally the father said, "Mike, I just worked as hard as I've ever worked in my life." The son replied, "Yeah?" Ike Richman nodded. "Yeah," he said. "I just convinced Wilt Chamberlain to play for the Warriors."

A man of big appetites, the Dipper liked adding notches in his belt. That's what all of those points were, and his women, too—notches—a way to define himself, a way to keep score of his manhood and put a sheen on his celebrity.

Chamberlain had learned about the pursuit of women from the masters, the Globetrotters. When they weren't trying to get laughs, the Globies were trying to get laid. Saperstein didn't want his players to date white women, fearing white fans might resent it. (The Globies sometimes dated white women, anyway.) They had their own terminology: blacks were *rocks*, whites were *you-alls*, and ugly women were *mullions*. If spotted with a mullion by a teammate, a Globetrotter fled or simply claimed later, "That wasn't me." The Dipper fell in step with them, happily and devotedly. He learned their tricks, and now, liberated by fame and wealth, he took them a step further. He had become bigger than the Globetrotters. He could do this solo now. He didn't need a team.

The Dipper was young and frisky, full of life, and full of himself. It seemed that everything belonged to him, and he took it. Women were attracted to him. He was famous. He had the aphrodisiacs of money, size, mystery. As a New York City high school basketball star then known as Lew Alcindor, Kareem Abdul-Jabbar was befriended by the Dipper. He became a regular at Big Wilt's Smalls Paradise and often visited his apartment near Central Park. There, he was awed by the Dipper's collection of jazz records and his collection of beautiful women, one more lovely than the last: once, a blonde, blue-eyed Dane, the next time a beauty in a form-fitting Danskin "with thighs that made me want to cry on the spot." Out on the town, the Dipper would place himself in a woman's view, make eye contact from

across the room, and hope she would come to him. Short of that, he would
send a go-between, ofttimes using a go-fer hanging by his side (a role filled
deftly at Smalls Paradise by Charlie Polk). The Dipper had his charm. Introduced to a woman whose affections he sought, he flirted and teased. He
kept her on the edge of not knowing what to say by being slightly rude. Self-
assured, and physically imposing, Chamberlain stood nearly two feet taller
than many women. He'd try to convince a woman that sex was an experience not to be missed. Here was the Dipper's theory: "If we lust in earnest
for each other, that's *real* and we should act on this, because how many real
things *are* there in life?"

His teammates rarely saw Chamberlain with women, not because he
wasn't with women, but because they rarely saw him at all. Gola had seen a
young white woman waiting for Chamberlain after a few home games.
Interracial dating in 1962 was widely considered social taboo—in sixteen
states, mostly in the South, interracial *marriage* remained against the law—
and his white teammates noticed that some of the Dipper's dates were
white. (In their telling of stories decades later, they considered this fact significant enough to point out.) The rookie Frank Radovich knew of Chamberlain's womanizing and heard teammates wisecrack about his peccadilloes:
"Guess we won't see Wilt until game time tonight. Hope he can still
walk . . ."

Once, Chamberlain's pursuit of women created tension with a teammate. On a flight back from the Midwest, he and Tom Meschery hooked up
with two white stewardesses. The women suggested a double date, the Dipper suggested Big Wilt's Smalls Paradise, and it was so arranged. They
would meet at the stewardesses' hotel. Though a rookie, Meschery, a.k.a.
The Mad Russian, had a game, linguistic fluency, and a heritage that impressed nearly everyone. Meschery (pronounced *Meh-shair-ree*) was infused
with the San Francisco spirit. He had a longshoreman's swagger and rough-
and-tumble attitude and an intellect to befit the bohemian café crowd. Born
in Manchuria and descended from Czarist Russian nobility, Meschery
counted on his family tree cousin Leo Tolstoy, who, it was said, had been
kicked out of the house by Meschery's grandmother because she thought
him godless. Meschery spoke French and Russian fluently (prompting Tom
Gola to say, "You don't hear *that* from the guys on the streets of Philadelphia!"), and he liked to discuss literature and world politics. A few of Mesch-

ery's white teammates heard about his planned double date with Chamberlain and teased him. They called him *Wilt's boy* and *Wilt's pimp.* Their teasing had a sharp metallic edge. There was a cutting message in it: *You've overstepped yourself, rook.* Meschery cared about perceptions within the team, particularly what the veterans thought. He felt mocked. He decided to back out of the double date; he gave Chamberlain a made-up excuse, and then the Dipper got a phone call from his date, canceling. Meschery showed up at the hotel at the appointed hour, anyway, because . . . well, there was still a stewardess waiting for him.

What happened next stunned him. Greeting his date at the hotel, Meschery saw, looming on the far side of the lobby, Wilt Chamberlain. The Dipper silently watched his every move. Meschery froze, unsure of what to do, how to proceed. He felt himself shrinking from the Dipper's glare. Suddenly, Chamberlain turned and walked out. The next day in the locker room, he confronted Meschery, not angrily or with shouted threats but with patience and forbearance. This was a side of the Dipper that Meschery had never seen. "Why did you do that last night?" Chamberlain asked. Meschery struggled to answer. Teammates, Meschery said, had pressured him and laughed at him. He didn't want to cause problems or friction. The Dipper listened. He thought Meschery had backed out for racial reasons. Finally he spoke. "I want you to look at this skin"—he touched his own hand—"and then look at your hand. Now look at my hand. We're exactly the same, just a different color." The Dipper did not raise his voice, made no physical threat. That would have been much easier for Meschery. This was worse, an intellectual threat, an intellectual shout-down. Chamberlain was scolding him as if he were an unschooled child who needed to be chastised. He seemed nearly sympathetic, as if he felt sorry for Meschery. He said, "I'm not angry with you." Sitting in the locker room, alone with the Dipper, Meschery was certain of only one thing—this was not one of his own finest moments. He interrogated himself: Was it that he was embarrassed to go to Harlem? Was it that he was unwilling to go out with a black man and a white woman? Or was it simply a rookie's buckling to the peer pressure of his teammates' whispered jeers, *Wilt's boy* and *Wilt's pimp?* Whatever it was, Meschery knew he had succumbed to it. The exchange brought him a deeper realization, an epiphany: His West Coast liberal façade was nothing more than that, a façade. Certain moments in life change you, Meschery decided, and cause you to grow up. This was one of them. He was indebted to Chamberlain for that. In a new way, Chamberlain had shown himself the bigger man. This experience "allowed us to be truthful with one another," Meschery would say. "Wilt and I became more friendly, not less friendly."

The Dipper's basketball exploits played against the backdrop of the larger drama of race in America. The Freedom Rides rolled across the South. The nation's black leaders cheered President Kennedy for his civil rights promises but complained about his slowness to deliver on them. Jackie Robinson, in his ghostwritten editorial page column in *The Amsterdam News* in Harlem, expressed his frustration: "We think that the President is a fine man, like we said. But Abraham Lincoln he ain't." In Philadelphia, 400 black ministers led their congregations in a Selective Patronage Program to boycott Tasty Baking Company pies and cakes and then Sunoco and Gulf gas until more African-Americans were hired to prestigious jobs. From Harlem, James Baldwin wrote, "For the Northerner . . . Negroes represent nothing to him personally, except, perhaps, the dangers of carnality. He never sees Negroes. Southerners see them all the time. Northerners never think about them whereas Southerners are never really thinking of anything else. Negroes are, therefore, ignored in the North and are under surveillance in the South, and suffer hideously in both places. Neither the Southerner nor the Northerner is able to look on the Negro as simply a man."

The race issue was aboil in America, and it pulsated, too, beneath the surface of professional sports. For black athletes, Jackie Robinson remained the standard-bearer. Robinson had persevered and come through the slurs and the rage, keeping his deportment, performing like an all-star. Robinson had, in his way, presaged King's nonviolent movement, putting a face on the black struggle for assimilation in America. Even as a businessman now, as director of personnel for a chain of coffee shops called Chock Full o'Nuts, Robinson remained, in the deepest sense, a race man. He gave speeches and raised funds for the NAACP, led civil rights marches in Washington, traveled to racially tense spots in the South, addressed discrimination in public housing in Rhode Island, and hosted his own radio show in New York City. He had supported Republican Richard Nixon in the 1960 presidential campaign, rising up against bigoted southern Democrats, but also had lobbied in the 1960 Democratic presidential primary in Wisconsin for the candidacy of

Hubert Humphrey, playing both sides, as perhaps only Jackie Robinson could. A week before the hundred-point game in Hershey, Robinson appeared at an NAACP rally before 4,000 in Jackson, Mississippi, where his most fervent hope of enlisting other famous black athletes in the civil rights cause finally came to fruition, with the participation of boxer Archie Moore and the young baseball outfielder Curt Flood. ("Is there a medal anywhere which is worth a man's dignity?" Robinson wrote.) Of course, Robinson had the protection of a supportive boss at Chock Full o'Nuts who effectively subsidized his civil rights work.

In contrast to Robinson's full engagement in the civil rights movement, the Dipper, like most young professional black athletes in 1962, was more a spectator of the movement than a participant. (Few white athletes at the time engaged in political or social issues, either.) In one instance when Chamberlain had become active, in spring 1960, he provided a caveat: Upon agreeing to serve as honorary chairman of the annual membership drive for the Philadelphia branch of the National Association for the Advancement of Colored People, he made clear to local NAACP leaders that he was lending only his name, not his time. Attorney A. Leon Higginbotham, president of the NAACP branch in Philadelphia, thanked the Dipper for serving as "titular head of the drive intended to make democracy a reality throughout America and throughout our State," and then reassured, "We hope to keep those contacts [with you] to a minimum." In another instance, he contributed in a quieter way: While building his Villa Chamberlain apartment complex in Los Angeles, he privately insisted that only black contractors and subcontractors be hired. In all ways, the Dipper did what he wanted, and from afar others decided what his action, or inaction, meant.

After his record-breaking rookie season, he had stunned the Warriors by announcing his retirement from the NBA, and he suggested race was partly to blame. Chamberlain insisted he had no problems with his teammates. But he said he was getting beaten up on the court by opposing players and that if he responded in kind and became embroiled in fistfights "it would reflect on me and then indirectly on my race."

This comment made Boston's Bob Cousy blanch: "In my ten years in the NBA, I never saw any evidence of racial prejudice. There are over one hundred Negro players who have either tried out or made positions with clubs in the league and I have never heard such a similar complaint from them. Chamberlain feels he's being pushed around more than anyone in the league. The guy has only averaged thirty-six points per game, broken rebound records and had more foul shots than anyone else. How easy does he want it? . . . Wilt is the biggest complainer ever to hit the NBA. Standing six feet one inch, it is difficult for me to feel sorry for a man seven feet tall." The Dipper's reply: "Maybe if Bill Russell said it, I'd pay attention. But Cousy has never encountered the problems that we have."

The Dipper had announced his retirement while sitting in the locker room, only moments after the Warriors had been eliminated from the playoffs by Boston. He expressed interest in touring again with the Globetrotters. Only days before this startling retirement announcement, over lunch, Gotty had offered him a new three-year contract, telling the Dipper he had earned it with his performance as the NBA Rookie of the Year and Most Valuable Player and also for increasing attendance at Warriors games by twenty-three percent. The Dipper's suggestion that he was retiring as a way to keep from discrediting his race was less than credible. Even Jackie Robinson, in a newspaper column, wrote, "If Wilt is worrying about the effect on anyone other than himself, I'd suggest that he forget about it. Great numbers of Negro athletes have had good years and bad years in their fields and the race has continued to progress. There have been fights before and there will be fights again." Besides, Robinson wrote, "I look for him to change his mind . . . I have a hunch that Wilt is not only a great basketball player, but a fine businessman as well. He is certainly in a position to use his tremendous draw as a means to exact more favorable terms for next season from the Warriors."

As it was, the Dipper retired for long enough to tour Europe with the Globetrotters. He returned to the Warriors in time for his second NBA season and signed a three-year contract with Gotty that rivaled the largest in all of professional team sports—Willie Mays's $85,000-a-year deal with the San Francisco Giants. Upon his return, the Dipper explained how he'd talked with family, friends, and "leaders of my race" and decided, "It would be better for me and I could do more good for my race if I played rather than if I retired."

Racial barriers remained in sports. In the college ranks, the South's three most prominent athletic conferences—the Atlantic Coast, Southeastern, and Southwest—had yet to desegregate. In the nation's capital, the

Washington Redskins remained the NFL's last all-white team. In Philadelphia, the Phillies had been the final team in the National League with a black player, a full decade after Jackie Robinson first joined the Dodgers. Even now, the NAACP branch in Philadelphia threatened to boycott the Phillies to protest the team's continuing use of a segregated motel at spring training in Clearwater, Florida. This arrangement relegated the Phillies' five black players to living in private homes in the black section of town.

A dozen years after the color barrier was broken in 1950, the NBA now had thirty-seven black players, roughly one-third of the total, and more than double the percentage of black players in either Major League Baseball or the National Football League. Referee Pete D'Ambrosio worked an NBA game in 1961–62 featuring the expansion Chicago Packers and noticed five black Packers on the court at the same time, something he'd never seen before. With the emergence of the black player, the NBA game was undergoing a cultural and stylistic shift. It was played faster, higher, and better than ever before. A new epoch was at hand, and it created tensions. For the NBA's black players, St. Louis, the league's southernmost city, remained the most difficult and racially intolerant place to play. (Bill Russell would call it "the loneliest town in the world.") In the middle 1950s, each NBA team typically had only one or two black players. Now, most teams had three or four. Privately, the NBA's black players talked about the league's quota, certain of its existence, even if team owners would not admit to it; when black players lost roster spots to inferior whites, they viewed it as the quota's evil work. Al Attles, who came to the Warriors in autumn 1960 from virtually nowhere (North Carolina A & T, a historically black college), learned that he had earned a spot with the Warriors from a black man who worked as a redcap at the Philadelphia airport. The redcap told him: "Woody Sauldsberry's gonna be traded." Attles thought the idea of trading his black teammate preposterous. After all, Sauldsberry had been NBA rookie of the year only two seasons before. But then Sauldsberry was traded and Attles did the math: That left four black players on the 1960–61 Warriors: the Dipper, Guy Rodgers, Andy Johnson, and Attles. He had heard about the quota—four black players per team, maximum. Now, here was Al Attles's proof.

In October 1961, during the exhibition season, the champion Celtics had been involved in a racial showdown in Lexington, Kentucky. Boston's black players left town hurriedly before their game against St. Louis after the coffee shop in the team's hotel refused to serve Tom Sanders and Sam Jones. Celtics owner Walter Brown fumed that the Celtics would never play another exhibition game in the South, or any other place, where they might be embarrassed. Back in Boston, Russell told newsmen, "I will not play any place again under those circumstances." One of Boston's white players, Frank Ramsey, who once played at the University of Kentucky, apologized to his black teammates on behalf of the entire state. "No thinking person in Kentucky," Ramsey said, "is a segregationist."

In Detroit early in the season, the Pistons' Ray Scott, an inquisitive and deeply introspective rookie, sought to understand the NBA and a black man's place—his place—in it. He found a mentor in Detroit assistant coach Earl Lloyd, who in 1950 had joined Nat "Sweetwater" Clifton, Chuck Cooper, and Hank DeZonie as the league's first black players. In hotel lobbies, on the Pistons bus, in restaurants and in nightclubs, Earl Lloyd explained to the rookie the way things were in the early Fifties in the NBA: how in St. Louis, restaurants would serve you on Styrofoam plates because "if you were black your order always was to go"; how he used to pick up Clifton or Cooper from their hotel and bring them back to his house for dinner and how "you felt responsible for each other. It was kind of you against the world"; and how Don Barksdale, another black pioneer in the NBA, once played a full quarter of an NBA game in 1953 without receiving a pass from his white teammates. (Later Barksdale would say, "I about wanted to cry.") Lloyd told the rookie that it was imperative for black players in the NBA now to carry themselves with a quiet dignity and strength and not step out too far unnecessarily. It was one thing, Lloyd explained, if you were Elgin Baylor or Bill Russell or Wilt Chamberlain. No one spoke for them. Their unique talents, to a certain degree, protected them. They could speak for themselves. But for the other thirty-four black players in the NBA the rules were different, more rigid: As a representative of the Negro race, you must wear a suit and tie. You must eat at the right places. You must conduct yourself as a gentleman at all times. Ray Scott listened carefully. He accepted all of it as gospel.

Of course, the Dipper remained his own man. "I'm not crusading for anyone," he said in 1960. "I'm no Jackie Robinson. Some persons are meant to be that way . . . others aren't."

His seeming shrug, or passivity, in public about matters of race in the early Sixties stood in stark contrast to the way he crushed in his fist any race-based impediments to his own self-definition. Rather than complain, the Dipper imposed his own impressive will. He sometimes dated white women, if discreetly; drove his Cadillac convertible at high speeds; and made more money than anyone else in the league. By averaging fifty points per game in 1961–62, he proved his physical superiority night after night and made a mockery of the league and its racial quotas and the notion that his white opponents were the best players in the world. He reduced to rubble the white-defined ideas of *fair play* and *sportsmanship,* which he knew as lies. Whites didn't want fair play; they feared it. The quota proved that. Beneath the veneer of public quiescence, the Dipper fought his own freedom struggle simply by being—aggressively, flagrantly, unapologetically—the Dipper.

CHAPTER 5

Second Quarter

EDDIE DONOVAN, THE KNICKS FIRST-YEAR COACH, had few options. These were the variables: his team trailing by sixteen points, his center, Imhoff, saddled with three fouls, Chamberlain with twenty-three points and ten rebounds . . . and the second quarter had yet to begin. Donovan's usual starting center, Phil Jordon, hadn't even made it to Hershey. Jordon remained thirteen miles away, at the team's hotel, sick and vomiting, the effects of the flu and yet another late night for which he was famous among teammates. (He'd been out with his postmidnight crony, guard Donnie Butcher.) Donovan looked at his reserve players on the Knickerbockers bench: a bare cupboard. Without size or bulk, he chose smoke and mirrors instead: rookie Cleveland Buckner, a shooter, not a defender. He was one of scout Holzman's proudest finds, with that peculiar shot of his, twisting, arms high over his head. "Like a swan with a broken wing," Jack Kiser wrote. Buckner had had difficulty adjusting—not to the NBA game, but to the big city. New York City wasn't Yazoo City. Sam Stith playfully teased Buckner for his Mississippi sound, calling to him, *"Hey, Cleeve-laaaaand!"* To teammates, Buckner seemed lonely. Johnny Green noticed that Buckner had lost weight since he'd started playing for the Knicks. "He was used to seeing country food and he comes to New York and doesn't see any of it," Green would say. Buckner could hardly afford any weight loss. He was a six-foot-eight Olive Oyl. Chamberlain had manhandled him earlier in the week, scoring twenty-eight points against him in a single quarter. For Donovan now, this was hardly a choice option. But he would get Buckner additional help. Whenever Wilt Chamberlain touched the ball, the coach said, every Knick in the vicinity was to descend upon him.

By force of habit more than strategy, Chamberlain kept moving directly to the same spot, down low, six feet to the left of the basket. When Attles or Rodgers lobbed the ball to him there, over the heads of the Knicks guards, Guerin and Al Butler, Buckner tried to get in the Dipper's way—as if that were possible. When the Los Angeles Lakers practiced in preparation to play the Warriors, a reserve center portrayed Chamberlain. Once, the ball was lobbed inside, the would-be Chamberlain turned toward the basket, and guard "Hot" Rod Hundley shouted, "Dip-per Duuuuuunk!" and the center defending the would-be Wilt, Jim Krebs, feigned fear, covered his head, and ran away. The Lakers broke up laughing and so did their coach, Fred Schaus. They understood, as did the Knicks, that once Chamberlain used his strength and bullied toward the basket, there was little that could be done.

But Chamberlain did not turn to the basket as often as Frank McGuire wanted. Chamberlain preferred a fall-away shot, stepping from the basket and shooting back over his right shoulder from a distance of ten to fifteen feet, banking the ball off the glass backboard. This was a shot a smaller man might use to overcome his opponent's height advantage, a shot described by Philadelphia sports columnist Sandy Grady as "a backward explosion like a whale breaching water, with the ball flipped off the apex of Wilt's jump." Paul Arizin became convinced that, with this shot, Chamberlain had an ulterior motive: He did not want to be considered a great player merely because he was tall. That, Arizin believed, "was the overriding factor in Wilt's whole psychology." It wasn't that the Dipper was denying his obvious size and strength advantage; it was merely an extension of that fact. Not only was he the biggest and strongest player on the court—anyone could see that—he was also *the best*. The Lakers' Tom Hawkins called it "the jolly giant's *fee-fi-fo-fum* syndrome."

His mammoth scoring achievements had prompted some of the nation's leading sports columnists to turn their backs on the game. "Basketball is for the birds—the gooney birds," Shirley Povich wrote in *Sports Illustrated*. "The game lost this particular patron years back when it went vertical and put the accent on carnival freaks who achieved upper space by growing into it. . . . Who can applaud Wilt the Stilt, or his ilk, when they outflank the basket from above and pelt it like an open city? These fellows are biological accidents who ought to be more usefully employed, like hiring out as rainmakers and going to sow a few clouds."

Chamberlain set out to prove that he could also do what smaller men typically did so well—dribble, run the floor, shoot. (Referee Earl Strom figured the fall-away carried an added bonus for the Dipper: Fading from the defense, he was less likely to be fouled, for him a good thing, since he despised shooting free throws.) The Dipper sought to prove himself multi-dimensional and well rounded in other ways, too. He had stunned his parents and siblings in 1960 by showing up on Dick Clark's *American Bandstand*. He drove to the television show's Philadelphia studio, and as the curtains parted there he was, in a five-button tweed Chesterfield with black satin lapels, standing before 150 teens screaming on cue. Chamberlain sang, *"By the river . . . 'neath the shady tree, Just my baby . . . Ju-hust my baby and me."* Dick Clark, just five-foot-nine, would later say, "I tried to interview the guy standing up and he was out of sight." The Dipper said, "My family's always laughed at me singing. I did this just to make 'em stop laughing." He added, "I did it to appease myself."

Now, in Hershey, the Knicks' Johnny Green lent aid to Buckner, down low. He crowded and shoved the Dipper. Green was six-foot-five, though he played taller because of his remarkable jumping ability. Stationed with the U.S. Marines in Japan years before, Green once saw "Jumpin'" Bill Manning dunk a basketball in a game played at the base. Green had never seen a dunk before. It left him speechless and eager to try it himself. He soon discovered that he, too, could dunk a basketball with ease. When Jumpin' Bill Manning left the base in Japan, fellow Marines began calling Green "Jumpin' Johnny," and the nickname stuck. "Hey, *Jumpin' Johnny Green!*" Chamberlain playfully called out during pregame warm-ups. "Betcha can't block this shot." Chamberlain turned and exhibited his fall-away jumper, kissing the ball off the glass. Green's smile masked a deeper truth. Chamberlain was right. There was no way he could block that shot. *But better the fall-away, Big Fella*, Green thought, *than the Dipper Dunk.*

Say this for Cleveland Buckner: the Knickerbockers rookie couldn't stop the Dipper, but he could shoot. Built like a stiletto and with that cockeyed over-the-head shooting style, Buckner kept the Knicks from disappearing altogether during the second quarter. This was Buckner's type of game, not much defense, high scoring, wide open. Quick off the dribble or out on the wing, running the fast break, Buckner found his range against the Warriors. Underneath the basket, he battled hard for rebounds. A streaky shooter, Buckner played about ten minutes on most nights; on this night, circumstances, and his own shooting accuracy, would get him thirty-three minutes. If Guerin or Naulls didn't take the shot for the Knicks, Buckner did. Holzman, the scout, had predicted Buckner would have breakout games such as this. On what would become the biggest scoring night of Cleveland Buckner's brief and obscure NBA career, hardly anyone in the crowd knew his name.

Teams couldn't compete with Chamberlain athletically so they tried to do it physically or psychologically. Typically, opposing centers came at the Dipper with pointed elbows and scowls, the guns and knives of their profession. Frank McGuire had never seen anyone hit in the mouth as often as the Dipper. Once, he saw Cincinnati's center, Wayne Embry, put a kneecap in the Dipper's crotch, and McGuire ran onto the court, screaming, "You can't let Embry do that!" but got no satisfaction from the referees. When referees weren't watching, opposing centers dug their fists into the small of Chamberlain's back or bounced him with a hard hip or stuck an elbow into his ribs in the belief that he wouldn't strike back. St. Louis's Clyde Lovellette used his own bag of sneaky tricks to annoy Chamberlain. Playing from behind, Lovellette thrust his right knee into Wilt's buttocks. He pinched Wilt's leg, side, or elbow. He even grabbed his shorts, forcing the Dipper to lower his hand to brush him aside. In his first battle with the Dipper in 1959 at Kiel Auditorium, Lovellette had determined not to be embarrassed by the rookie sensation. He threw a wicked elbow that struck Chamberlain in his mouth and dropped him to the floor. Philadelphia players searched the hardwood for Chamberlain's missing two front teeth before realizing they remained in his mouth—impacted upward, deep into the gum.

Chamberlain's coaches long had pleaded with him to strike back, the way George Mikan always had. Mikan knocked his tormentors into the bleachers. But Chamberlain was not, by nature, confrontational. Once he began to respond, though, the unprovoked attacks against him diminished. Boston Celtics players secretly discussed starting an altercation with a Philadelphia player in the belief that Chamberlain didn't like fights and didn't play well after one broke out, whether he was directly involved or not. Boston Coach Red Auerbach, perhaps more than anyone, mastered the art and science of getting inside Chamberlain's head. He had coached the Dipper one summer at Kutsher's resort in the Catskills where outdoor games were played to entertain guests. Walking into a bungalow at halftime, Auerbach found the Dipper, just graduated from high school, reclining on a bed. "You get your ass out of that bed and sit up and pay attention!" Auerbach growled. "You are not *that* good!" That's what Auerbach said, but what he thought was, *Yes, you are* that *good*. Now in the NBA, Auerbach fancied chasing the Dipper from his courtside conversations with referees during Boston timeouts by hollering, "What's this boy doing here? Get him out of here!"

Of course, none of these tactics worked. In 1958, Detroit's George Yardley became the first player to surmount 2,000 points in an NBA season. Yet on his own scoring climb, Chamberlain had transformed Yardley's total into his base camp. The Dipper scored a record 2,707 points as a rookie (37 points per game) and then 3,033 points in his second year (38 points per game). By midseason of his third year, there were whispers that Chamberlain might reach 4,000 points, doubling Yardley, though he would have to average 50 points a game to do it. The numbers startled. Syracuse's Johnny "Red" Kerr walked into a local bar once after playing the Dipper. "How many did ya get, Red?" the bartender asked. "Thirty-six," Kerr replied. "Well, then, set 'em up," the bartender exclaimed, happily. "My boy got thirty-six!" Delivering the beer, the bartender asked, "How many did Wilt get?" Sheepishly, Kerr said, "Sixty-two, I think." Kerr was silently thankful his complimentary drinks already had been delivered.

Earlier in the 1961–62 season, Walt Bellamy had tried a gentler approach. The new rising star among big men in the league had his own ideas how to stop the Dipper as he walked out for the opening tip on November 19, 1961, at the International Amphitheater in Chicago—all sweetness and tact.

"H'lo, Mister Chamberlain. I'm Walter Bellamy."

A six-foot-ten jump-shooter and member of the 1960 U.S. Olympic team, Bellamy was scoring nearly thirty points a night for the expansion Packers. On the court, he often referred to himself in the third person ("Mister Bellamy"). Once his third-person bellyaching prompted referee Norm Drucker to blow his whistle and say, "Mister Bellamy, please tell Walt that he just got himself a technical foul." Bellamy's first NBA meeting with Chamberlain was greatly anticipated. The Dipper elevated his intensity when playing Bill Russell or Elgin Baylor; to that short list he added the name of Walt Bellamy.

He reached for Bellamy's hand at center court. "Hello, Walter," the Dipper said. Then, he told the rookie, "You won't get a shot off in the first half."

What followed was Goliath's wrath. The first nine shots Walter Bellamy took from inside the free-throw line, Chamberlain blocked. Big Bells couldn't score. He couldn't breathe. Everywhere the rookie turned . . . Chamberlain. The Dipper didn't often play defense so fervently. When he did, the results could be terrifying. One NBA assistant coach watched as Chamberlain sent shots flying back past Bellamy's ear that night and said, "It was sad, man." On offense, Chamberlain scored over Bellamy on an array of fall-away bank shots, put-backs, and dunks.

When the two centers met for the second-half tip, Chamberlain looked at the shell-shocked rookie. "Okay, Walter," Chamberlain said, as if to a child, "*now* you can play."

When it was done, he had outscored Bellamy fifty-one to fourteen. The Warriors had won going away. Sweetness and deference proved no better than elbows and scowls.

Already in Hershey, the Dipper's visage was sweat-soaked, like raindrops clinging to a pane of glass. Typically, he guzzled water during timeouts to keep hydrated, yet still lost about seven pounds per game. The Knicks heard Paul Arizin wheezing as he moved up and down the court, same as always, like an old man. Guy Rodgers, unwilling to shoot, kept sliding fancy passes to Chamberlain and Arizin. So rapid was the pace of this game, so meager the defense being played, by night's end the teams would attempt a combined 233 shots, or nearly five shots per minute. At that rate, they could have used a twelve-second shot clock.

Working his cigarette at the Hershey Sports Arena press table, Jack Kiser did not see anything out of the ordinary from Chamberlain during the second quarter—except his free throws. The Dipper kept making them. Kiser knew free-throw shooting was the weakest part of his game. He was the worst free-throw shooter on the team, among the worst in the league, making barely more than half during his three seasons. The Dipper wasn't sure what the problem was. Maybe his hands were too big or he was just too tall or weightlifting had made him too strong or perhaps it was simply in his head. He'd practiced different methods of shooting free throws: one-handed, two-handed, from three feet behind the line, a jump shot, a fall-away, even blindfolded. Now the Dipper shot his free throws underhanded, same as Arizin and Rodgers and others in the league. He dipped down low, spreading his knees wide. "*Anybody* can make a free throw," Jack Kiser barked at the Dipper, blowing like a windstorm into the Convention Hall locker room after a game, pen and notepad in hand. "I mean *anybody.*"

With his southern accent that one sportswriter would term "cornpone, kind of like an addled Jerry Lee Lewis," Kiser taunted anyone, even Chamberlain, though in truth he was the Dipper's great defender in print. Loud and caustic, Kiser even wrote with a smirk. He didn't think much of the Knicks. "You can find better benches in Central Park," he wrote. About the Warriors' recent loss to the Knicks, Kiser had written, "It was, honestly, the most pathetic offensive show put on by a Warrior team in years." And then, upon further consideration, a paragraph later, "It was, honestly, the most pathetic defensive show put on by a Warrior team in years. New York should have been a pushover." NBA referees knew Kiser as "Poison Pen." Referee Earl Strom, smarting from Kiser's criticism, once scuffled with him as they entered an arena. On another occasion, Kiser yelled at referee Norm Drucker from his courtside seat at Convention Hall, "You're dumping, you're shaving points, Norm!" Drucker attempted to throw him out of the game. "But you can't throw me out," Kiser said. "Why not?" Drucker asked. "Because," Kiser answered, "I'm not *in* the game." Gottlieb intervened. "What's the matter?" he asked Drucker. "He said something that's unbecoming of a newspaperman," Drucker replied, adding, "Get him out or you'll forfeit the game!" Gotty had nearly a full house, not the usual occurrence. To placate Drucker, he moved Kiser to another seat.

Yet Chamberlain rather liked Jack Kiser, especially his directness, and played cards with him on airplanes, even if Kiser mocked him publicly for his poor free-throw shooting. The Dipper had an uneven relationship with the media; a few sportswriters in New York, such as Leonard Lewin and Leonard Koppett, liked the Dipper and wrote favorably of him. But, as Kiser would write, "too many writers around the league like Wilt personally about as much as they do a typographical error." They thought him aloof. He thought they put words in his mouth. "Seeing as how this is a sportswriters' dinner," the Dipper had said, upon receiving his league MVP and Rookie of the Year honors in Philly in 1960, "I don't want to be misquoted, so I'll just say, 'Thank you.'" Sitting in the audience, sportswriter Jack McKinney of *The Philadelphia Daily News* was moved to write, "Wasn't that a lovely acceptance speech? . . . It was then that we of the press and radio realized how we have wronged the poor fellow. When Chamberlain played with the Globetrotters, the writers insisted on tipping off the public. Record-breaking crowds invaded his privacy and all Wilt got for the discomfort was $65,000." McKinney termed it "the terrible price he must pay for being tall, talented, famous and rich."

But Kiser became the Boswell of the Dipper's biggest season, smart-alecky, all knowing, precisely what *The Philadelphia Daily News* wanted. When sports editor Larry Merchant, only twenty-six years old, arrived to *The Daily News* from New York in 1957, he all but planted sticks of dynamite into the staid and predictable nature of Philadelphia sports journalism practiced by the morning *Inquirer* and *The Evening Bulletin*. Merchant brought color, controversy, and Jack Kiser. *The Daily News* had nearly folded in 1956. Then Walter Annenberg, publisher of the rival *Inquirer*, bought the paper in 1957, killed its Sunday edition, and transformed it into an afternoon paper. The newsroom was set in a former warehouse without air conditioning on 22nd and Arch Streets. Through open windows trains blew soot that speckled copy paper. Columnist Sandy Grady, an elegant stylist widely respected in Philadelphia by athletes and journalists alike, quickly recognized that *The Daily News* managing editor J. Ray Hunt had two obsessions: Notre Dame football and women's breasts. Grady heard Hunt roar to his front-page editors, "Bazooms! Give me more bazooms!" In the sports department, Merchant instructed his writers to get raucous and raise hell for *The Daily News*'s 285,000 readers. Dig into what happened on the field and then tell why it happened; bring the readers closer to the sports personalities. Merchant had been raised on *The New York Post,* a real sportswriter's paper, and tried to emulate it in Philadelphia. *Tummeling* is what he called it—Yiddish for having a little fun. In the years that followed he built one of America's finest sports sections.

He originally hired Kiser to work the late-night desk, on the recommendation of Grady. Grady and Kiser had worked together at *The Charlotte News.* Grady knew that Kiser was a quick study, understood layout techniques, and was underpaid. In his green Volkswagen Beetle, Grady drove Kiser up to Philadelphia. For Kiser, this was a risky job move, Grady believed, "because Jack didn't have standout writing talent, and *The Daily News* was an insecure paper." Yet almost at once, Kiser fit right into *The Daily News,* a working man's paper, popular in the river wards because of its edge.

Certainly, once Kiser moved off the night desk and onto the Warriors beat, he showed his own edge. He wrote: "Eddie Gottlieb pays $1,000 [per game] to see Wilt Chamberlain score points. That makes Mister Gottlieb an extremely rare creature because there are millions of people in the immediate vicinity who won't pay $1.25 to see the tall Warrior center score points." In his three-dot sports columns, Kiser spread rumors, often trades he imagined. Editors at competing papers in town instructed their own writers to follow up on these rumors. They unnerved players and galled writers. His columns were prickly, sarcastic, fun.

With Convention Hall attendance what it is of late, why doesn't Gotty run the Warrior–Chicago game as a preliminary Saturday night and have the Eagles play the Colts in the feature?

•　　•　　•

Wouldn't it be fitting and proper for Red Auerbach to give part of his salary to Bill Russell? With Big Bill out of the lineup, Auerbach is just a 1-5 coach. With him in action, Red is a 37-8 mastermind. . . .

•　　•　　•

Wasn't the ignoring of Sam Jones in the all-star selection the biggest miscarriage of justice since they disqualified me out of a $745 daily double? . . .

Thin, pale, and ingratiating, Kiser was formidable in his way. Merchant would say, "There was something very intense about him. There was a sense that maybe there was another side of Jack I didn't know, some darker side, nothing I could ever put a finger on. That very same thing that made him a good reporter and brick thrower, like a lot of newspapermen, came from some background that was always looking to take on the establishment. There had to be a hard edge there."

At times, Kiser became a part of the Warriors season narrative. He had quickly befriended the Dipper, listening to his tales with admiration. Following a two-point loss to the Knicks at Madison Square Garden on November 14, a lackluster performance by Chamberlain, reporters crowded Frank McGuire outside the locker room. In his story, Kiser transcribed the exchange: *Reporters:* "Why didn't you take Wilt out when he was going so bad?" *McGuire:* "Who do you mean? Wilt? Well, because we haven't been taking him out, that's why." *Reporters:* "Does this mean you'll never take him out?" *McGuire:* "I'm no fortune teller. I can't answer that question." *Reporters:* "If any other player wasn't helping the team like that, would you have taken him out?" *McGuire:* "I don't think that's a fair question and I won't answer it. I don't know what you guys are trying to do, but if you're trying to get me to put the rap on Wilt, then you're wasting your time. I've never criticized a ballplayer—either one of mine or one on the other team—and I'm not going to start now." *Reporters:* "Do you think Wilt was giving 100 percent?" *McGuire:* "Yes. Definitely." *Reporters:* "Do you think it was his worst game?" *McGuire:* "You are the ones that must determine that, not me. . . . Everybody has a bad game once in awhile. DiMaggio struck out a few times and Mantle struck out a few times, didn't they?"

Kiser had his own explanation for this interrogation: competing reporters out for blood, not only Wilt's but Jack Kiser's. He wrote the next morning in *The Daily News:* "Why the intense attack? Maybe it was because they were so accustomed to New York losing that they could not believe the win had been earned by merit on the Knicks' part. Maybe it was because Chamberlain is so great and it's always a good story to expose some failing in greatness. But more likely it was because most of the reporters in the squad [outside the locker room] remembered a day over two years ago when the opposition paper beat them bad with a story on Chamberlain's retirement (a short-lived one, it turned out). They didn't think the manner in which the story was obtained was entirely kosher, and they'd been waiting for Wilt to make a misstep."

Indeed, nearly two years before, in February 1960, as Chamberlain's rookie season had neared an end, Kiser broke the story that the Dipper was considering quitting the team to participate in a series of worldwide track and field exhibitions in an attempt to break the world decathlon record. This story, which had significant shock value, obviously had been in the works between Chamberlain and Kiser for some time; it was the first in a lengthy series that stretched across five days and thousands of words with articles about the Dipper's boyhood and college years. Vintage tabloid stuff, it was filled with hyperbole and sensational headlines such as THE MAN WHO WAS NEVER A BOY and FELLOW PLAYERS STUNNED BY WILT'S STATEMENT and WILT DENIES DENYING OUR STORY. The series drew attention to Chamberlain and Kiser, a winning proposition for both. (When the Dipper actually retired the following month, he claimed race as part of the reason, and he left for the Globetrotters not track and field; even so, Merchant, in a column, later crowed of Kiser's scoop, "Even if Chamberlain was . . . bluffing for a raise, it was still a remarkable story.") Of course, the lengthy series infuriated Gotty, who upon signing the Dipper to a three-year deal before his second season made certain to phone Jim Heffernan of *The Evening Bulletin*. Heffernan believed that Gotty handed him this page one story "just to show Kiser that he didn't know everything."

Not until December had the Warriors, and Chamberlain, found their own formidable stride. They won seven of eight games before Christmas, seven in a row in January, and then thirteen of nineteen in February. The team's patterns and tendencies were clear: the Dipper took nearly forty shots per game, and Arizin, with his determined drives to the basket and accurate jumpers, took about twenty. The playmaker Rodgers suffered bouts of inconsistency with the worst shooting percentage of his career, missing nearly two of every three field goal attempts. The absence of the oft-injured forward Tom Gola exposed a weak bench. The Warriors struggled against the league's top two teams, losing six consecutive games to Boston and winning only twice in eight games against Baylor's Lakers. Chamberlain brutalized every team, averaging fifty-six points against St. Louis and forty-eight points per game against Syracuse, with the league's other teams falling in between statistically, except Boston. In a dozen games against the Celtics in

1961–62, Chamberlain averaged forty-one points. Russell remained his most tenacious opponent.

As the season progressed, criticism against the Dipper and his unprecedented scoring mounted. Syracuse coach Alex Hannum contended referees protected Chamberlain. "Nobody can breathe on him without getting a foul called," Hannum said. Chicago Coach Jim Pollard said, "They've created a monster. . . . He's nothing but a scoring machine. The idea of the game isn't to score points. The idea is to win." Syracuse veteran Dolph Schayes concurred: "How do you think the other [Warriors] players feel? They want to feel important, to feel needed. Some of them are treated like garbage. They're pawns. Wilt doesn't help them. Nobody can play full speed 48 minutes. What's he trying to prove?"

As the Warriors' home attendance declined, Kiser defended Chamberlain: "Now that Wilt Chamberlain has gone cold at the gate, wouldn't the Big Dipper have to perform as well as three $25,000 players to earn his big check? And isn't he?" When others, like Schayes, criticized Chamberlain for shooting too often, Kiser countered, "At last glance Wilt was hitting 49.3 percent of his shots, the rest of the team was hitting 40.2. Nuff said." In mid-December, Kiser wondered about falling attendance in Philadelphia: "It could be that all of Chamberlain's dunk shots look alike, all his jump shots look alike, and once you've seen one of them you've seen them all. The big guy could score a hundred in a game and few would be surprised, or willing to see him try for 101 the next time out. Didn't he go into last night's game with 300 points in a five-game period that has to go down in history as the hottest streak of all time?"

Kiser's devotion to Chamberlain was exceeded perhaps only by his devotion to controversy. When the Warriors arrived in Boston to play Detroit in the first game of a doubleheader on January 19, six weeks before Hershey, they were greeted by this headline in *The Boston Traveler:* STILT STUNTS NBA GROWTH. Sportswriter Hugh Wheelright's story amounted to a blistering attack against Chamberlain for the way "he pads his bank account" as a scorer. Wheelright contended that Chamberlain's seventy-three-point game against Chicago on January 13 "nauseated everyone who saw it" for his steadfast refusal to pass to his teammates who knew "they must pass to Chamberlain or sit on the bench." Wheelright charged that Chamberlain had "cussed out little Al Attles for shooting a layup with no one within 40 feet of him. 'You should have waited for me,' was the expurgated version of Superman's remarks," Wheelwright wrote, before adding, "A Philly writer observed: 'Wilt accomplished nothing but to drive away more fans. His and the Warriors' behavior made a travesty of the game. It was a disgrace.' "

What none of the Warriors could have known then was that the source of Wheelright's material was . . . Jack Kiser. Wheelright and Kiser were friends who loved nothing more than to toss a Molotov cocktail onto their own sports pages. They swapped material often. Wheelright, a 1949 Harvard graduate with a degree in international law, was known to the Boston Celtics as something of a card shark. He counted Cousy and trainer Buddy LeRoux as gin rummy partners and Tom Heinsohn as his insurance man. Wheelright had verified Kiser's material, as best he could, in conversation with an NBA referee and timed the release of his story for the Warriors' arrival. Kiser could not use the material himself, he told Wheelright, for fear that it would alienate the players he covered.

Reading Wheelright's story, McGuire erupted. He read it aloud to his players in the locker room before the game and conducted his own question-and-answer session. McGuire asked, "Has anybody on this club been told to feed Wilt or else he would be on the bench?" Heads shook. "Al," McGuire said to Attles, pointedly, "did Wilt curse you for not passing to him?" Attles shook his head. "Is anybody on this team unhappy?" McGuire asked. A chorus of emphatic *No's* filled the room. "Well," McGuire said, "it looks as if the whole world is against you. Now is the time to pull together, to play together. To show the people who don't know the truth that this is a bunch of lies." The Warriors went out and crushed Detroit in the opener, an aroused Chamberlain scoring fifty-three points and playing, Kiser wrote, "the kind of defense his worst critics insist he should play every second." Kiser added, "The unintentional hero is Hugh Wheelright, a sports reporter for *The Boston Traveler.* And a half-glad, half-mad McGuire asserted later, 'Mr. Wheelright deserves an assist on this one. He helped us to win the game.' "

After the victory, McGuire called for Wheelright. Entering the Boston Garden locker room, Wheelright heard McGuire's volcanic roar. "It was a malicious, vicious article, Hugh," McGuire yelled. "Full of untruths, one based on fantasy rather than facts. It's all lies!"

"Is that so, Frank?" Wheelright replied. "What's a lie?"

"It's all lies!" McGuire said.

Wheelright did not back down. "Let's start with one specific thing, Frank. Name one lie for me."

From across the room, Wheelright heard Attles shout, "It's yellow journalism!" Wheelright puffed out his chest. "Well, that's a word I never expected to hear in this dressing room—'Yellow.'" (Wheelwright knew the Warriors had been called "yellow" for their inability to beat the Celtics.) McGuire grabbed Wheelright by the wrist and pulled him from the locker room, saying, "Come on, you'll get killed in here."

Outside the locker room, sportswriters crowded McGuire as he berated Wheelright. "It's not true! You weren't even at that game, Hugh! How did you even get that stuff? Huh? *Where did you get it, Hugh?*" Wheelright felt himself in a corner now. He couldn't, and wouldn't, give up Kiser as his source. Before he could answer, though, Wheelright saw a head bobbing up and down in the crowd, behind McGuire, and heard a southern accent, filled with a mock anger, shouting, "Yeah! *Where did you get that stuff, Hugh?*" It was the conniving Jack Kiser. Wheelright stifled a laugh. The secret remained theirs to keep.

Now, Kiser fingered a cigarette at the press table in Hershey, his face clouded by smoke. Guerin began to find his range in the second quarter, penetrating the middle, leading the Knicks back into the game. Philadelphia led at halftime 79-68, and though Chamberlain had scored forty-one points, it was his free-throw shooting that struck Kiser. The Dipper had made thirteen out of fourteen. Just like Kiser had said: Anybody can shoot free throws.

Eddie Donovan had bigger worries. His Knicks were within eleven points, and a career night blossomed for Cleveland Buckner. But there was still the small matter of how to stop the Dipper.

CHAPTER 6

Gotty and the Zink

GOTTY DROVE TO HERSHEY EARLIER that evening, which is to say he had Dave Zinkoff drive him there. They were quite a pair, two Jewish bachelors, together since the middle Thirties, a promoter and his sidekick getting by on instinct and shtick. Gotty, sixty-three years old, was known as the Mogul, a nickname he once defined: "A mogul is a top banana." Zinkoff, fifty-one years old, was, like Gotty, born on the other side—Russia—but raised in west Philadelphia where his parents owned a deli. He had a difficult first interview with Gotty, then searching for a public address announcer. "Get over to that corner there—and shout!" Gotty instructed. Zinkoff did. Then Gotty said, "Now lower your voice," and Zinkoff did that, too, his tone gravelly even as a young man. (At this point Zinkoff was thinking of Gotty, "He's *meshugs.*") But Gotty said, "Pretty good," and hired him for $5 a game. Years later, Gotty hooked up Zinkoff with his friend Abe Saperstein, and he traveled the world with the Globetrotters as their p.a. announcer. Zinkoff liked to refer to himself in the third person, as in, "The Zink don't drink." For all but four years during World War II when the Zink served in Iceland, the two men seemed inseparable.

They spoke their own language, Gotty and the Zink, much of it through nods and inference, though their conversation was mostly one-sided. Gotty talked, the Zink listened. Of course, Gotty paid the Zink to listen, and to sell ads for Warriors programs, and to serve as his colorful game announcer, and to drive him in his big Cadillac, and to send out his trademark Christmas gift each year, one-pound Hershey chocolate bars.

They liked to tell stories about themselves: The Zink once in the 1930s asked for a raise, contending that some fans came to games merely to hear him. Gotty said no to the raise, so the Zink quit. For three Saturdays, capacity crowds kept coming to games. Gotty waited, the Zink came back . . . then Gotty gave him a raise, from $5 a game to $7. Once, the Zink spoke about the Warriors at a local orphanage. He felt sorry for the orphans and invited thirty to a game as his guests. Gotty was furious. "Why the hell did you do that? What do you think we're doing here? This is a business! How are we gonna make money if you invite everybody you meet to a ballgame? We're professionals!" Red-faced, the Zink went home and wrote out a check for thirty tickets. He handed it to Gotty. "What the hell's this?" the Mogul shouted. He tore up the check. "What are you, a wise guy?"

The Zink seemed to know everyone in town—the politicians, newspapermen, cops—largely from his charity work. He often organized shows for veterans at service hospitals and brought along pretty young women from Police Athletic League shows and various organizations to greet the patients and to hand out gifts; "waitresses," he called them. Surrounded by such women, the Zink would explain his enduring bachelorhood rhetorically, "Why buy a cow when milk is so cheap?" Gotty never came close to marrying, either. "Now maybe the girl thought she came close," Gotty once said. "I wouldn't know about that." From his courtside seat at Warriors games, the Zink didn't always watch games closely. He was too busy talking to one of his waitresses; occasionally a Warriors official had to tell him which player had just scored. On the p.a., though, Zinkoff was an original with his flourishes and trills. When the former Warrior Jack George scored, the Zink had called out, "By George!" After a Tom Gola basket he called "Gola Goal!" and after a Chamberlain stuff, "Dipper *Duuuuuuuunk! Chaaaam-ber-lain!*" It was all part of the show.

The show, of course, belonged to Gotty. The man who brought the

Dipper into the NBA was a founding father of Philadelphia basketball, a practical, pear-shaped man in a gray suit, a watch fob dangling from his vest. Gotty used his vest and pants pockets like filing cabinets, cramming them full of notes and game tickets. The New York sportswriter Red Smith decided Gotty was "about the size and shape of a half-keg of beer." To the rookie Tom Meschery, Gotty "looked like a bloodhound, a wonderful face with big John Huston jowls." "What do you mean, what does a promoter do?" Gotty once responded to a writer. "He promotes! He gets the game up, he puts it together, he advertises it, he supervises it; he nurses it. He promotes!"

As a boy, Gotty lived in an area of New York City that later became Spanish Harlem, and there his father, Morris, ran a candy store. When Morris Gottlieb died, Gotty was only nine, and his mother moved the family to south Philly. He later attended the Philadelphia School of Pedagogy and taught a few years at a junior high before moving into sports promotion and later coaching. He promoted entertainers, too; in 1937 he gave the comic Joey Bishop his first job, in Wernersville, Pennsylvania, $25 a week for the Bishop brothers trio. Joey Bishop thought Gotty meant $25 for each brother. The first week the Bishop brothers got $8 apiece. Joey Bishop complained. Gotty thought about it and replied: "I'll tell you what. We'll do your laundry, too."

The Mogul's team now was his life and it was strictly a seat-of-the-pants operation. Gotty paid his bills immediately and preferably in cash since that saved him three percent. Arizin once saw Gotty chase after a boy who had picked up the basketball as a game ended at Convention Hall: As Gotty ran, jowls flapping, belly roiling, he looked like an egg rolling across a table. He ripped the ball from the kid's hands. Over the years, Gotty had developed an uncanny ability to walk into an arena, gauge a crowd, and guess its size, invariably within a hundred of the correct number. He didn't pay his players much, Chamberlain notwithstanding, but they liked and respected him anyway. His dour expression disguised an essential decency and sharp intellect; when he made friendly bets with them, the stakes always were the same—a prune Danish.

He made up the NBA's schedule of games each season on a yellow legal pad; to do it, he said, "takes a certain kind of mechanical brain." In the old days, when he owned the South Philadelphia Hebrew Association team known as the SPHAs (pronounced *Spahz*), his players joked that Gotty paid them in the dark so that as he slapped the bills into their hands they couldn't read the denominations. His SPHAs players all were Jewish—Joel "Shikey" Gotthofer, Inky Lautman, Moe Goldman, Cy Kaselman. The team's players wore Hebrew letters across their chests—samekh, pe, he, aleph—and the Jewish star; Gotty had designed the uniforms himself. One of the original SPHAs, Hughie Black, would say, "Half [the fans] would come to see the Jews killed and the other half were Jews coming to see our boys win."

The SPHAs became champions of their home city, won two of three games in 1925–26 over the Original Celtics, barnstormed across the northeast, and played in the Eastern League and then the American League, winning many titles in the semiorganized professional ranks. On road trips to Trenton and Camden and Reading, Gotty drove his eight-seat Ford touring car, his seven players seated and the Zink (who handled SPHAs promotions) stretched out on the floor in between the seats. Not that the Zink minded; he was young and flexible then. The Zink slipped a lucky number into the SPHAs game programs, and the winner got a $20 suit from Sam Gerson's store. Gotty staged many SPHAs games on a ballroom floor at the Broadwood Hotel, corner of Broad and Wood streets, the games usually followed by a dance. One of his SPHAs players, Gil Fitch, rushed into the locker room after games to change into a tuxedo and then led his band, accompanied by singer Kitty Kallen. SPHAs games became a social staple in Philadelphia's Jewish community. "Many a fella met his wife there," Gotty would say. "Many a fella met somebody else's wife there, too." The Zink put it like this: "Man, those were the days! Basketball and girls, what a combination! The Zink had a lot of good times then. That's how the Broadwood got its name. Some broads wouldn't and some broads would."

In his bow tie, Gotty had been a fiery coach, quick to chew out his players, both with the SPHAs and then, after the war, with the Warriors. That's when arena owners in the big cities formed the Basketball Association of America, progenitor of the modern NBA. After one disappointing road loss late in the 1940s, his Warriors met the next morning at the airport where Gotty organized a team meeting—in the men's room. His players formed a semicircle near the urinals. Shouting, Gotty asked each player, "And what's *your* problem?" All heads bowed until a knock on the door. Gotty cracked open the door and peered out. "WHAT THE HELL DO YOU WANT?" he shouted. A man outside said he needed to use the bathroom. Gotty scared him off.

Sitting in the back seat during the ride to Hershey was Jim Heffernan, beat writer for *The Evening Bulletin,* a solid, stable, and mainstream newspaper, which each day congratulated itself with the masthead motto, "In Philadelphia, Nearly Everybody Reads The Bulletin." Heffernan loved to listen to Gotty and Zink. They were like Damon Runyon characters, he thought, colorful and quirky and, in Gotty's case, cheap. Heffernan had driven to New York with Gotty and Zink several times before and finally realized that Gotty timed their departures so they would arrive at Madison Square Garden just after 6:00 P.M. when the parking meters expired. If they arrived before 6:00, Gotty instructed the Zink to drive around the parking lot until the meters went off. To the Mogul, time wasn't money. Money was money.

  Listen, I've got news for you. That was how Gotty began many sentences, as in, *Listen, I've got news for you: You don't deserve a raise. You already make too much money.* Early in the 1961–62 season, Gotty had startled Meschery and the other Warriors rookies by standing at the hotel check-out desk and informing each player how much he owed for telephone calls from their room: Usually it was twenty cents, sometimes a few nickels more. When St. Louis Hawks general manager Marty Blake phoned and asked to attend a Warriors playoff game against the Celtics at Convention Hall in March 1960, Gotty replied, "Marty, we're sold out. Just bring your own chair." And he meant it. So Blake followed instructions. He brought a folding chair on a train, carried it into Convention Hall, and set it beside the court; after the game, Blake carried his chair back home. Of course, Gotty himself always sat courtside to intimidate referees, who knew of his power in the league. Referees understood that with one phone call by the mighty Gotty their careers could be history.

The Warriors and the Knicks came to Hershey—an hour's drive north of where Pickett charged and Lee failed at Gettysburg—for a simple reason: Gotty put them there. It was Gotty, and Gotty alone, who drew up the NBA schedule; he knew when every train, plane, and bus departed from each NBA city. Gotty loved Hershey. His team had trained in Chocolate Town each autumn for years, and he had personal friendships there. But Gotty, ever the promoter, had more in mind than his relationships or his chocolate cravings. Potentially there was money to be made in Chocolate Town. Hershey had a big arena and plenty of basketball fans within driving distance, fans who typically might attend weekend games in the Eastern League, a vibrant independent association with fine talent, including dozens of black players unable to crack the NBA quota and others banned by the NBA for involvement with gamblers. The Eastern League featured teams across Pennsylvania, in Allentown, Wilkes-Barre, Sunbury, Hazleton, Williamsport, and Scranton. Further, the NBA was trying to expand its audience by luring new fans. During the 1961–62 season, the Boston Celtics played a few games in Providence, Rhode Island; the Cincinnati Royals in Dayton, Ohio; and the Syracuse Nationals in Rochester and Utica, New York. Out west, the Lakers played a game in Portland, another in Seattle. This was the Warriors' third game of the season in Chocolate Town. They drew 4,800 fans the first time, 4,400 the second. The way Gotty had it figured, his Warriors were spreading their wings for the good of the league, and if nobody showed up at the game in Hershey, at least he could pick up a few extra crates of chocolate bars.

Back in 1949, two years after Jackie Robinson had broken baseball's color line, New York Knicks owner Ned Irish told the NBA's Board of Governors that he wanted to sign the league's first African-American player, the Globetrotters' Nat "Sweetwater" Clifton. Gottlieb was nearly apoplectic. He didn't have big money, but Gotty had big ideas and a promoter's well-honed instincts. He had been a part of the game from its urban Jewish origins, first as a player and later as coach and now as franchise owner. For years Gotty also had promoted Negro League baseball teams such as the Homestead Grays and the Baltimore Elite Giants. He understood the way sports fans thought.

Or thought he did.

A business pragmatist, Gotty believed that white customers wouldn't pay to see an NBA game if too many players were black. "Our players are going to be seventy-five percent black in five years," Gotty said at the 1949 meeting, not as a prediction but a warning. "We're not going to draw people to the game. You're going to do a disservice to the game." Further,

Gotty said, to steal Sweetwater Clifton was to risk angering Abe Saperstein. His good friend Saperstein, he reminded the board, was a good friend to the NBA—and a gold mine. A Globetrotters appearance virtually guaranteed sellouts at NBA doubleheaders. So Gotty posed the question: If we steal Saperstein's players, what happens if he stops bringing his Globetrotters to NBA arenas? Then what? It would cost the NBA its top drawing card. Without two guaranteed Globetrotters sellouts a year some NBA teams might not make it. This was the dark heart in Gotty's fast-talking charm. He was out to turn a buck, and if necessary to do that, he would perpetuate segregation. Gotty had grown up scrambling and scuffling, and as owner of the Warriors he was still scrambling and scuffling. As he would explain years later, "This was my blood; this wasn't a tax gimmick. If I lost $50,000, it was $50,000 that I lost."

Gotty was persuasive. The Board of Governors turned down Irish. Six months later, though, Irish came back. He said his Knicks needed a big man. He still wanted Sweetwater Clifton. Irish banged his fist on a table and presented his ultimatum, gently: If I don't get Sweetwater Clifton, I don't know if the Knicks can stay in this league. The NBA would have to choose its poison: lose Abe Saperstein or lose its franchise in New York. The vote passed, and Sweetwater Clifton went to the Knicks in 1950, breaking the NBA's color barrier. As Carl Bennett, the Fort Wayne Pistons' general manager, walked to the door after the Board of Governors meeting, an outvoted Gotty snarled at him, "You dumb S.O.B. You've just ruined our league." Five NBA teams would sign black players before Gotty. Not until 1954 did Gotty sign his first, Jackie Moore of La Salle.

A year later, in 1955, Gotty finagled league rules to his own advantage, using the integration of the NBA, which he had fought so passionately, to enrich himself. The NBA permitted its teams territorial picks; that is, in return for giving up a first-round selection, a team could select, without challenge, a college star who played in its immediate geographical area. Team owners hoped that drafting local college players would intensify loyalties with fans and help draw bigger crowds. So Gotty claimed Wilt Chamberlain as the Warriors' territorial pick even though the Dipper was yet in Overbrook High School. NBA owners winced. These owners knew that territorial picks did not apply to high school players. But they respected Gotty, who was after all a good league man. Because they felt they owed Gotty for his fidelity to the league, they allowed him to bend the rule, stipulating only that Chamberlain couldn't enter the NBA until his college class graduated, which meant the 1959–60 season. His power play a success, Gotty said he was willing to wait and somehow managed to keep a straight face as he said it.

In the fall of 1959, the specter of the Dipper playing for his Warriors thrilled Gotty. "Wait until the people in Convention Hall see Wilt dunking that apple," Gotty said. The crowds were large for Chamberlain at first; he was the talk of the league, as Gotty had predicted. But now, in his third season, attendance had fallen, especially at home, from an average of 7,000 fans per game to fewer than 5,000—this even as Chamberlain's point production grew. With ratings and sponsor interest in decline, NBC considered not renewing the league's television contract. Only 2,891 fans attended a Warriors home game against Syracuse in December, and Gotty confessed that even that number was padded since he'd counted the Syracuse University football team. "And they were here as guests," he said. Even so, Gotty lashed out at critics. "Would we draw better without Wilt? Could the team win without Wilt? Is it riskier to play with him or without him? If the people don't want to see him, then we've got to do something else, but I can't think of any other city where the people wouldn't pour out to see him.

"If Bellamy scores forty and Jerry West gets sixty-three, then Wilt should get one hundred and sixty-three some day.

"What should we do, chop his head off, or his arms off because some people think he has an unfair advantage?"

CHAPTER 7

McGuire and His Warriors

THE DIPPER'S COACH, FRANK MCGUIRE, had the chesty confidence of an old-time ward politician. In his fine tailored suit and with his hair slicked back and parted just so, he looked like a millionaire. Before the game, McGuire had stood near the Warriors bench, relaxed and congenial, posing for a picture and kibitzing with the Hershey crowd. He was a rookie NBA coach, though hardly a coaching rookie. He'd been a college stalwart at St. John's and then the University of North Carolina, posting a 267-93 combined record and taking both schools to the NCAA title game. Years later, he would joke that his biggest responsibility while coaching the Warriors was "to see that Wilt made the plane on time." Brought in from the college game to help close an eleven-game deficit to the Celtics from the previous season, McGuire arrived in Philadelphia already a star. He drove a big car, attended mass with devotion, and had a beautiful wife from a proper family. McGuire had *married up,* as the saying went, and his lovely wife had polished his rougher edges to the point where soon he was buffing his fingernails and being named by the Barbers of America as one of the nation's ten best-groomed men. With his expensive suits he set a new standard of couture among NBA coaches. One of thirteen kids of an Irish-cop father who died young, McGuire had walked the New York waterfront as a boy and later worked on it. He played for a few years during the Depression for the Brooklyn Visitations of the old American League, building a name on his defensive skills. When the Warriors flew into New York late at night, McGuire stopped by police precincts to visit old friends till the wee hours of morning; a few of them had patrolled the streets with his father. To his players, he defended his old friend Carmine De Sapio, chieftain of the Tammany political machine in New York, against charges of bossism. ("It's a bum rap," he insisted.) McGuire joked that in New York he needed two sets of complimentary tickets for games: On one side he'd put the cops he knew, and on the other the robbers. His Warriors players heard him talk about his friend, the President, another handsome Catholic with chesty confidence. Articulate, robust, and above it all: That was Frank McGuire.

Meschery fell under McGuire's motivational spell and came to believe that his coach was part basketball, part Barnum & Bailey circus. Even so, Meschery liked and respected the man. McGuire was also a big spender, his legend at North Carolina tarnished only by bloated expense accounts. He carried himself as if he'd known wealth forever, though he retained a soft spot for working people. In New York restaurants, McGuire dropped names and money, greasing palms, a ten-spot to the hatcheck lady and a twenty to the maitre d'. He made quite a pair with Gotty. According to one sports journal, the Warriors owner and coach were "as dissimilar as a bagel and a steak." The coach lived at the Cherry Hill Inn, an expensive place in New Jersey, and drank J & B Scotch Mist. The owner's miserly ways caused him to chafe. The Warriors once ran out of tape in Syracuse and had to borrow some from the Nationals. McGuire was incredulous. *Wilt's making all this money and we've got no tape for his ankles?* During exhibition games on the road, McGuire, with no assistant coach or equipment manager, had to look after his players' valuables. He put their wallets and watches and as much as $10,000 in expense money and gate receipts in a bag and placed it beneath his spot on the bench. (The Dipper once cracked to his coach, "I don't want you to worry about what I am doing on the court. I'd rather you worry about my cash and my rings.") Finally, McGuire snapped. Waiting for the team bus before an exhibition game in Oklahoma City, he saw a converted camper pull up. Small and cramped, it had a makeshift bed in back. Gotty's players had long known such bargain-basement vehicles. But Frank McGuire hadn't. He stood in the stairwell of the camper en route to the arena that night, steaming mad. Early the next morning, he sat beside Attles and Rodgers in the hotel coffee shop and said, "You lost your coach last night. I quit." McGuire explained that the team's accommodations were not acceptable. They were not conducive to self-respect or to winning. At Chapel Hill, he'd grown accustomed to going first-class. ("It costs twenty-five cents more on the dollar to go first-class," McGuire often said.) Never had he envisioned this. But Gotty convinced him to stay.

At his hiring, McGuire was awarded $20,000 a year for three years, the added title of vice president, and only one guiding instruction—this was Wilt Chamberlain's team, make sure he scores a lot of points.

And so McGuire did.

At training camp in Hershey, McGuire had applied his well-rehearsed oratorical skills in his first meeting with players. He proclaimed the Dipper the most dominant force in basketball history and said the Warriors would beat Boston by getting the ball to Chamberlain "two-thirds of the time." The established stars of the team translated his talk differently. Paul Arizin heard McGuire say, "We should win the pennant—with Wilt." Tom Gola heard McGuire say, "We're ahead 50-0 at the start of every game," and Gola read between the lines, believing that what McGuire really meant was, *Okay, Wilt's got his fifty points, now what are you other guys going to do?* Guy Rodgers knew that players' salaries were determined by their scoring averages so, leaving nothing to chance, he asked, "Coach, whatever you say is fine, but will you sit in with us when we go to talk contract [next season] with Eddie Gottlieb?" McGuire smiled and said he would.

McGuire did his Wilt research carefully. His predecessor, an all-star Warriors player turned coach, Neil Johnston, had lost his job in large part because of his inability to get along with Chamberlain. During halftime of a game they would lose to Syracuse, Johnston had chastised Chamberlain in the locker room for not playing defense. "Wilt, [Johnny] Kerr has made five shots from the corner. Go out and get him. His name is *Kerr*." Chamberlain snapped back: "My name is *Chamberlain*. I'll go get him when I want to." This exchange, carried out in front of his team, effectively neutered Johnston. McGuire had heard about this. He considered it a cautionary tale. He spent hundreds of dollars on phone calls inquiring about Chamberlain.

From Kansas, Coach Dick Harp advised, "Wilt responds to leadership by someone he respects." Six seasons earlier, as Chamberlain's sophomore season at Kansas began, McGuire had been quoted in Chapel Hill, saying, "Chamberlain will score about a hundred thirty points one night and the other coach will lose his job. There might be somebody in the penitentiary who can handle him, but I guarantee you there is nobody in college." McGuire was coach of the North Carolina team that defeated Kansas and Chamberlain in the 1957 NCAA title game. McGuire had placed one player in front of Chamberlain, the rest in a zone designed to collapse around him whenever he touched the ball. He also tried a psychological ploy or two. He used five-foot-eleven guard Tommy Kearns for the opening jump against Chamberlain. Naturally, Wilt won the tap, but McGuire hoped to let the Dipper know he had a few new tricks in his bag. North Carolina won that title game in triple overtime, 54-53, and limited the Dipper to just six field goals and eleven free throws, in all twenty-three points. That victory fortified McGuire's reputation as a winner and Chamberlain's as a great individualist unable to win a title.

Now, as Warriors coach, McGuire spent considerable time with his star center, explaining himself and his expectations. "How long do you want to play?" McGuire asked. "Forever," the Dipper replied. "No," McGuire said, "I mean how long each game." The Dipper said, "When you take me out, I'm sitting next to you. I'm not scoring or rebounding. And when I go back in, it takes another three minutes to get this body going." McGuire determined to play him every minute of every game. He brought Chamberlain to his summer home at Greenwood Lake in New York. There, Wilt played with Frankie, McGuire's ten-year-old son born with cerebral palsy. Always a soft touch with kids, Chamberlain let Frankie tug on his mustache and chin hairs. Chamberlain warmed quickly to his glib new coach. Gola realized what was happening: All of the Dipper's previous coaches had given orders to him as to what to do, but McGuire didn't and Wilt responded to him. When McGuire suggested that Chamberlain, having missed 500 free throws the previous season, try shooting his foul shots underhanded, Chamberlain willingly tried it—and stayed with it. (He converted sixty-one percent of his free throws for the season, nothing to brag about, but still the highest such percentage during his NBA career.) On another occasion, after an overtime loss in Los Angeles, Gola saw the Dipper sitting in the locker room with football's Roosevelt Grier, smoking a cigarette in clear violation of one of McGuire's rules. *Wait'll Frank sees this!* Gola thought. Just then, McGuire appeared, walked past the Dipper. "Tough game, Wiltie," McGuire said and kept walking without another word.

The respect was mutual. Chamberlain once saw McGuire alone in his hotel room, quietly despondent about being away from his wife and children, especially Frankie, and became for his coach a sympathetic listener. The Dipper asked, "What's wrong?" McGuire replied, "Look at this room." In the postmidnight darkness it looked especially tiny. The Dipper said, "I got a room twice this size at the end of the hall, Coach. It's all yours." He gave the coach his room key.

In the fall of 1961, their relationship and their season taking flight, the Dipper and McGuire stood together on the cover of *Sports Illustrated* beside a mocking headline: PROBLEM FOR A NEW COACH. In his cover story, sportswriter Ray Cave saw dramatic implications in their relationship: "[McGuire's] challenge is to develop further and properly use the game's greatest individual talent—and toughest problem—Wilt Chamberlain. And his eventual effect may be to measurably change the character of professional basketball from the brawling, hustling, cigar-in-your-face and eye-on-the-till game it has been for decades to the major league sport which it longs and deserves to be."

The Warriors bus had departed in midafternoon from the Sheraton hotel in Center City where Gotty kept his office. As the bus crossed the Schuylkill River, the Philadelphia skyline receded. Bumpity-bumping down the two-lane highway on a two-hour drive, past signs pointing toward Allentown and Reading and into the Pennsylvania heartland, the Warriors soon were staring at fat Dutch barns, orchards, and grazing livestock. The driver kept turning over his right shoulder to yammer at no one in particular. No glamour here: bags thrown across ceiling racks, players' long legs stretched across aisles. With Gola at home and the Dipper traveling separately, only nine players made the trip, plus a few game crew officials and ball boys, which meant a lot of empty seats. It was a team of Catholics, African-Americans, and a veritable Rushmore of homegrown Philadelphia basketball heroes—Chamberlain, Gola, Arizin, and Rodgers. Gotty also liked having four rookie players, not because it made for a stronger team (it did not), but for a cheaper team.

Al Attles was closer to Chamberlain than the other Warriors. A quiet fellow, deep ebony in complexion, and only a shade over six-feet tall, Attles was, in personality, the antithesis of the Dipper: deferential in conversation, never overreaching. Raised in an integrated section of Newark, Attles attended Weequahic High, the alma mater of novelist Philip Roth, who in *Portnoy's Complaint* recalled the school's predominantly Jewish student body and the football team's fainthearted cheer: *"White bread, rye bread, / Pumpernickel, challah, / All those for Weequahic, / Stand up and hollah!"* On the court, though, Attles was hellfire on defense and the consummate team player on offense. He played every game as if it were his last. His nickname, The Destroyer, grew from a collision, in which he and others dove for a loose ball; his opponent emerged with fractured facial bones and Attles with a don't-mess reputation.

Attles always knew when Chamberlain was around: The bus would resound with the Dipper's deep voice and the playful challenges he issued. Earlier in the season, as the Warriors flew over the Midwest, the pilot announced, "We're passing over Toledo, Ohio." Hearing this, Chamberlain had turned to Attles: "How many people you think live in Toledo?" Attles raised a brow. "I'm not a census taker, Big Fella. I don't know," he said. "Take a guess, my man," the Dipper insisted. Attles sighed, then guessed, "Four hundred thousand." Chamberlain said, "You're wrong." Attles said, "How many do you think?" Chamberlain said, "Three hundred ninety-nine thousand nine hundred ninety-nine." Attles rolled his eyes. The Dipper said, issuing yet another challenge, "I'll bet you that I'm closer." Attles played along. "Okay, how much should we bet?" Wilt: "Six thousand dollars." Attles's salary was $5,500. "Unh-uh," he said, shaking his head. "Okay," Wilt said, "if you don't take the bet then I win." Attles said, "Fine, you win."

Such kindred moments with Attles, friendly as they were, were the exceptions in the Dipper's relationship with his teammates. For the most part, even in their presence, he seemed beyond their reach. They would exchange quips with him, listen to his Globetrotter stories, or play cards on a team flight, usually a five-card rummy game called Tonk. But the Dipper was guarded, self-protective, didn't let anyone too close. After three seasons, his teammates hardly knew him—certainly none of the eight white players did.

At best they could only imagine what it would be like to be the Dipper, and even that was a stretch. In public, Chamberlain drew attention, crowds. Rookie Ted Luckenbill grew tired of fans rushing at the Dipper to ask, "How's the weather up there, Stilt?" Once, Luckenbill heard it from a particularly obnoxious fan. Wilt answered, "I've got a phone in my ass. Why don't you call and find out?"

Each night there was a statistical sameness for these Philadelphia Warriors: Chamberlain rolled out his big numbers, unprecedented totals, dropping fifty-seven points on the Lakers' Ray Felix or fifty-eight on Detroit's Walter Dukes or sixty-five on St. Louis's Larry Foust, his unique athleticism making the Knicks' Phil Jordon or the Nationals' Swede Halbrook seem weak, doltish. The Warriors played in Convention Hall, a cavernous auditorium on 34th and Spruce Streets, thick with cigarette smoke and the cold echoes of Wendell Willkie's acceptance speech at the 1940 Republican Convention. Their upstairs locker room seemed an afterthought, more like a storage room. A small room with clean-scrubbed white walls, it had space for eleven folding chairs but no lockers, the kind of room Willkie might have used to be alone with his thoughts for a few moments before facing the cheering crowd and the specter of Franklin Roosevelt. During games, Warriors players draped their clothes over the chairs and put their shoes beneath them. Afterwards, the water boy brought towels, the first always to Wilt. There the Dipper guzzled a bottle of 7-Up followed by a large bottle of milk, talking to a reporter or two.

To his teammates, there was something disquieting about Chamberlain. It wasn't so much that the Dipper thought himself a great player or that he was as great as he believed or even that he was great in a way they never could be. These were incontrovertible facts. It was simply his overwhelming presence. It was as if when he was in the room, they weren't. He made them feel their inadequacy and smallness. He was large, luminous, and occasionally loud, at the center of every moment. Not one of them had ever known anyone quite like him. His white teammates knew only that he had an apartment in New York and a nightclub, and they heard rumors about women and an entourage in Harlem. He existed apart from his team, orbiting in his own glittery realm. The Dipper's teammates saw him only at practices and games, and then, just like that, he was gone again. Their friends

would ask: "What's Wilt Chamberlain *really* like?" His Philadelphia Warriors teammates would only shrug and show their palms to the sky.

Paul Arizin had seen it all, teammates coming and going, for more than a
decade. At thirty-three, his hairline sharply receded, Arizin was in the final
weeks of an NBA career that had started a dozen years before. Though he
lost two seasons of his prime to military service, his professional career had
been remarkable. Arizin had been around the NBA so long that he not only
had played against George Mikan, he stole the league scoring title from
Mikan in 1952, and then won it again in 1957. The idea of Arizin and Chamberlain in the same lineup now seemed incongruous: a merging of disparate talents and personalities from disparate NBA eras, like Ulysses S.
Grant fighting alongside George Patton. When Arizin joined the Warriors
as a rookie in 1950, the Dipper was in junior high school—both players
stood six-foot-four then. At that time, Arizin played against an army of set-
shooters, NBA players whose shooting style harkened to those described in
Walter E. Meanwell's 1922 book *The Science of Basketball for Men*. Meanwell
described the game's three defining shots as the "Two-Hand, Underhand
Loop Shot" (feet spread, fired from the waist up), the "Overhand Loop
Shot" (shot with two hands from the chest in the set position) and the "One-
Hand Push Shot" (jumping toward the basket while shooting). Arizin
played hard, yet always under control, and made himself into one of the
great players of the NBA's first decade. Married, with kids, he would shortly
begin a new career in sales at IBM. The Warriors rookies looked to Arizin
almost as a wizened uncle.

He was still scoring twenty-one points a game, still hanging in midair
too long for most defenders, still shooting his jump shots without arc, still
looking at his open palm after scoring a basket (a nervous tic Ruklick had
detected), and still wheezing up and down the court, the result of a breathing ailment many thought was asthma. When Boston's Red Auerbach heard
Arizin gasping for breath on the court, he believed it all a trick, because once
Arizin got the basketball in his hands he streaked past the Celtics and scored.
Auerbach even told his players not to feel sorry for Arizin: "Don't pay attention to his breathing. He's got asthma? So what? I've got asthma, too!" Unlike his teammates, Arizin didn't want to talk about basketball away from

the court. It made him fidgety. He preferred to be alone, working *The New York Times* crossword puzzle or reading a book, a mystery by Agatha Christie or Raymond Chandler or perhaps a biography. On the road he spent time with Gola and veteran forward Ed Conlin but most often he stayed to himself. He brought his seven-year-old son into the locker room on occasion. Little Michael Arizin got along handsomely with the Dipper. He talked with him more than his father. Paul Arizin hardly knew Wilt Chamberlain. In three years as teammates they never had a meaningful discussion. That was due, in part, to Arizin's personality—serious, sober, much as you might expect from someone raised in his grandparents' south Philly funeral home. Funerals were held in the living room, and sometimes the young Arizin walked past an open casket as he headed upstairs. It's no wonder he developed a lifelong aversion to flowers.

His Warriors teammates thought Tom Meschery, the Mad Russian, unusual in the way all Californians were unusual. Meeting him for the first time, Sportswriter Stan Hochman of *The Philadelphia Daily News* noticed it instantly: "Meschery was a guy who looked slightly offbeat. You could see he had the makings of a flower child." Meschery was six-foot-six and boxy, had a nice jump shot and a short fuse that lit whenever he opposed Boston's sneering Tom Heinsohn. Meschery fought willingly, if not competently; much of the blood spilled was his own. "Tired of his guff," Meschery threw a first punch at Heinsohn in a late-season game and walked off the court a bloody mess, saying, "My only regret is that I missed the punch."

Certainly, he had a fighter's bold lineage. Meschery's maternal grandfather, Vladimir Lvov, was of Russian nobility, had owned thousands of acres of timberland east of Moscow, and was said to have been nearly seven-feet tall. Lvov had been a senator in the Duma, the Russian national Parliament convened and dissolved four times between 1905 and 1917, and once lived in the old home of the mad monk Rasputin. Lvov had served as chief procurator of the Holy Synod, the lay head of the Russian Orthodox church. Tom Meschery had heard the family stories over the years—always from his proud, talkative mother, Masha, because his father, Nicholai, like most Old World men, said barely a word. Meschery also had read some of the old letters his family kept. Alexander Kerensky, the Social Democrat who led the Provisional government, had viewed Lvov as a nettlesome meddler, centrally involved in a military conspiracy to overthrow him. As part of the conspiracy, Lvov had been the one to ask Kerensky to step aside. "You must be joking, Vladimir Nikolaevich," Kerensky said. Lvov replied, "I certainly am not." Kerensky had him arrested and jailed in the Winter Palace. Lvov bribed his way out, and his fate never was entirely certain to the young Meschery, who inherited his lost grandfather's impressive size.

Tom Meschery's father had fought as an officer with White Russians on the western front with Admiral Kolchak and later fled with so many others across the border into China, settling in Harbin, Manchuria. There he met and married Lvov's daughter. In Harbin, Tom Meschery was born (ergo, a second NBA nickname, "The Manchurian Candidate," title of a 1959 Cold War novel and 1962 hit movie with Frank Sinatra). Three years later, in 1941, his father, having sailed away and settled in San Francisco, sent word for the family to join him—too late. Pearl Harbor turned the family's world upside down. The Japanese sealed the harbors, which kept three-year-old Tom Meschery, his older sister, and mother from leaving. They spent the next several years in an internment camp in Tokyo for women, children, and displaced persons. From missionaries there, Tom Meschery first learned English. Their camp was bombed—a church next door took a direct hit—and as fires spread, the Mescherys left in a hurry through a cellar door. When the atom bomb fell on Hiroshima in August 1945, the Mescherys were walking the streets of Tokyo, young Tom on his mother's back. After the war, through the Red Cross, the family reunited on the docks of San Francisco. As the McCarthy era unfolded, his father changed the name from Mescheriakoff to "Meschery" because it sounded less Russian. Kerensky would come to America to lecture at Stanford University. Meschery's father hadn't forgotten the past. He and some of his Russian friends, with a little too much to drink, crashed a car into a wall near the university. Inside the trunk of their car, police found a loaded pistol, two swords, and a photograph of Czar Nicholas the Second.

Tom Meschery had a wonderful laugh that his teammates loved; it was deep, genuine, and infectious. But his ambitions were difficult for them to grasp. Meschery had an affinity for history and wanted to travel the world. Entering St. Mary's College near San Francisco, he had wanted to join the U.S. Foreign Service, perhaps working in Russia, but his curiosity about basketball interceded. Basketball became his mission. *Two years,* Meschery told himself, upon his selection as a first-round draft pick of the Warriors. That was his time frame—to make it as an NBA player for at least two years. But now that he was producing twelve points and seven rebounds per night, the rookie was modifying that time frame. He was having fun, making good money, and watching the Dipper's heroics. The Foreign Service, he decided, could wait.

Meschery played every minute of every game as if proving himself as an athlete and as an American. Onto the court he carried a fighter's spirit: a loaded pistol and two swords.

Arizin believed every team could be subdivided into three categories: "There are the real drinkers and the woman chasers. Then there are the guys who are milk-shake drinkers who never drink [alcohol] at all. Then there is a 'middle class' in between them." He might have added that for the Warriors, as with the nation, there also was a racial divide. These Warriors subdivided socially into four cliques: white veterans, white rookies, black players, and Wilt Chamberlain. (The Dipper was the only Warrior to room alone on road trips, a contractual perk.) On the road, roommates Attles and Rodgers, the only other black players on the team, went out with Chamberlain to dinner or a movie, but only occasionally; with white teammates that never happened. The white teammates simply rode Chamberlain's coattails on the court, some willingly, some reluctantly; all gladly pocketed the extra playoff money he earned them.

What little frivolity broke out in the Philadelphia locker room usually was the work of the chatterbox Rodgers. Good-looking and glamorous, Rodgers had the gift of gab and was the most animated Warrior. He might even sing Bobby Darin's version of "You Must Have Been a Beautiful Baby" or "Mashed Potato Time," the number-one hit by Philadelphia's Dee Dee Sharp: *"Mashed Potato, feel it in your feet now, / Mashed Potato, come on get the beat now . . ."*

Chamberlain was restrained in the locker room, except to argue small points or to spin tales about his poker winnings, the Globetrotters, or his driving skills. As Meschery would say much later, "Wilt did everything in grandiose proportions. Even his truths were larger than truths." Hearing Chamberlain boast loudly about how fast he had driven his Cadillac—from New York to Los Angeles in thirty-six hours, nonstop—Guy Rodgers took him on. "Let me get this right, Dip," Rodgers said, licking a finger as if it were an imaginary pencil. "You would've had to average about a hundred miles per hour, is that right?"

"Hey, my man," Chamberlain said, "there's no speed limit in Kansas." In Kansas, it seemed, the Dipper hit 120 miles per hour.

"You ever stop to take a leak?" Rodgers asked.

"Not once," Wilt said, proudly. Nor did he stop to eat; he packed sandwiches and bottles of 7-Up. As for refueling the car, he said, "My Cadillac's got *auxiliary gas tanks.*"

These Warriors came to know Chamberlain's playful embellishments and bluffs—those cropped up in poker games on airplanes where Chamberlain refused to fold, always upped the ante, and usually won because, as Meschery realized, "he had a lot more money than we did." Because his stories sometimes seemed exaggerated (and often were, for effect), a few Warriors didn't believe his claim to have scored ninety points in a thirty-two-minute high school game. (Chamberlain had newspaper clippings to prove it.) He talked often about the Globetrotters and told his stories with fervor. To ask, "How would the Trotters do against an NBA team?" was to prompt him to up the ante. Chamberlain boasted that the Trotters could beat any NBA team. "And the Trotters play baseball, too," he would say, "and I'm tellin' you *they could beat the New York Yankees!*"

After his rookie season in the NBA, Chamberlain had visited Russia with the Globetrotters—Gotty even joined his old friend Saperstein on that trip—and his Moscow story was a richly textured classic. In a hotel lobby, the Dipper told teammates of how the Trotters had played nine games in seven days, sold out Lenin Stadium every time, and he said about fourteen million people watched on television. By the final night, he said Russian musicians were playing "Sweet Georgia Brown," the Trotters' theme song. The Politburo invited the team to dinner, he said. That night waiters kept bringing more bottles of vodka to the table. The Dipper was not a drinker, but he said he couldn't disappoint the Kremlin, after all. He clinked glasses, even proposed a few toasts. *And Khrushchev says, "Nobody leaves until only one man is sitting up straight!"* One by one, Chamberlain explained, the Trotters' heads dropped, falling gently against their arms on the table, defeated by vodka. Meanwhile the Politburo members, wearing their blue suits with little medals hanging from their lapels, began to drop, too. Chamberlain's own head throbbed at the temples. *Now, it's the next day.* He said the Trotters and Politburo members slept at their chairs. *There are only two of us left. Just me . . .* , the Dipper paused for story-telling effect, *and that motherfuckin' Khrushchev!* His teammates howled with laughter. The Dipper could tell a tale.

Each Warrior understood his role—McGuire made certain of that—even obscure players who had no roles at all during games. Backup center Joe Ruklick was the Kennedy liberal from Northwestern University. He rarely played, though he had his fun. A smoker of L & M cigarettes (the cigarette of choice, he'd heard, of First Lady Jacqueline Kennedy), Ruklick made his contribution to the team by practicing hard against Chamberlain and by stirring animated conversations in hotel coffee shops and on trains, planes, and buses, with Catholics such as Gola and Conlin. Inwardly intense and intellectually curious, Ruklick riled up these teammates by waxing passionately about the Democrats (especially galling to Gola, a Nixonian) or by philosophizing about oral sex (Gola, blushing, insisted it was a venial sin) or by reading Henry Miller's *Tropic of Cancer,* the bestselling memoir of an American expatriate in Paris published in the United States in 1961 to great fanfare and banned in some libraries as obscene. "This is not a book in the ordinary sense of the word," Miller wrote. "No, this is a prolonged insult, a gob of spit in the face of Art, a kick in the pants to God, Man, Destiny, Time, Love, Beauty . . ." Ed Conlin, Ruklick's roommate, thumbed through *Tropic of Cancer* in their hotel room. Of a Parisian prostitute Miller wrote: "Perhaps it wasn't so pleasant to smell that boozy breath of hers . . . but the fire of it penetrated her, it glowed down there between her legs where women ought to glow . . ." Ed Conlin, once a star at Fordham, a Jesuit school, growled at Ruklick, "Your mother would *kill you* if she knew you were reading this."

Ruklick had been an all-conference player at Northwestern, a big man with a deft little hook shot, but Chamberlain played every minute of every game, so no one got to see Ruklick and his deft little hook shot. Instead, he became a keen observer of the team, sitting on the bench with forward Frank Radovich, a couple of Midwestern sentinels, joking and staring at pretty women in the crowd. Once at the Boston Garden, seeing a gorgeous woman, so gorgeous Ruklick swore she must have been a Kennedy, Radovich advised, "Joe, you sit at the end of the bench tonight because I want a better look at that girl. She's got a short skirt on." During another game, there came a shrieked catcall: "Hey, Radovich, you and Ruklick ever do anything besides cheerlead?" Radovich turned and yelled, "Yeah. We screw your wife!" Ruklick scrunched down low and said, "Frank, you're going to get us killed."

The sentinels agreed that part of their role was to protect the Dipper if a fight broke out on the court. Ruklick couldn't forget the first time he'd seen Chamberlain, at a luncheon in the student union in Lawrence, Kansas, in December 1956, the day of the Dipper's first college game against . . . Joe Ruklick. The anticipation on campus had been merely huge: Phog Allen, just forced to retire as Kansas coach by age restrictions, saying of the Dipper, "He is the best that has ever been." When the Dipper walked into the student union, dipping his head beneath the doorway, Ruklick saw his sweater with a deer and a snowflake on it. Ruklick cringed and thought, *My God, Wilt skis, too.* Ruklick scored twenty-two points that night, but the Dipper produced the biggest night of his college career with fifty-two points and thirty-one rebounds in an 87-69 victory for Kansas. *Newsweek* magazine put it like this: "Chamberlain's great performance came under the pressure of an unparalleled build up. The national consensus: For better or worse, basketball is stuck with what looks like an unstoppable scorer, who may eventually affect his game as radically as Babe Ruth affected baseball." That night Ruklick had been even more direct, saying, "It's just ridiculous. He made me feel like a six-year-old kid." And, lo, six years later, the Dipper still made Joe Ruklick feel like a six-year-old.

Ruklick arrived to the team with the Dipper in 1959 and had served as his backup ever since, rarely playing. Three years later, Chamberlain still called him "Rookie," in part because he struggled in pronouncing the name, "Ruh-da-lick." Ruklick noted how his white teammates, particularly the veterans, rarely talked to Chamberlain, even during games in courtside huddles. It was, Ruklick decided, a freeze-out. He saw his white Warrior teammates speaking more freely and frequently to white players on opposing teams than to Chamberlain. Once, during Wilt's rookie season, Gottlieb walked into the Convention Hall locker room, his players sitting on their folding chairs. Gotty handed each player a sheet of paper. "A bonus check, Mogul?" forward Joe Graboski had cracked. Gottlieb shook his head. "Just read it." What the players found in their hands was a ballot for the NBA all-star team. They were not permitted to vote for teammates, only for players on other teams. Ruklick approached Gola. "Why don't we vote for [Phil] Jordon at center or [Jim] Krebs or Larry Faust," Ruklick said, meaning anyone but the Celtics' Bill Russell. That way, Ruklick suggested, Chamberlain might get more total votes than Russell and be named to the NBA all-star first team. He saw Gola's face harden. Gola reminded Ruklick that he was only a rookie, and rookies like Ruklick needed to keep their mouths shut. Gola, a solid citizen, was a locker room Gibraltar. He told Ruklick the integrity of the ballot was "to vote your honest opinion." All of the Warriors heard the exchange, including Chamberlain, who said nothing. Ruklick didn't push it but felt embarrassed, chagrined. He voted for Phil Jordon, anyway. And Russell won the players' vote over Chamberlain.

Ruklick came to believe that his white teammates didn't like Wilt Chamberlain because they didn't know or understand him. Nor did they want to. They had absorbed the ethnic, working-class racial prejudices of their fathers formed early in the century. Of course, Chamberlain's personality didn't do much to bridge the divide. He did not freely reach out to his teammates. That wasn't his style. He didn't seek friendship from them, only the basketball. Sometimes he would refer to himself in the third person, as "Norman." Teammates didn't get it as first. He set them straight: "Wilton *Norman* Chamberlain." He could be aloof, funny, boorish. Once McGuire called a practice strictly for free-throw shooting. Players understood this was McGuire's way of saying, "Wilt, you've got to improve your free-throw shooting." The Dipper showed up, reluctantly, and brought two big dogs with him. He strung their leashes around the backboard post. He didn't even change from his street clothes. He practiced free throws at the distant end of the court, alone. None of his teammates wanted to rebound for him because they feared the dogs. McGuire watched it happen and practice broke up quickly. Throughout Chamberlain's most remarkable season, his white teammates watched him with acute fascination. They might as well have looked through a telescope for the Big Dipper, so far from them was he.

There were precious few private moments that provided teammates real insights into the complexity of Chamberlain and what it was truly like to be the Dipper.

Ruklick once saw Chamberlain sleeping on a train, from Syracuse to New York City, in a driving snowstorm, crammed into a six-foot berth, and it seemed a metaphor for his basketball life—the Dipper was too big for the small-time NBA. As a rookie in 1959, Ruklick carried onto the Warriors bus a copy of James Joyce's *Ulysses,* a seminal novel about a day in the life of working-class Dublin that used the structure of the Homeric *Odyssey.* As Ruklick passed down the aisle, the Dipper noticed the book and said, "Yeah, I saw that movie"—a reference to the 1955 Kirk Douglas adaptation of Homer's epic poem. Ruklick suppressed a smile and kept walking.

Attles connected with the Dipper on a playful level. When the Dipper challenged him to enter an empty boxing ring before an exhibition game, they sparred, danced, and popped their fists into the air, laughed out loud, make-believing they were Archie Moore and Cassius Clay.

Luckenbill had shared an elevator with him during training camp in Hershey, just the two of them. In a frisky mood, the Dipper playfully slammed his elbows into the elevator's back wall. *Bam! Bam!* Why he did that Luckenbill didn't know, but when the Dipper stepped from the elevator the rookie from the University of Houston noticed two dents in the wall. An NBA greenhorn raised in Elkhart, Indiana, Lucky learned plenty from the Dipper. He had arrived for one team flight wearing shirt, slacks . . . and white socks. The Dipper shook his head and said disdainfully, "You're not in college anymore. Here, take these," and handed Luckenbill a pair of colored socks from his own bag. Now, Luckenbill thought about the dents in the elevator wall and returned to the elevator minutes later. Alone, he stepped inside, let the elevator door close and then slammed both of his elbows into the wall, same as the Dipper. *Bam! Bam!* He searched but found no new dents. Then a new cognition—pain! His elbows hurt. That was the day Luckenbill realized not all men were created equal.

After several games in the 1961–62 season York Larese rode with the Dipper on mostly empty trains back to New York. Larese, a rookie guard, had played for McGuire at Chapel Hill and had only signed with the Warriors in December after the expansion Packers waived him. He was a pure shooter who once set a school record by making twenty-one consecutive free throws in a game against Duke. (Larese shot his free throws quickly, as soon as the referee handed him the ball. Once, referee Mendy Rudolph didn't have time to get out of the way, and Larese's free throw skimmed off the top of his head. "Why did you do that?" Rudolph growled. Larese apologized and said, "That's just the way I shoot.") Some of his Philadelphia teammates, including Meschery, couldn't help but notice how Larese "spoke like Frank and even walked like Frank," and slicked back his hair like Frank McGuire, too—never mind that both hailed from Greenwich Village. Cynically, they called him "Frank's boy." On these train trips Larese discovered how keenly aware the Dipper was of being observed. Once Chamberlain carried a stack of books onto the train. Larese noticed the one on top and asked, "What the hell are you doing with a French book?" Chamberlain replied, "I'm taking French as a language." Larese said, "You're kiddin' me?" He wasn't. The Dipper told Larese that many people didn't think he had an education, or any intelligence for that matter. Chamberlain knew many whites thought he couldn't write or even *talk*. He genuinely wanted to learn how to speak French, but he suggested to Larese it was also important that people *saw* him with a French book in his hand.

Of course, the Dipper's interest in learning to speak French was well known to the team. During one plane flight, a teammate called out to Meschery for help on a crossword puzzle. Boisterous by nature, even in his fluent French, Meschery shouted the answer—the credo of the French Revolution—down the plane's center aisle: *"Liberté, Egalité, Fraternité."* Rodgers knew the Dipper was studying French and turned to him to ask, "What's he sayin', Dip?" The Dipper had no idea so he said, "He ain't saying shit."

En route to Hershey, the team stopped amid a triad of Lancaster County towns known as Paradise, Bird-in-Hand, and Intercourse, at a Dutch country inn that was a favorite of Gotty's; the inn's owner was a Warriors season-ticket holder. In his big, cozy front room, he had laid out quite a spread: chicken in the pot, dumplings, corn fritters, Schnitz and Knepp (dried apple slices and ham cooked in a round bread dumpling), chow chow, and shoofly pie, the rich harvest of the Pennsylvania countryside. The game wouldn't start in Hershey until 8:45 P.M. Some of the Warriors gorged themselves. As the first tangible proof that this night would be like no other, Gotty had earlier sent word that he would pick up the tab.

CHAPTER 8

Halftime

HALFTIME BELONGED TO THE ZINK. "Please turn to your Wig-wam program," he said on the public address system. On the program's cover was a smiling Indian dribbling a basketball and a picture of the Dipper. Gotty once called the Zink "the only p.a. announcer I've ever known who could take on a crowd of 18,000 and out-shout them," to which the Zink replied, "It isn't that I out-shout them. I *work* the crowd." Now, in Hershey, the Zink worked the crowd with his usual halftime fan giveaway. "Our gift prizes tonight," the Zink began, and he read from his list: a box of New Phillies Cheroots cigars, a souvenir rubber basketball autographed by the Warriors and, as ever, "those delightful kitchen favorites . . . Formost salamis."

Standing near half-court, microphone in hand, the Zink said, "Your lucky number is on page twenty-two. Tonight's lucky number is 2638."

A fraternity boy from Bucknell University in Lewisburg, Pennsylvania, reacted at once, Arnie Skaar shouting: "I won!" There, on page twenty-two of the thirty-five cent program in Skaar's hand, was "No. 2638." This number was even certified on the page in blue ink by the Zink's handwritten signature. But a Theta Chi brother, George Dirkes, raised a brow and said,

"Excuse me? That's *my* program!" Skaar replied, "You *gave* it to me." Dirkes said, "You asked to *look* at it." Skaar marched down the aisle to the waiting Zink. Dirkes followed him. The Zink, real bubbly, said, "Looks like we've got *two* winners!" The Zink gave them a choice: the Formost salami or the Seamless brand rubber basketball autographed by the Warriors? A difficult decision. (Two more Theta Chi brothers watching from the seats craved the salami; they were hungry.) Skaar took the ball. Away from the microphone, the Zink told them, "Here's the ball. You two guys figure it out." The Zink offered Dirkes and Skaar seats behind the Warriors bench during the second half. Moving to those folding chairs, Dirkes told Skaar, "You can *hold* the ball . . . for now."

The locker rooms in the belly of the Hershey Sports Arena were dimly lit holding cells; there, for a quarter century, minor league hockey coaches had exploded in tirades. The furnishings in the Warriors locker room were spare: a solitary wooden bench lining each wall, metal hooks from which to hang a shirt or slacks, three oversized brown metal lockers, a sink, a toilet, two urinals, and a tiny shower room with three shower heads too low for anyone taller than five-foot-ten. Into this locker room space the Warriors' Guy Rodgers carried a bubbling enthusiasm and a halftime message: "Let's keep getting the ball to Dip. Let's see how many he can get." Frank McGuire liked that idea. Meanwhile, Ruklick had played briefly, at forward, and once banged hard against the lithe Cleveland Buckner. Ruklick thought, *God damn, that guy's in shape.* The two players squared off, ready to fight, until the referees separated them. Ed Conlin, the veteran forward, congratulated Ruklick: "I'm glad you didn't back down from that. . . ." Conlin's voice trailed off. Ruklick understood it was about race.

Across the way, the Knicks knew that Chamberlain had scored forty-one points in the first half. It meant little to New York's players. They were accustomed to this. Jerry West already had put up sixty-three points against them earlier in the season, and a year before Baylor had scored seventy-one against them. The Knicks always seemed the perfect foils for somebody's big night. Besides, for Chamberlain, forty-one points at halftime was merely at the upper reaches of his own usual superior range.

Every year when the Knicks broke training camp, Willie Naulls saw in

his teammates a look of quiet resignation. It came from knowing their team didn't have championship material. In Hershey, as with most games, the Knicks were competitive but fighting uphill. They were outmanned, as ever, and knew it.

Sweetcakes. That's what Bill Russell called Willie Naulls, in part, because he was uncommonly smooth and handsome. These qualities were impossible to miss. "Willie Naulls was a guy I wanted to be like," the Pistons' Ray Scott would say years later, "because I wanted to appear flawless on the court, too. Willie had a movie-star personality. He did what handsome guys do. [Off the court,] he stood around and looked handsome."

At the NBA all-star game party in a St. Louis nightclub in January, Naulls had accepted a challenge from Walt Bellamy and Oscar Robertson in a Twist contest. A New York sportswriter described Naulls on the dance floor as "suave, smooth, experienced and well under control," an apt description for his game, too. Women noticed him. The Knicks' guard Sam Stith saw Naulls's small black book, in which he kept phone numbers, many of them, Stith surmised, the numbers of attractive women. Stith once asked, only half-kidding, "Willie, if you ever get traded, can I have your black book?" Stith estimated Naulls's black book to be two inches thick, and years later he laughed and pretended to thumb through each page of that book, reading aloud the imaginary names: " 'Miss America, Miss America, Miss America.' "

On the court, Naulls was a pure shooter, a six-foot-six forward with a breezy, unaffected sense. He wanted the ball, as scorers always do. He was having his best professional season, scoring twenty-five points a game, exceeded on the Knicks only by Guerin's twenty-nine-point average. Naulls had been named captain of the Knicks, a remarkable achievement for an African-American athlete at the time—it was a first for the Knicks—though Guerin was the player who, by dint of personality, captained the team on the floor. Naulls respected Guerin. They were two candles in the Knicks' otherwise dark season. Guerin had proven his decency to him, inviting Naulls to his home, and, on another occasion, sharing his salary figures with him. That, Naulls believed, was the sign of a true teammate: a willingness to talk business.

Naulls counted the Dipper as a great friend. He often saw him at Big

Wilt's Smalls Paradise. Naulls had first met Chamberlain in college, while driving through Lawrence, Kansas. That day the Dipper had treated him as if they'd been best friends forever. The Dipper was funny, easygoing, and knowledgeable about sports, especially boxing and track and field. Naulls liked him instantly. Now, he was especially inspired by the way Chamberlain seemed to be investing his money: a nightclub, an apartment complex, a portfolio of stocks. Naulls felt solidarity with the Dipper, and also with Bill Russell, with whom he often dined in Boston, and with Earl Lloyd, one of the NBA's black pioneers and now a Pistons assistant coach, who took Naulls to hear the Temptations and other Motown groups when the Knicks visited Detroit. Naulls understood that race often trumped team affiliation in determining friendships in the NBA. On this night, the Dipper had invited him to drive back to New York with him after the game, and Naulls had accepted.

Long ago Naulls's mother had told him, "Nobody is better than you," and that belief had sustained him through a childhood marked by segregation, and it sustained him still. His family had moved from Texas during the war to Los Angeles where his mother worked as a domestic, his father as a pipe fitter in the Long Beach shipyards. Even now Naulls returned to Los Angeles each off-season and played summer games at the Dinker playground against other black stars such as Woody Sauldsberry, Andy Johnson, football's Eugene "Big Daddy" Lipscomb, and many other lesser-known but hugely talented players. At the Dinker playground, Naulls believed, the talent far exceeded that in the NBA; the Dinker playground players were quicker and superior ball handlers.

Naulls knew that the thirty-seven black players in the NBA now were only the tip of an iceberg that ran deep and wide into America's urban core. That relatively few had broken into the NBA was, he felt certain, the fault of NBA team owners who "looked at what your parents gave you versus what God gave you." Over the next decade, a new generation of black superstars, with their on-court innovations and luminous nicknames, would storm the league and revolutionize the game, the likes of Earl "the Pearl" Monroe with his spinning crossover dribble and Connie "the Hawk" Hawkins with his acrobatic swoops.

Naulls understood he could've been stuck in St. Louis. As a rookie he had played only a few games for the St. Louis Hawks in 1956. After being re-

fused service at a segregated diner during the team's training camp in Gales-burg, Illinois, he had nearly quit. A team physician talked him into staying. Naulls was thankful for the trade to the Knicks, thankful to leave a St. Louis team that one year later became the last all-white champion in NBA history.

Yet six years into his Knicks' career, the New York press still didn't really know Willie Naulls or ask about him. Writers and broadcasters had picked up on his nickname from his pudgier days at UCLA, Willie the Whale. Once he was referred to as Willie the Black Whale. Naulls would say, "I was just 'a big black guy.' I prayed that I would never mirror the rage I felt for writers and fans. I was raised to withstand it. Most black athletes were." On New York radio, he answered sportscaster Howard Cosell's questions honestly only to hear Cosell misconstrue his answers and say, "There, you heard it here first: Willie Naulls is retiring." *Did I say that? I didn't say that.*

Naulls found inner peace and contentment in Harlem. Unlike Dallas or Los Angeles, in Harlem he met many black professionals, third- and fourth-generation teachers and businessmen and physicians, urbane and sophisti-cated, thriving in a warm cocoon. He met Sidney Poitier in Harlem and Duke Ellington. He saw Roy Campanella's liquor store and decided he'd never seen a place owned by a black man that was so big. Living in Mont-clair, New Jersey, Naulls met baseball's Larry Doby and football's Marion Motley and heard them talk about the old days in Cleveland and the way things were there for black people and how they'd gotten along. At Madison Square Garden, he'd met other black luminaries. Once, Ralph Bunche, United Nations diplomat, and schooled at UCLA, embraced Naulls before a game and thanked him *for what you are doing* for the race. Naulls met Jackie Robinson, who also had attended UCLA. At the Knicks bench, Naulls had told Robinson that he was a big Dodgers fan and loved to watch Sandy Kou-fax and Don Drysdale pitch and more importantly that "I really, *really* re-spect you."

Now, as the halftime stat sheets made their way into the Knicks locker room in Hershey, Naulls noticed the Dipper already had converted fourteen of twenty-six shots, a full night's work, and more, for any other NBA player. Naulls disregarded criticism of the Dipper's game. *Is Wilt selfish because he thinks he can make every shot? 'Course not. Shooters always think they are about to make ten in a row.* Naulls also noticed that Chamberlain had made thirteen of fourteen free throws. *Hmmm. That's a new one.*

· · ·

On the prowl, as ever, Kerry Ryman and his scamp buddies didn't listen to the Zink's halftime giveaway. Besides, they hadn't bought a program, let alone tickets to the game. So the boys meandered over to the arena's arcade. Ryman typically had his heart set on popcorn and pinball or perhaps the bowling machine where he slid a hard-rubber puck into mechanical pins. The boys emptied their pockets and pooled their coins. On some Saturdays, Ryman worked at the Community Center bowling alley, setting pins, earning a dime per game, maybe two dollars for a hard day's work. As halftime neared an end, the boys moved near the spot where hockey players sharpened their skates, to steal a few glances down the back hallways, same as they did at Hershey Bears games, hoping for a close-up look at the players and referees. The boys carried their winter coats, not having bothered to leave them on their seats. Those really weren't their seats anyway, and if they were no longer available when the third quarter began, not to worry. They'd scope out better ones, nearer the court, and claim them as their own. It was all part of their game.

Help each other out on defense, Eddie Donovan emphasized in the Knickerbockers locker room during halftime. He was talking to his players about Wilt Chamberlain, how to surround him inside, down low. Naulls knew his primary role was to cover Tom Meschery, a strong rebounder and a fine jump shooter, while keeping an eye on Chamberlain. Naulls was to make certain Meschery didn't get the ball into the big man. If he failed at that, Naulls knew at least not to get into Wilt's turning motion. *You do that and you take your life into your own hands.* Naulls had made that mistake once long ago. The Dipper had nearly knocked him out cold, his elbow catching Naulls flush on the forehead. In Hershey, Sweetcakes wouldn't make that same mistake again. He would play hard and shoot often, as he usually did. Then, much later, on the drive home, he would ask his friend the Dipper about his stock portfolio.

CHAPTER 9

Imhoff, Guerin, and the Knicks

IT WAS PART OF THE CURIOUS ODYSSEY of Darrall Imhoff's brief career with the New York Knicks that he played opposite Wilt Chamberlain on the hundred-point night. The usual late-night merrymaking, combined with the flu, had rendered the customary starter, Phil Jordon, unfit to play. Sweating and shivering, Jordon remained at the Hotel Penn Harris in nearby Harrisburg. Eddie Donovan gave Imhoff words to play by in Hershey: "You're all I've got tonight. Try not to foul out." Imhoff's goal in Hershey was to go it alone against the Dipper, for as long as he could, being mindful not to commit too many fouls. This was a humble goal, but of course, there was much for Darrall Imhoff to be humble about. When he'd gone off to college Imhoff was six-foot-eight and really not even a basketball player. But he had possessed one great gift—he was tall and growing taller—and so he was made into a basketball player. Back in 1955, when the Dipper scored ninety points in a high school game, Imhoff was body surfing in southern California, wearing white duck pants (which were then in vogue) and feeling lucky to have even made the Alhambra High School varsity basketball team. As high school players, the Dipper and Darrall Imhoff

were as different as west Philly and the West Coast: one would change basketball, the other could barely hold one.

In Hershey, Imhoff's NBA career was but seventeen months old and
now he would be matched against the greatest scorer in league history. So
intent was he on creating his own humble history in Hershey, Imhoff could
hardly have known that this game, and his role in it, was a part of a larger
sweeping history, a defining moment in the metamorphosis of the pro
game. Together their portrait in Hershey would be rich in symbolism:
Chamberlain and Imhoff stood alone on the trembling tectonic plates of
their sport. They symbolized pro basketball's accelerating generational shift
writ large: the agile black athlete, swift and strong, moving freely against a
white opponent who, though young, earnest, and determined, seemed out-
moded and immovable, a handsome blond shrine to a bygone era when all
of the players were white, dating back to George Mikan in his steel-rimmed
glasses and to the even more remote days when the game was played inside
a chicken wire cage (ergo, the term "cagers") that protected surly players
from unruly fans.

So much for humility and being mindful of not committing too many
fouls. Darrall Imhoff had committed three and so No. 18 had returned
quickly to the bench in a state of exasperation. By season's end, Imhoff
would foul out of ten games (only five players in the entire league fouled
out more frequently). Remarkably, he would record more fouls in his second NBA season than baskets.

And to think, Imhoff had arrived in New York to the sound of trumpets,
gussied up with glory. He had marched behind Rafer Johnson and the American flag into the 1960 Summer Olympics in Rome and then marched out
with a gold medal around his neck. The Knicks' newest big man, Imhoff
was a six-foot-ten golden boy with golden hair from the Golden State and
now he had his gold medal, too. Defense and rebounding, that was Imhoff's
forte, and he was a pretty passer from the low post, too. An NCAA title already was his, earned at the University of California, Berkeley. The Knicks
picked him third overall in the 1960 NBA draft: Oscar Robertson, Jerry
West, Darrall Imhoff. Heady company. He got a two-year, no-cut contract,
at $12,500 per. He faced big expectations.

But a message awaited the rookie Imhoff in New York and so did the last-place Knicks. New York's star guard Richie Guerin delivered that message at training camp. He did it privately, his words superheated. Born in the Bronx, raised in Queens, and schooled at Iona, Guerin personified New York City: all panache and puffed-up bravado, a great intimidator of smaller men and of bigger men with a smaller sense of self (their knees buckled under his glare). Guerin was tired of starting over, tired of finishing in last place, tired of new Knicks centers. He saw Imhoff's jug ears and subtle swagger and the way he seemed to commit every act on the court with his left hand. Guerin's message cut along a knife's edge: "If you want the ball," he told Imhoff, "then get it off the boards."

That simple. Richie Guerin was not passing the ball to the straitlaced rookie.

The golden boy would have to prove himself.

The sound of trumpets was not heard again that season.

Or the next.

Guerin was a gladiator. Five last-place finishes (and four different coaches) in six seasons in New York might've dulled the spirit of other players. Not Guerin: all those losses fueled his competitive rage. He performed well at every aspect of the game—shooting, passing, defending, and fighting, especially fighting. He threw tantrums, elbows, and fists, carrying the 1950s spirit of the league into the 1960s. Fighting was at the center of his reputation. Guerin charged once, fists raised, at Rod Hundley, the Lakers guard. Hundley did what made sense: He turned and ran. When the referee stepped in, Hundley was backpedaling and screaming, "Get that sucker away from me!" (Then, when passions subsided, Hot Rod Hundley said, purring like a kitten, "Hey, Richie, I don't want any part of you, my man.") Guerin was, at six-foot-four, too big for most opposing guards to handle, an advantage he seized at every turn. Guerin could score and inflict pain while doing it. Backing in, working his elbows, he turned his body into the defender, knocking him out of the way and drawing a foul at the same time, a brutally effective move. Guerin regularly annihilated the Celtics' Bob Cousy in the low post, Cousy pleading, "C'mon, Richie! I'll give you whatever you want from the outside. Just get out of here!" Each night Guerin wanted his Knicks teammates to play as hard and as well as he. That rarely happened.

At twenty-nine, Guerin was at the pinnacle of his career. Only Robertson and West, among guards, scored more, and by only a fraction. Guerin had produced big nights himself this season, scoring fifty-one points, fifty, forty-seven, and forty-six; two of those games came against the Warriors. A fiery ex-Marine, Guerin treated every game like the battle for Corregidor. He wouldn't shy even from Bill Russell; he drove into the teeth of the Celtics' great defensive front. That was Richie Guerin's style, on the court and off.

The rookie Donnie Butcher admired Guerin's moxie. They were friends; their wives sat together at games in Madison Square Garden. Butcher would go on about his friend Guerin: Richie knew people in every city. Richie could walk into a restaurant in L.A. that had a two-hour wait and get a table right away. A sold-out Bing Crosby concert, you say? Not a problem: Richie will get you front row seats. Richie had the smile. Richie had the style. Richie liked a good party and, boy, could Richie dance. Richie was dashing in his full-length coat. Richie knew Mickey Mantle and Whitey Ford and Richie could throw down a few at Clete Boyer's place, too.

Guerin was a crowd favorite, a star—and he knew it—and he got royal treatment.

A year earlier his close friend, Knicks Coach Carl Braun, had tried and failed to transform Guerin into a playmaker. Guerin was a splendid passer— only he wanted to shoot. He spent nearly two hours a day in the off-season working on his two-hand set shot. Joining the team from St. Bonaventure University for the 1961–62 season, Eddie Donovan said of Guerin, "A new pro coach like myself appreciates having him around." His teammates stepped lightly on the court around Guerin and so did the referee Pete D'Ambrosio. Once in New York, D'Ambrosio had whistled Guerin for a foul and heard Guerin growl at him, "I'll get you outside." Then D'Ambrosio heard Guerin say, "I'll punch your head off." He cited Guerin for a technical foul. Later, D'Ambrosio mentioned the incident to another referee, Sid Borgia. "Yeah," Borgia said, "Guerin said the same thing to me once."

That rookie season had passed ignobly for Imhoff. He didn't play much. When he did, his game stuttered. Not enough experience, too much left hand. Sometimes, he showed up at games only to learn that he was not among the Knicks' eleven players suiting up. He watched in street clothes.

Every day was a learning experience for Imhoff: One day Knickerbockers veteran Johnny Green bet him $20 that he could dunk a basketball ten times in fifteen seconds. Imhoff looked at Green, then at the basket. "No way," Imhoff said; the bet was made. Imhoff watched Green work like a machine, dunking with his left hand and catching it with his right, then doing it again and again. Green made his ten dunks with a few seconds to spare. He looked at Imhoff and said, "Gimme twenty, rook." That the Knicks, in mid-season, had reacquired Jordon from Cincinnati (they'd sold him to Detroit three years before) did not boost Imhoff's confidence. Several times the rookie Imhoff had scored baskets near the end of a game at Madison Square Garden and heard boos from the hometown crowd. It confused him until Knicks veterans explained that gamblers were upset the Knicks beat the point spread.

Few realized how far Imhoff had traveled. The game of basketball had not come naturally to him. He'd gone to it, clumsily, in part because he kept growing. He wore size thirteen shoes at age thirteen and size fifteen shoes at age fifteen. His family joked that you could *hear* him growing. He had long wondered about his size, where it came from. His parents were of modest height. Not until 1973, when his lengthy NBA career was ending, did his mother approach him, box of tissues in her hand, to say, gravely, "Darrall, there's something we need to talk about." Imhoff feared his mother was about to tell him she had a terminal illness. Instead, she startled him with other news: She told him the man he'd known as his father was not his biological father. She had been married once before, briefly, to an actor in Hollywood, a Norwegian named Petersen; as their marriage was ending she learned she was pregnant. Against the wishes of some, she had the baby in 1939, a boy she named Darrall Tucker Petersen. Soon after, she married Clark Imhoff, who proudly and lovingly adopted and raised the boy. Early on they legally changed his name, to Darrall Tucker Imhoff. Stunned by what he was hearing now, Imhoff hugged his mother and told her that he loved Clark Imhoff even more for what he had done thirty-four years earlier, for being as devoted as any father could be. As an aside, Imhoff's mother mentioned that Petersen, the actor, was six-foot-eight.

Darrall Imhoff had figured his basketball days ended long before that when an Alhambra High School teammate snapped him with a towel in the locker room. Imhoff gave chase, slipped and fell and broke his elbow, ending his senior season. He might have become the tallest park ranger in American history—if not for an aunt. He trudged off to college to major in forestry. His aunt, Vivian Tucker, a professor of humanities at Berkeley, helped him search for a place to live on campus. She phoned Cal basketball Coach Pete Newell. "I'm not a housing director," Newell said, politely. "I'm a basketball coach." But Vivian replied, "He's six-foot-eight and a half, Pete." Newell's interest was piqued. "What's his name?" Though Imhoff made the Cal team as a walk-on, he didn't play much the first two years. But he kept eating, kept growing: up to six-foot-ten. Newell had a way with words. "Son," he told Imhoff, draping his arm around his shoulder during one practice, "I never yet have had a player who didn't learn from his mistakes. And you are going to learn a lot." But Pete Newell was patient, and with Imhoff, his patience would pay off. The turning point came during Imhoff's junior year when he finally received a scholarship, though to earn it, he had to sweep out the Berkeley student union at 6:30 on most mornings. Trailing the play in a game against San Jose State, Imhoff swept in from behind to block the opposing center's layup, pinning the ball against the glass.

It shocked the crowd, and Newell, even Imhoff. He built himself into a defensive stalwart and rebounder and served as passing hub of the Bears' reverse action offense. Newell kept him well grounded. As his confidence and his performance improved, Imhoff once stalked angrily to the bench during a timeout, muttering that teammates wouldn't throw the ball to him. "What they ought to do," Newell howled, "is throw a *rock* at you." Imhoff would lead California past Oscar Robertson and the University of Cincinnati in the NCAA semifinal and past Jerry West and West Virginia University in the final to capture the national collegiate championship.

As his game matured during his second season with the Knicks, so did Imhoff. Naulls became his first African-American roommate and introduced him to the jazz music of Dave Brubeck and his odd-meter masterpiece album *Time Out*. Imhoff and Naulls got along famously and certainly never had a cross-cultural moment as laughable as when Knicks teammate Dave Budd mistakenly used the tightly bristled hairbrush of roommate Johnny Green to clean his shoes. In games, Imhoff did not shoot well, though he played effectively on defense, blocking shots, picking up a teammate's lost man, vocally directing coverage—aspects of the game that didn't show up in box scores. But he was neither Robertson nor West, his fellow first rounders, and the New York press reminded him of that often.

Yet there were a few shining moments. Leonard Koppett, who covered the Knicks for *The New York Post,* wrote as the 1961–62 season entered its final month that few Knicks fans grasped how much Imhoff had improved during his second year in the league since most of his best efforts had occurred on the road. Imhoff was only twenty-three, after all, and Koppett wrote, "His potential is such that every team in the league would like to have him on the squad, but up to now it has remained mostly potential."

Of course, as the game in Hershey approached, Leonard Koppett was far, far away. On a sunny morning in Fort Lauderdale, Florida, he joined other baseball writers in the swimming pool at the Yankee Clipper hotel. Koppett could hardly believe it. The world champion New York Yankees had arrived for spring training, and so had he. The creation of the expansion New York Mets had forced *The New York Post* and other dailies to send a second writer to Florida. It was a plum assignment, a badge of honor among sportswriters, a quantum leap up from the NBA. On his first morning in the Florida sun, Koppett looked around. *Could this really be late February? Where is the snow? Where are the Knicks?*

To the last question Koppett knew the answer: last place. He'd predicted as much in *The Post* before the season opener. Even with their overnight remaking, a new coach and a fifty percent roster turnover, the Knicks faced "the bleakest outlook in their history," Koppett wrote. "Nothing indicates sufficient strengthening to make up 17 games on Syracuse." If the Knicks made the playoffs, Koppett wrote, "It would roughly astonish everyone in the NBA."

Koppett had covered the Knicks for most of their sixteen-year history, initially as a stringer in 1946 chronicling the Basketball Association of America for *The New York Herald-Tribune* and then on staff for *The Post.* He had watched the downward spiral of the Knickerbockers, a name that originated in the 1600s with the Dutch settlers in the area and the trousers they wore rolled up just below the knees. Attendance at Knicks games in 1961–62 fell twenty percent, to 8,000 per game, the lowest such figure in franchise history, which meant nearly 10,000 empty seats at the Garden.

Koppett had seen the team's more successful years in the early 1950s. But even in those successful days, to make room for bigger ticket events like the Ice Capades or the circus, team president Ned Irish pushed the Knicks out of the Garden and into the 69th Regiment Armory. Not that Koppett had criticized Irish for that. Irish, after all, had been the originator of the college basketball doubleheader at the Garden, a brilliant idea during the Depression that gave customers real value for their money: three hours of entertainment, same as a night at the movies or a baseball game. That had been a problem for the NBA in its earliest years. Basketball fans had grown accustomed to seeing two games, not just one, and so doubleheaders became common in the NBA; on those nights, half the league was in the same building. (NBA players liked the Garden doubleheaders; afterwards, twenty players or more gathered at an Eighth Avenue tavern called the Everglades, leaving bags from four different teams in a pile by the bar.)

Koppett had seen the Knicks dissolve in the late 1950s under coaches Vince Boryla, and Fuzzy Levane, and Braun. Now it was Eddie Donovan's turn. Koppett liked Donovan, the thirty-eight-year-old coach, though it seemed hardly anyone in New York watched the Knickerbockers anymore. There was no radio coverage for most Knicks road games. WINS Radio, with Les Keiter handling play-by-play, couldn't secure a sponsor. The Knicks' performance hadn't helped: a losing record against every team in the league, even the expansion Chicago Packers. "Did the Knicks set any records this year?" a kid at a summer camp would ask Johnny Green. The Knicks forward looked at Sam Stith and Willie Naulls, smiled, and replied, "No, but a lot of people set records against us."

The New York press treated the Knicks with indifference or sarcasm. Columnists such as Red Smith of *The Herald-Tribune* and Arthur Daley of *The Times* and Jimmy Powers of *The Daily News* preferred football, boxing, baseball, dog shows . . . anything but professional basketball. Powers referred to pro basketball's big men as "freakish" or "praying mantis types." Red Smith's boss at *The Herald-Trib,* Stanley Woodward, a bloated six-foot-four press-box legend who wore thick-lensed glasses and had played football at Amherst while studying Latin and Greek, considered basketball a necessary evil. "I have strong reservations," Woodward said, "about the masculinity of any man who plays the game in short pants." Of course, Koppett knew that his own paper, *The Post,* an afternoon tabloid, was important to

The young Dipper, a soft touch with kids, sits on a street corner in August 1960, chatting with four of his fans. *(Temple University Libraries, Urban Archives, Philadelphia, PA)*

At Big Wilt's Smalls Paradise, a historic Harlem nightclub, Wilt Chamberlain often greeted guests. "Twist" dance contests on Tuesday nights were the rage in 1962 as taxis and limousines triple-parked in front of the nightclub on Seventh Avenue. *(© Bettmann/CORBIS)*

The signing of Wilt Chamberlain in 1959 had Warriors owner Eddie Gottlieb looking up. He chortled, "Wait until the people in Convention Hall see Wilt dunking that apple." *(Temple University Libraries, Urban Archives, Philadelphia, PA)*

Gottlieb was a tireless promoter. But when hardly anyone showed up to see his Warriors play a game in 1961, it caused Gotty to slump. *(Temple University Libraries, Urban Archives, Philadelphia, PA)*

Coach Frank McGuire, new to the pro game, meets with his Philadelphia Warriors at training camp in Hershey, Pennsylvania. *(Temple University Libraries, Urban Archives, Philadelphia, PA)*

McGuire gathers with a veritable Rushmore of homegrown Philadelphia stars *(left to right):* Tom Gola, Guy Rodgers, Paul Arizin, and Wilt Chamberlain. *(Temple University Libraries, Urban Archives, Philadelphia, PA)*

Richie Guerin, the Knicks' all-star guard, played with a competitive fury. *(Temple University Libraries, Urban Archives, Philadelphia, PA)*

The 1961–62 Philadelphia Warriors. Seated *(left to right):* Owner Eddie Gottlieb, Paul Arizin, Al Attles, captain Tom Gola, York Larese, Guy Rodgers, Coach Frank McGuire. Standing *(left to right):* Ted Luckenbill, Joe Ruklick, Wilt Chamberlain, Frank Radovich, Tom Meschery, Ed Conlin. *(Courtesy of Joe Ruklick)*

The New York Knicks struggled to avoid another last-place finish. Among the team's key players *(left to right)* were Willie Naulls, Phil Jordon, Johnny Green, Dave Budd, and Darrall Imhoff. *(© Bettmann/CORBIS)*

The chocolate baron Milton S. Hershey and his wife, Kitty, with no children of their own, created a school for orphan boys in 1909. Here, in 1923, he holds a student. (*Courtesy of Hershey Community Archives, Hershey, PA*)

The Hershey Arena opened in 1936. Its monolithic barrel shell roof was state-of-the-art, a technology brought over from Europe. (*Courtesy of Hershey Community Archives, Hershey, PA*)

Dave Zinkoff produced *The Wigwam* game programs for the Warriors. Showing foresight, he placed Wilt Chamberlain's picture on the cover for the game against the Knicks on March 2, 1962. (*Courtesy of Hershey Community Archives, Hershey, PA*)

During the first quarter, the Dipper swept around flat-footed Darrall Imhoff for a finger-roll. Paul Arizin trails the play. (*The Patriot-News of Harrisburg, PA*)

The Dipper scores his final basket to reach one hundred points. His voice rising, Bill Campbell told his WCAU Radio listeners, "He made it! He made it! He made it! A Dipper dunk!" *(AP/Wide World Photos, Paul Vathis)*

Teammate Ted Luckenbill and young fans congratulate the Dipper, exhausted yet energized by his climb to one hundred. *(AP/Wide World Photos, Paul Vathis)*

In the postgame locker room in Hershey, Warriors publicist Harvey Pollack, thinking photo op, penned "100" on a borrowed sheet of paper. The Dipper, trademark rubber bands at his wrists, held the paper in his hands and smiled sheepishly. This photograph has become the most enduring image of the famous night.
(AP/Wide World Photos, Paul Vathis)

the NBA. *The Post* had a liberal Jewish readership and basketball, a city game, remained popular with Jews; in the century's first decades, immigrant Jews in New York City had been drawn to the gritty game (as well as boxing) and produced many of basketball's earliest star players.

One of the Knicks' biggest problems over the years had been the college draft. Jerry Izenberg, covering for *The New York Herald-Tribune,* had noticed that each player the Knicks selected had some physical deficiency. But the Knicks' party line usually went like this: "Yeah, Johnny Green is only six-foot-five, but he plays like he's six-eight." Or: "Yeah, Cleveland Buckner is skinny, but he plays like he's 230 pounds." So Izenberg sidled up to Ned Irish in 1961 and asked, "Ned, is it possible for the Knicks to draft somebody *who is six-seven* instead of someone who plays like he's six-seven?"

What these Knicks had, to their credit, were three members of the 1961–62 NBA all-star team: Johnny Green, Naulls, and Guerin, that is, a jumper, a shooter, and a fiery leader. To Hershey, the Knickerbockers would bring five black players, the most (along with expansion Chicago) of any team in the league—three starters (Naulls, Green, and guard Al Butler) plus Buckner and Stith. At the team's first practice in training camp, Donovan had gathered his team and then pointed to Guerin and Naulls, saying, "You've been around longer than I have. I'm going to rely on you two guys to help me out." Stith heard this and thought it a mistake, a sign of Donovan's inexperience; playing for Donovan at St. Bonaventure, Stith had never heard him show such softness. Between them, Guerin and Naulls dominated the Knicks offense, combining for nearly fifty shots a game. Green, an extraordinary leaper whose primary job was rebounding, produced sixteen points and thirteen rebounds a game. Occasionally, Green grabbed Guerin's shots from above the rim and dropped them into the basket—which was good for the Knicks but irritated Guerin, who was credited with a missed shot on such plays. Guerin reciprocated by passing the ball—selectively. "A lot of times you would be open," Green would say years later, "and Richie wouldn't pass the ball in close to the basket. He was having a great year and a lot of times he'd be selfish with the ball because he was trying to feather his own bed." A long-simmering tension between the two all-star players bubbled over in a locker room fight. Green, a former Marine himself, lunged at Guerin and threw him to the floor. Startled Knicks players, who had never seen the easygoing Green so enraged, pulled him from Guerin, whose face reddened with fury. Donovan was in shock. "This is not to leave the dressing room," Donovan warned his players. Later that night Guerin let bygones be bygones, calling to Green, "What's the matter? You're not playing cards with us tonight?" Green replied, "I'll be right there," and he joined the card game in progress.

Now, at 10:00 in the morning in Fort Lauderdale, a Cadillac convertible delivered Whitey Ford, Mickey Mantle, and Roger Maris. The New York sportswriters quickly toweled off. Maris was their big story. He had hit sixty-one home runs the previous year to break Babe Ruth's single-season record. Unsigned for the new season, Maris sought a raise from $29,000 a year to $80,000, or $2,000 less than Mantle. Only two other Yankees in history had ever earned so much, Joe DiMaggio and Babe Ruth.

The writers crowded Maris: "What's doin', Rog?"

Maris told Koppett and the others he had reached an agreement and would sign his Yankees contract in a few hours. To the morning papers, this news would have to wait until tomorrow. But *The New York Post* was alive with editions yet to come at 11:00 A.M., 1:00 P.M., and 3:00 P.M.

Koppett retreated to his room at once to phone his sports editor, Ike Gellis. He broke the news. Rog would sign for $72,000.

Koppett considered his great fortune. Here it was only 10:30 in the morning, the sun was shining, he'd already talked to Rog, Mick, and Whitey, and his news story for the day was done. The swimming pool awaited him. This was the big time. No snow, no half-empty arenas, no hard-earned story of his buried next to the tire ads. The Knickerbockers' record was 27-45. Last place, still.

No wonder none of the New York papers cared enough to send a writer to the game in Hershey.

Two days before Hershey, Imhoff stared into the waters of Jamaica Bay as the Knicks took off on American Airlines Flight 51 from New York's Idlewild Airport en route for Chicago.

Below, Imhoff saw the crash site where workers searched for bodies. Only a day before, an American Airlines jet had crashed into the shallow waters. Ninety-five people were killed, and more than $60,000 floated in the Atlantic. One of Dwight Eisenhower's friends, W. Alton "Pete" Jones, a seventy-year-old oilman, was a passenger headed for a fishing trip with Ike.

Apparently, Jones liked to have cash available on trips. In his pocket he carried $16,500, including a $10,000 bill; his briefcase held another $46,000, wrapped in plastic. Now, as the Knicks' plane banked in the sky, almost instinctively Imhoff leaned left, as if to help lift the plane away from the tragedy below.

With eight games remaining, this had not been the season Imhoff hoped for. Two days earlier, in Philadelphia, Guerin had poured in fifty points against the Warriors and the Knicks won only their second road game in twenty-two attempts. Phil Jordan had been thrown out of that game by referee Norm Drucker for abusive language (not uncharacteristic for Jordon), and Imhoff once again had fouled out. In the fourth quarter of that game, with the Warriors too far behind to catch up, Chamberlain was matched against Buckner and scored twenty-eight points, an NBA record for most points in a quarter. The Dipper's points were meaningless, though later they would be seen as a portent of Hershey. Chamberlain finished with sixty-seven points. *Poor Cleveland,* Imhoff thought as he watched that day from the bench. Buckner was so thin he nearly disappeared from sight when he turned sideways. At a disadvantage of five inches in height and fifty pounds in weight against the Dipper, Buckner had seemed a thin reed snapped by gale force winds. The Knicks returned home to the Garden the next day to play Syracuse, whereupon they squandered a sixteen-point lead and lost.

Imhoff and Jordon had failed to solidify the Knicks center position. It only made matters worse that they played for an Eastern Division team, meaning they were matched against Russell and Chamberlain a combined twenty-four times a season. The Knicks scout, Red Holzman, had planned to select Walt Bellamy with the first pick in the 1961 draft, but that pick was awarded by the league to the Chicago expansion team and with it went Bellamy.

The playing styles and personalities of Imhoff and Jordon could not have been more different. A Native American from the state of Washington, Jordon was in his sixth NBA season. He had not yet lasted with the same team for consecutive full seasons. Though well-liked by teammates, he was odd, quirky, and often practiced without energy or purpose. He'd bounced from the Knicks to Detroit to Cincinnati and back to the Knicks, lasting about a year and a half at each stop. Earlier he'd played at Whitworth College in Spokane but only after the local Spokane Kiwanis Club had granted his widowed mother a place to live as part of its Homes for Widowed Mothers program; naturally, this generated a recruiting controversy. (Jordon hadn't lasted long at Whitworth, either.) "Like a tall pencil in shoes," is how the broadcaster Les Keiter described him. Jordon brought to the NBA in 1956 a delicate outside shooting touch, especially for a six-foot-ten player, and a keen devotion to his nightlife. Often he went out on the town after road games and his teammates wouldn't see him again until the next morning at the airport. His favorite late-night friendships were with Guerin and Butcher. The rookie Butcher didn't think Jordon took basketball seriously enough. "If I don't play, I don't care," Butcher heard Jordon say.

Bleary-eyed, the Knicks gathered in the lobby of the Bismarck Hotel in Chicago at 6:30 A.M. on Thursday, March 1. Guerin's thirty-four points had carried the previous night in a neutral-court victory over Detroit. Imhoff had played evenly against Walter Dukes as Jordon, complaining of a sore shoulder, did not play. The Knicks later watched from the crowd as the Dipper mauled Bellamy for sixty-one points in the second game of the double-header. Now they would fly to Pittsburgh and catch a connecting flight to Harrisburg. The season seemed interminable. Even Bob Cousy of the first-place Celtics complained: "The last two months of the National Basketball Association regular season were practically a waste of time." Cousy estimated that, by the end of the playoffs, his Celtics would have played 116 games, including exhibitions. "I'm told it figures out to four and a half games a week and sixty thousand miles of travel, an endless procession of hotel rooms and one-night stands. That's not basketball. It's vaudeville," Cousy said. "I don't believe anyone—owner, player or fan—will argue that the caliber of play in the NBA in March is equal to that of November or December. . . . At the finish there's not much more to the game than running up and down the court and shooting. Defenses are out of gas." Cousy estimated that thirty percent of NBA players were injured. "The last time I noticed Syracuse was dressing seven men. Seven out of eleven." Cousy had heard complaints that scores now were too high in the NBA. "The contention is that the big men who can reach the basket standing flat-footed are squeezing the little men out (which they are) and taking the premium off the field goal (also true), and the fan is sick of huge scores and the indefensible dunk shot. Well, first of all you can't legislate against the seven-footer. It's bad enough that he has to go through life with everybody staring at him. He should not be discriminated against in his chosen field, too. If you raise the baskets he will still be twelve inches closer than the six-footer." Cousy offered two solutions: Shorten the NBA schedule and reemphasize defense. "The good defensive player is lost today under the deluge of points, points, points," he wrote. "He gets little credit."

In Harrisburg, the Knicks set up at the Hotel Penn Harris, a fine and stately place not far from the state capitol. Though scheduled to room with Butcher, Jordon spent Thursday afternoon and early evening in guard Sam Stith's hotel room. He brought a case of beer with him. Jordon knew that Stith's wife was expecting their first child at any moment. "I'm staying right here," Jordon said, beer in hand, "until that baby of yours is born." He meant it, too. The hours and the beers passed in Sam Stith's room, Jordon drinking alone happily, occasionally picking up Stith's phone and dialing his buddy Guerin just to inquire, "Richie, how ya doin'?" Stith mostly listened to Jordon; this was only his first year with the Knicks so Stith thought it best to keep quiet, though he did have a passing thought of no small concern: *What if Donovan walks in and sees all of this beer?*

His beer done at last, Jordon left Stith's room and spent a late night with Butcher in Harrisburg. It made the next day, Friday, March 2, that much more difficult for Jordon. From behind the closed bathroom door in their hotel room, Butcher heard Jordon groaning and vomiting. He asked Butcher to get Pepto-Bismol to help soothe his stomach. Butcher stopped at a nearby pharmacy to get it. As the Knicks bus prepared to leave for Hershey, Jordon said to Butcher from behind the bathroom door, "Butch, tell them I can't go. I've got to stay here."

And that's how it happened that the Dipper was Darrall Imhoff's to cover on March 2 in Hershey.

CHAPTER 10

Third Quarter

HERE NOW WAS A TEMPO that mirrored Willie Naulls's own preferred style of play: "Run, jump, beat the ball down, and get it on." For both the Warriors and the Knicks in the third quarter, baskets came in bunches, a combined eighty-four points, the game's pace caffeinated and at times breakneck. The Zink was getting a workout on the microphone—if only Gotty had paid him by the syllable. The Zink called out on his p.a. system, "Air-uh-zun" and "Gair-un" and "Nauuuuullsss" and—ten times in the third quarter alone, with a noticeable increase in pitch—"Chaaaam-ber-lain!" It was just as Bob Cousy had said: By March, the last month of a long NBA season, *there's not much more to the game than running up and down the court and shooting. Defenses are out of gas.* For the Knickerbockers, Guerin created his own opportunities, while Naulls needed to be more inventive, using picks and screens set by forward Dave Budd, Buckner, or Al Butler. Naulls was piling up his points on free throws. When Naulls first joined the Knicks in 1956, he had despised the team's slow, walk-up style of give-and-go plays and two-handed set shots. It was tortuous, confining. Not like this.

•   •   •

Only the Dipper thought to occasionally slow down the game's pace, and he had his reasons. Pulling down rebounds on the defensive end, Chamberlain did not look to start fast breaks. Instead, he shimmied his body to bump away the Knicks as he held the ball aloft. Then, and only then, did he hand it to one of his guards, Attles, Rodgers, or Larese. His guards then waited for the Dipper to get down the court. This was not a new strategy for the Warriors. This was often their way. To the Celtics' Red Auerbach, Chamberlain's refusal to whip the ball down the court after a rebound proved that he was not, like Bill Russell, a true team player. Hogwash, Frank McGuire thought. In a calculated effort, McGuire let the Dipper be the Dipper.

Now, from the free-throw line Chamberlain shot underhanded. He bent low, his knees spread wide—his least athletic move on the court, like a grown-up trying to sit in a kindergartener's small chair. The flimsy rim vibrated as it jiggled: He made the free throw. The Zink announced to the crowd that the Dipper had fifty points. The Knicks' Jumpin' Johnny Green didn't need to hear it. Green *felt* it, like the earth moving. No matter how hard the Knicks tried to slow Chamberlain, they could not do it. They met him in force above the free-throw line, throwing guards and the weak-side forward into the mix to help Buckner and Dave Budd. They banged on Chamberlain and pulled on him. Attles, Meschery, and Rodgers kept lobbing the ball to him. If the Dipper couldn't get to his favored position, he moved to the right side of the basket or passed the ball back outside and burrowed deeper into the Knicks defense, until finally he got to his preferred position, on the left side, down low: home. Then the ball came back to him. Overmatched, the Knicks seemed in full retreat.

Chamberlain once dribbled the ball down the court. From the Knicks bench, reserve guard Sam Stith shielded his eyes. Chamberlain dribbled the ball so high, Stith thought it made for an easy steal, but the Knicks were backpedaling. Stith cast a look at Eddie Donovan, his coach, sitting at the distant end of the bench. Donovan bit his lip, a nervous tic Stith well knew from their years together at St. Bonaventure. Angry, embarrassed, and flabbergasted, Donovan was enduring an uncoachable night. Without weapons, what could he do? Stith wished the game would end now, in the third quarter. *Just get us on the bus and gone.*

At the WCAU Radio table, Bill Campbell seemed less than enthralled by what was transpiring on the court. Campbell didn't say what he was thinking, that the last-place Knicks were terrible. His statistician, Toby Deluca, repeatedly slid pieces of paper to him, game facts and biographical morsels, such as "Imhoff won a gold medal for the 1960 U.S. Olympic team." Deluca was music director at WFIL Radio in Philadelphia—Dick Clark's *American Bandstand* desk was in his station's library—and he'd watched Chamberlain sing in the studio on *Bandstand* a couple winters before. "A gimmick," Deluca called it. "Schlock." Watching him on the court now, though, Deluca was awed. This was total domination. On his score sheet, Chamberlain's points, written in black ink, crossed over into the Guy Rodgers column. So Deluca pulled out a different pen to change Rodgers's points into red ink. He slid another tidbit to Campbell: "Chamberlain has made fourteen of fifteen free throws tonight." *What?* Campbell gave a quizzical look at his statistician, as if to say, Can this be right?

There was, of course, a good explanation for Chamberlain's fine free-throw shooting, more than *just one of those nights.* After all, he'd had *two of those nights* at the Hershey Sports Arena already this season. In victories over the Lakers and Hawks at the arena, Chamberlain had made a combined twenty-seven of thirty-eight free throws, nearly seventy-two percent. He would make all eight free throws in this third quarter, which meant twenty-one for twenty-two overall. How does a sixty percent free-throw shooter throughout the season convert ninety-five percent on a night in Hershey? The Knicks' Donnie Butcher figured it had to be those flimsy rims, same as the ones he'd seen in Kentucky coal mining towns, weakened from years of local kids showing off by hanging from them. To Tom Gola, listening on radio at his neighbor's house in Philadelphia, the Hershey arena *floor* was bad enough—one of the Lakers had broken through it in December when several boards gave way beneath him—but the rims in Hershey were, well, like magnets. Basketballs typically ricocheted off tight baskets, but these rims weren't tight. They were old, soft, and forgiving; to put the ball near the hoop in Hershey meant, with a good roll, it was apt to fall in. Both teams were easily exceeding their customary shooting accuracy: the Warriors were converting nearly fifty-five percent of their field goal attempts, the Knicks forty-eight percent.

Seated with a few of his buddies down near the court, Kerry Ryman knew exactly why Hershey's rims had grown flimsy. Donnie Butcher had it just right. When the circus came to Hershey each year, clowns used red, varnished springboards as part of their act. Ryman and his friends had borrowed those springboards a few times. They used them to slam dunk balls into the baskets that had been pushed to the side of the arena, the same baskets being used now by the Warriors and Knicks. With long running starts and the benefit of the clowns' springboards, Ryman and his friends rose through the air, feeling as tall as Wilt Chamberlain. Trouble was, they were only five-foot-four, or thereabouts, and needed to hang from the rim after each dunk in order to gain their balance before falling catlike to the floor. After a while, arena workers chased them away. Ryman and friends figured those rims were old and bent, anyway. When they got another opportunity with those springboards, they would do it again.

The game offered smaller moments and images that, even without the Dipper, would've given fans in the Hershey arena their two dollars and fifty cents' worth: Jumpin' Johnny Green (only six-foot-five) rising for a rebound, his wrist fully above the rim; the old pro Paul Arizin, head faking and then driving for a one-handed runner; Sweetcakes Naulls releasing jump shots from eighteen to twenty feet, classically elegant; Rodgers, a whirling sensation, leading the fast break as stylistically as Bob Cousy ever did; and Leatherneck Guerin, without the injured Gola in his way, backing the smaller Attles into the lane, an executioner at work. The game in Hershey straddled two NBA eras with isolated images of the game's past and future. Perhaps as an offering to basketball traditionalists, Guerin and the Warriors' Ed Conlin attempted a few set shots.

The metallic *rat-a-tat-tat* at the press table came from Harvey Pollack's Olivetti manual typewriter. Like his Olivetti, Pollack was ink stained and indefatigable. Some called him the Octopus because he always seemed to be working eight jobs simultaneously; Pollack mailed Christmas cards each year that featured an Octopus on the cover, each of its arms identified by one of Pollack's jobs. Pollack worked full-time for the city of Philadelphia's recreation department, cranking out news releases each time a new park, playground, ice rink, or swimming pool was built or dedicated. Four blocks away, Pollack also worked part-time for Gotty as the Warriors' publicist and game statistician. Since few in the media seemed to care about the game in Hershey, Pollack had added three more jobs to his list on this night: In the newsman's parlance, he served as a *stringer* for two national wire services, the United Press (his usual account) and the Associated Press (short-handed on this night), and also for his city's leading morning newspaper, *The Philadelphia Inquirer*, whose own beat man, John Webster, didn't make the trip.

To Hershey, Pollack had brought his trusted Olivetti, a ditto machine (to make purplish-red copies of statistics), and his fifteen-year-old son, Ron, who during the game ran his father's typed pages to the Western Union desk for transmission to *The Inquirer*. Of course, Harvey Pollack barely had time to type. Watching the game intently, he recorded the official statistics and at each timeout banged out a few paragraphs on his typewriter. On this night, the Octopus was more like a centipede. Ron Pollack kept a running score for his father, handwriting on yellow Western Union pages the game's play-by-play, such as, "Wilt fade-away, 14 feet [56]" or "Wilt dunk [58]," the bracketed numbers representing the Dipper's running point total. Apparently someone on *The Philadelphia Inquirer* sports desk was tuned in to Bill Campbell on WCAU because Harvey Pollack was handed a note from *The Inquirer* during the third quarter: "Please detail for us every field goal that Wilt gets." *I need this like I need a hole in the head,* Harvey Pollack thought. Now the Dipper reached sixty points. The NBA's all-time single-game record of seventy-eight points—his own, set in the triple overtime loss to the Lakers—was within reach.

Pollack was cocksure, pugnacious, and very good at his work, though Chamberlain wasn't so sure. He'd complained once to Gotty that Pollack undercounted his rebounds. One night Gotty asked Vince Miller, Chamberlain's childhood friend, now a high school teacher and part-time Warriors scout, to keep track of the Dipper's rebounds. When the game ended, Gotty privately asked Miller and Pollack how many rebounds they'd awarded Chamberlain. Then he approached his star. "Wilt, whose number do you want, Harvey's or Vince's?" Without hesitation, he said he wanted his friend's. Gotty said, "Okay, but Harvey gave you more rebounds than Vince." That was the last time Chamberlain ever questioned Harvey Pollack.

A timeout. Pollack's Olivetti sang: *rat-a-tat-tat,* a lonely journalistic tune on this night. No New York beat writers had shown up. Only two Philly sportswriters attended the game: Jack Kiser from *The Daily News* and Jim Heffernan from *The Evening Bulletin,* and they brought no typewriters since their deadlines were much later; they wouldn't write until they returned to Philadelphia. Reporters from local papers such as *The Lebanon Daily News* and *The Harrisburg Patriot* would dictate stories by phone. After the game, Pollack would have many chores and little time. He would file a lead paragraph to *The Inquirer* by way of Western Union, then add up game statistics and crosscheck them with the official scorer, Dave Richter, and fill out the official box score. Then he would go to the Warriors locker room to facilitate postgame interviews. Next he would use a pay phone to call the United Press, dictating a story off the top of his head; his son then would replace him on the line to provide the box score information as Pollack moved over to another pay phone to dictate a different lead to the Associated Press. Then, after everyone had left, Pollack would return to his Olivetti to type a new story for *The Inquirer's* later editions. A juggling act is what it was, every tentacle of the Octopus at work.

Bill Campbell didn't understand why Frank McGuire never removed Wilt Chamberlain from games. *Why play a big man forty-eight minutes every night, even when you're winning by twenty points with two minutes left?* Campbell figured that Gotty or McGuire had cut a deal with the Dipper before the season: If they wanted him to break scoring records, certainly he would score more points on the court than on the bench. Chamberlain had missed only eight minutes, thirty-three seconds of play during the season's first seventy-five games. He missed that entire time against the Lakers thanks to referee Norm Drucker. Chamberlain so vigorously argued a call that he earned three technical fouls and an ejection. The harangue was a rarity, Drucker knew, because the Dipper respected referees. (By the end of the eighty-game regular season, Chamberlain had committed just 123 fouls, an average of one and half per game.) As lead official, Drucker reported the incident in Los Angeles in a telegram to President Maurice Podoloff at NBA headquarters in the Empire State Building. Drucker explained that fellow referee Earl

Strom gave Chamberlain a technical. "At this point," Drucker wrote, "Mr. Strom informed me that Chamberlain had made reference to Earl Strom's old mother." He added, "Before the foul was shot, Chamberlain yelled at Strom that he must be gambling on the game. This was in earshot of all the front row spectators. I immediately applied another technical." Drucker and Strom recommended a $300 fine for the Dipper; Podoloff settled at $150.

Bill Campbell knew there was no chance the Dipper was coming out of this game. When Chamberlain hit sixty points, Campbell wondered how high this might go. His own boyhood romance with radio had led him here. In 1937, he'd heard Ted Husing broadcast the remarkable five-set Davis Cup tennis final between the American Don Budge and Germany's Baron Gottfried von Cramm. Husing, sitting too close to the court, had distracted the players with his call. He agreed to speak more quietly. Listening from his father's Buick as they drove through Philadelphia, Campbell heard Husing whispering—whispering for an hour and a half. It was chilling, mesmerizing. It was so dramatic that when he arrived home, Campbell brushed aside his father, saying, "Not now, Dad," and ran into the living room to turn on the radio. Husing's fine work merely reinforced Campbell's desire to enter the radio business. A summer intern in 1940, Campbell heard a dreadful radio call of a rowing race between two lifeguards in Atlantic City. His boss at the radio station asked if he could have done better. Campbell said yes and was put to a test in the studio. "Describe this room," his boss said. Campbell did his best, giving small details about the curtains, the chair, and the table and even the microphone he was using. He got the job.

Campbell later moved on to Lancaster, Pennsylvania, where he recreated minor league baseball games on radio. He read the pitch-by-pitch recap on the Western Union wire and then described games as if he were actually there. He moved on to WCAU Radio in Philadelphia, where in October 1948 he interviewed baseball legend Connie Mack:

> *"This is Bill Campbell speaking to you live from the ballroom of the Warwick Hotel in downtown Philadelphia where tonight the Reciprocity Club of Philadelphia is honoring Mister Connie Mack, celebrating the completion of Mister Mack's 48th season as a manager of the Philadelphia Athletics. . . . First of all let me paint a picture of this magnificent ballroom for you, ladies and*

gentlemen. . . ." He introduced Mack: "It's awfully good to see you, Mister Baseball." Connie Mack replied, "Why, it's just a great pleasure to be here."

Campbell was the Warriors play-by-play broadcaster during the middle 1950s and on road trips roomed (on Gotty's tab) with Coach George Senesky, a calm, pragmatic man. Both Senesky and Campbell dreaded Gotty's late-night calls but came to expect them, especially after defeats. Once, Senesky handed over the phone, saying, "Gotty wants to talk to you, too." That night the Hawks' Bob Pettit missed several free throws in the game, and Campbell had told his WCAU listeners, including Gotty, "Pettit, usually a very, very good foul shooter, is off his speed tonight." Pettit made the next free throw. So now Gotty was on the phone, saying, angrily, "What did you have to say that for? If you'd kept your mouth shut, he would've missed that one, too!" Campbell brushed it off. That was just Gotty. What a piece of work.

When the players of this game had grown old and gray, they would yet light up in conversation remembering the way the young Dipper ran the floor on a fast break. They would speak about it with a hushed reverence, as if they'd seen something otherworldly, like aged Plains Indians recalling their first sight of the steam locomotive. Guy Rodgers would remember playing against the Dipper in practices, telling a writer, "You'll never know what it looked like to be backpedaling and see Wilt Chamberlain fill the lane." Attles, sitting back in his office chair decades later, would remember the cadence of the Dipper's breath at full throttle, like the huff-and-puff of a mighty train, and that the Dipper never ran on the break too far to the outside and that, "You better get out of his way otherwise you are going be run over." Ruklick would remember that the Dipper accelerated and screeched to a halt like no one of his size any of the Warriors had ever seen and that as the Dipper raced down court on the fast break he made it seem so effortless, never gritting his teeth or clenching a fist or bowing his head to get a jump start. More than once in Hershey, it happened like this: Rodgers accepting the outlet pass and dribbling to the middle, Attles racing in quick little steps to his left, and the Dipper to his right covering eight feet of hardwood with each elongated stride. On the fast break, he was exquisite to watch—in the mind's eye, the other players on the court dissolved around him. The Dipper made the court seem shorter, and he made it *his*. "It was as if he were an enlarged version of a smaller guy," Ruklick would say, still marveling at the memory, "as if when he thundered through a gaggle of players he was a superimposition of disproportionate dimensions on them." Among those precious few signature images that qualify among the defining best in NBA history—Russell's shot block, Cousy's dribbling, Jabbar's sky hook, Erving's swooping dunk, Magic's no-look pass, Jordan's midair majesty—is the Dipper, at twenty-five, out on the right, running the floor.

In the winter of 1962, as Chamberlain moved toward Hershey, the writer John McPhee watched eighteen-year-old Bill Bradley play for Princeton's freshman basketball team for the first time. He loved the way Bradley played the game, moving without the ball with a grace and simplicity, no extraneous motion, always anticipating his next move. In his book *A Sense of Where You Are,* McPhee wrote:

> *My own feeling for basketball had faded almost to nothing over the years because the game seemed to me to have lost its balance, as players became taller and more powerful, and scores increased until it was rare when a professional team hit less than a hundred points, win or lose; it impressed me as a glut of scoring, with few patterns of attack and almost no defense any more. The players, in a sense, had gotten better than the game, and the game had become uninteresting. Moreover, it attracted exhibitionists who seemed to be more intent on amazing a crowd with aimless prestidigitation than with advancing their team by giving a sound performance. . . . After watching Bradley play several times, even when he was eighteen, it seemed to me that I had been watching all the possibilities of the game that I had ever imagined, and then some. His play was integral. There was nothing missing. He not only worked hard on defense, for example, he worked hard on defense when the other team was hopelessly beaten. He did all kinds of things he didn't have to do simply because those were the dimensions of the game.*

If Bill Bradley had mastered the dimensions of basketball as it once was, Wilt Chamberlain mastered the dimensions of the new game that would replace it. What Chamberlain was doing to the old game was much like what

Elvis Presley had done to traditional American popular music. He didn't destroy it; he simply placed it in a new context. The old pro game was more regimented and patterned, much like the lives of the men who played it. The new game was faster, more spontaneous and inventive. It was played increasingly above the rim and with a more luminous athleticism. Wilt Chamberlain scored more points in 1961–62 than the entire Philadelphia Warriors team, a division winner, scored during the 1947–48 season. Many basketball fans could not identify with the new game. In the new game they could not *see* themselves. Players were taller—too tall, as some fans saw it—and much faster, and many of the greatest stars were black, a breakthrough that was part of a larger societal revolution.

The advances made by African-Americans in the NBA were swift and stunning: For the first time, in 1961–62, the league's four highest scoring averages were recorded by black players (Chamberlain, Baylor, Bellamy, Robertson). Since Mikan, and before, basketball big men had been called *pituitary freaks* or *glandular goons*, but in some of the new criticism there was racial coding, as well. There were suggestions that the new NBA stars didn't appreciate or understand the game, its patterns, and its pure intangible qualities. The new stars were showboats, stars only because of physical advantages, which were unearned and unfair. It was so unlike baseball. "Baseball's time is seamless and invisible," Roger Angell would write, "a bubble within which players move at exactly the same pace and rhythms as all their predecessors." The Dipper and others were changing the speed and the geometry of their game.

The criticism of the new game came from predictable sources—the traditionalists, those who were being one-upped or replaced; no one had ever accused their game of being electrifying. They resisted the new game for its individualism, its blackness. The new game had been incubating for years on urban asphalt, including each summer at the Rucker Tournament in Harlem. There, black players from college and the NBA and street legends whose careers had ended prematurely played in the park on outdoor courts, fenced in, local fans packed tight, with some watching from perches in nearby trees. By design, the Rucker game was a cultural spectacle, the talent kaleidoscopic, all bravado and strut, slam dunks and crossover dribbles that raised the crowd to near hysteria.

In the summer of 1962, a team from Brooklyn would play a team from

New York in a celebrated Rucker game. Brooklyn featured the Hawk (Connie Hawkins), the Czar (guard Eddie Simmons, who was said to *rule the court*), Big Bells (Walt Bellamy), and the jumper Jackie Jackson (who was said to have once plucked a half-dollar from the top of a backboard, though Wilt wondered aloud, "Well, who put the half dollar up there?"). In addition to Chamberlain, the New York team included Celtic Satch Sanders and the former Knick Cal Ramsey. The Hawk showed up late, a rumble passing through the crowd as he appeared, the Czar gently leading him by the hand, saying, "Let's go, baby!" Early in the game, Brooklyn's Jackie Jackson performed a double-pump dunk as Wilt trailed the play, sending the crowd into a delirium. Connie Hawkins, a stylistic genius at work, scored on a finger-roll over Wilt. Then the Dipper awoke. He blocked Hawkins's next shot and Dipper-dunked, again and again and again. *Did the Dipper make dunks on eight consecutive possessions or was it nine?* The last, he slammed with such force the ball bounced over the eight-foot fence, which stopped the game until that ball—the only ball—could be retrieved. Fans held their heads in disbelief and shouted as the Dipper jogged slowly down the asphalt, nodding, still king of the court.

Sports columnist Sandy Grady, rising to Chamberlain's defense six weeks before Hershey, wrote in *The Evening Bulletin,* "To the anti-basketball skeptic, Chamberlain's massive scoring may be ridiculous, but it is no more outlandish than Roger Maris's homer orgy." But on the day before the hundred-point game, Temple University Coach Harry Litwack, at the weekly Basketball Writers Club luncheon in Philadelphia, predicted baskets soon would be raised above the ten-foot level in the colleges and perhaps in the NBA, too. Litwack hated to see a team work hard and patiently for a basket and then, at the other end, "some goon stands under the basket and taps in a missed shot and that's two points, too. I never thought that was fair."

When he wasn't hearing about his unfair height advantage, Chamberlain was hearing, ad nauseam, about Bill Russell. On the night of the hundred-point game, Russell and his Boston Celtics were playing, and losing, in St. Louis. Yet Russell's spirit loomed in the Hershey arena as it loomed wherever Chamberlain played. No matter how superior Chamberlain's individual scoring achievements during his third season, he was reminded constantly of how Bill Russell, at six-foot-ten, the greatest shot-blocker and defender in basketball history, had played five seasons and already won four NBA titles, and how Bill Russell once had won an NCAA title at the University of San Francisco *and* an Olympic Gold medal in Melbourne, Australia, *and* an NBA title . . . all within thirteen months. Bill Russell was considered the consummate teammate, the game's greatest winner. His style of play harkened to the game McPhee revered: integral. While Chamberlain ferociously swatted opponents' shots ten rows into the grandstands, Russell blocked shots and somehow managed to keep the ball on the court in hopes of starting a fast break. That was Russell—all for the team.

To see them side-by-side—Chamberlain was nearly four inches taller, forty pounds heavier—made Russell appear the underdog, a ridiculous notion the Celtic center gladly embraced. Of course, Russell had five teammates in 1961–62 who one day would join him in the Hall of Fame while Chamberlain had just two (Arizin and Gola). In Red Auerbach, Russell also had the game's superior coach and game tactician. "I respect Russell and he's my friend," Chamberlain said in December 1961. "But people don't understand one fact—he's with Boston, I'm with Philadelphia. He's got the greatest team in basketball around him. That's not my opinion, but fact. Bill doesn't have to carry a scoring load. If he doesn't score a point, Boston can win. Bill's out there to play defense and rebound. Now when I go on the floor for a game, I know I've got to hit forty points or so, or this team is in trouble. I must score—understand? After that I play defense and get the ball off the boards. I try to do them all, best I can, but scoring comes first. If I were with Boston, maybe I would be a different player. I don't know. Maybe it's lucky that Russell and I are where we are, but I wish people would understand that our jobs are quite different."

Auerbach derived great pleasure in publicly needling Chamberlain—it seemed Auerbach's favorite pastime—suggesting that the Warriors center cared not about winning, only his own statistics, and also that he didn't always play hard, especially on defense. (The latter criticism was true, but could be easily explained: the Dipper in 1961–62 played an unheard-of 3,882 minutes, averaging forty-eight and a half minutes per game, including overtimes. Playing all those minutes every night, it would've been impossible for a seven-foot-one center to go full bore at every moment.) At times during the season, even as the Celtics won eight of twelve games against Philadelphia, Chamberlain dominated Russell, overpowering him with his strength. Russell was, at best, an ordinary shooter, making just forty-four percent of his shots, most from in close. Chamberlain could have skipped the final forty-four games of the 1961–62 season and still outscored Russell; he scored more points in thirty-six games than Russell did in eighty. It is true that Russell limited him to roughly a forty-point average in head-to-head meetings in 1961–62, ten points below his season average, the league's only center to limit him to less than thirty points in a game (twenty-eight and twenty-six points), the best defensive effort staged against the Dipper by any center or team (Chamberlain scored fifty-three and fifty points against Boston in two other games Russell missed due to injury). But, seen differently, it is also true that, in 1961–62, Chamberlain averaged nearly forty points a game against the greatest defensive center in history—an average that, alone, would have led the league in scoring.

Russell was famous for his rebounding skill, yet Chamberlain outrebounded him during the season. In one game in November 1960, Chamberlain also had grabbed a league record fifty-five rebounds—against Russell. Chamberlain was chastised for playing forty-eight minutes every night in 1961–62, as was Frank McGuire for allowing it, yet Russell averaged forty-five minutes per game that season. Chamberlain was chastised for his sixty-one percent free-throw shooting percentage, yet Russell made just fifty-nine percent of his free throws that season. Indeed, in their college days, Russell at USF and Chamberlain at Kansas, Coach Pete Newell of the University of California had learned the essence of both players: They conquered in their own unique ways. With his devastating shot-blocking skill, Russell put a trauma on Newell's shooters that lasted several games. Russell didn't block shots from merely one spot; he moved laterally in a wide arc, using his quick leap to block shots from behind or from the side. Newell discovered that his most confident shooters suffered nightmares during subsequent games, somehow imagining that Russell would emerge from the shadows to block their shots anew. In two games against Chamberlain and Kansas, Newell tried to be creative. He had seen other college teams gang up on Chamberlain, to no avail. Newell hoped Chamberlain would shoot his fade-away, rather than turn toward the basket, so he advised his own center, just six-foot-five, "Tell Wilt when he shoots that fall-away shot what a great shot it is. Tell him you want him to teach you that shot." That's what the Cal center did, but with only a limited payoff. With Wilt scoring twenty-three and nineteen points, Kansas won both games.

The two cities, Philadelphia and Boston, founded as William Penn's Quaker town and John Winthrop's Puritan "city on a hill," had developed a fierce rivalry through the generations. Chamberlain versus Russell fit neatly into this charged competition. Referee Norm Drucker, working Warriors-Celtics games, made sure never to stand near the visiting team's bench during timeouts at the Boston Garden or Convention Hall for fear he'd get hit by eggs or coins thrown from the crowd. Gotty loved the city-to-city rivalry and especially the Chamberlain-Russell hyperbole. Whenever possible, Gotty stoked the embers of it. In the newspapers, he decried Russell for his criminal goaltending on defense while privately pulling Russell aside in the locker room to say, "I assume you're not paying any attention to all that stuff about goaltending. It just helps to keep our seats filled and our flock growing." Then Gotty went back out and howled some more.

What fans saw in the Chamberlain-Russell wars in 1961–62 was less than the full truth. The men shared a friendship; while in town to play the Warriors in November, Russell ate Thanksgiving dinner in the home of Chamberlain's parents in west Philly. The two players dined together in Boston, too, sometimes with Attles or Sam Jones. McGuire warned the Dipper that Russell was trying to soften him up before games. The Dipper didn't believe it. Their personalities defined their style of play and how they treated opponents: Russell confrontational and defiant, the Dipper anything but, relying more on finesse with his fall-away shot. That Chamberlain never fouled out of a game in his fourteen NBA seasons can be explained in part by his preference to avoid confrontation. When the Celtics' black players had talked about boycotting the exhibition game in Lexington, Kentucky, Russell had led the discussion. That was not Chamberlain's way. About the broader issue of civil rights, the Dipper said only, "The best way to help integration is to live a good, clean life." This comment—straight-faced, banal, flat—typified the Dipper's public position on the issue at the time. His private life, of course, was a different matter.

Traveling to Boston guaranteed the Dipper would face jeers and derision. At the Boston Garden in January, the public address announcer facetiously told the crowd that Chamberlain had broken the arena record for most shots taken in a quarter. The crowd erupted in laughter. McGuire, in a red-faced fury, raced over to the p.a. announcer's table. "Is this the way you build up basketball?" he asked, shouting. "Why does everyone want to ridicule him?" McGuire would say, "I'd like to see Russell play Wilt all alone. People think that's what happens. When he got his sixty-two [points] Sunday, Wilt was playing against Russell, Tom Heinsohn, Tom Sanders, and Bob Cousy, sometimes in a collapsing zone. It isn't Wilt versus Russell but Wilt versus the world."

End of the third quarter: Chamberlain with sixty-nine points, including nine during the final two minutes of the quarter, the Warriors holding a nineteen-point lead, Pollack typing furiously on his Olivetti, Campbell wondering aloud how high the Dipper's scoring total might go. *The record, yes, but how high?* Sitting with his ten-year-old son on folding chairs near the court, the Associated Press photographer Paul Vathis wasn't taking any chances. He told his son, "Wilt's going to get eighty. You stay right here. I'll be back." Vathis went outside to his car and pulled his MamiyaFlex 2¼-inch camera from his trunk. The previous spring, he captured JFK and Ike walking alone even as press secretary Pierre Salinger announced to waiting photographers, "Okay, boys, that's it. Lids on." Now, he reentered the Hershey Sports Arena, a mere spectator no more, and planted himself beneath the Warriors basket. Something special was about to happen. He took the lid off.

CHAPTER 11

Ryman of Chocolate Town

FROM THE MOMENT OF HIS FIRST AWARENESS, Kerry Ryman understood that his world was shaped by chocolate. It dominated his senses: every second of his life he could see, taste, touch, and, most of all, smell it.

Ryman was a typical Hershey kid. Born in Hershey Hospital, he attended the Hershey public schools, his father worked at the Hershey chocolate factory, and his family lived in a rented row house on Chocolate Avenue. It was difficult for young Ryman to make it more than two or three sentences without mentioning *Hershey* since nearly everything in his town— every aspect of his existence—was infused, in fact, in spirit, or in scent, with that name. Ryman's mother once had been a cheerleader at Hershey High and as a young girl often saw Mr. Hershey from afar, smoking his cigars on the porch of his lovely mansion, Highpoint, as she and her girlfriends picked violets on the hillside below. The old man always waved to them. Lucille Poorman Ryman liked to tell people that she had chocolate in her veins, and when Milton Hershey died in 1945, she had been moved to write a poem entitled "Our Founder":

> *His ambition, generosity and success,*
> *Brought to the unfortunate happiness . . .*
> *He was equally kind to the great and small,*
> *And commanded respect and love from all,*
> *The good deeds of this Philanthropist are seen today,*
> *And the memories of Mr. Hershey shall not fade away.*

Ninety miles northwest of Philadelphia, Hershey sat in the lush Lebanon Valley, surrounded on three sides by an amphitheater of mountains. It was a neat and orderly town of nearly 6,000, the Amish and the Dutch craftsmen close at hand, where the sound of the crickets on summer nights was drowned out by the screams of kids at the amusement park riding The Comet roller coaster.

Was it a town surrounding a chocolate factory or vice versa? To read *The Hershey News,* published twice a month in 1962, it was difficult to tell since much of its news—nearly always good news—was about the Hershey Chocolate Corporation: a proposed split of the corporation stock, or its women's bowling team, the Chocolettes, bound for the state tournament in Erie. Certainly, it was a Republican town whose partisan leanings were evident in 1953 when President Dwight Eisenhower came from his farm in Gettysburg to celebrate his sixty-third birthday. Ike's motorcade swept down Chocolate Avenue where five-year-old Kerry Ryman (with a broken leg) was set up by his mother in a chaise longue and received a wave from the passing president. That night Eisenhower and his wife, Mamie, drove a horse-drawn buggy into the Hershey arena and 7,000 locals chanted, "We Like Ike, We Love Mamie!" and lit candles in the darkness and sang "Happy Birthday" to the president.

An eighth-grader like Kerry Ryman could learn a lot in Hershey in 1962 just by listening. At school, in current events, he could learn about the heroic astronaut, Lieutenant Colonel John Glenn, or the evil Mr. Khrushchev and his nuclear missiles. In the neighborhood, he could learn the latest buzz from the chocolate factory from workers in printing or in molding or in longitude (where chocolate paste was machine-blended into a smooth liquid). At home, he could learn from his parents about just how lucky he was. "You're growing up like a rich kid," they told him, "thanks to Mister Hershey." Seventeen years after his death, Mr. Hershey still made possible the Ryman family home—rented to a factory worker's family for $16 per month. He also made possible Kerry Ryman's daily after-school entertainment at the Community Club. An Italian Renaissance structure, elegant and U-shaped, the club featured a swimming pool, basketball courts, trampolines, slate pool and billiards tables, a library, a social room, and an ornate 1,900-seat theater with stylized balconies and a Pompeian lobby of marble grandeur. Kerry Ryman's full-year club membership cost his parents three dollars.

Because of Milton Hershey, Kerry Ryman didn't have to travel to see the world. The world came to him. Broadway shows. First-run movies, *The Magnificent Seven* and *Lawrence of Arabia,* watched in opulence and splendor on Friday nights, "Movie Night," at the Hershey Theater, and for only a dime. Dick Clark's Caravan of Stars: Paul Anka, Chubby Checker, the Shirelles. Ryman's own local favorites, the Hershey Bears of the American Hockey League. The Philadelphia Eagles in training camp each summer. Ryman had even carried the helmets of Eagles Chuck Bednarik and Pete Retzlaff from the dressing room at the Hershey Sports Arena across the street to the practice field at Hershey Stadium. He had seen the great (if sometimes wobbling) Sonny Jurgensen entering the Oyster Bar on Cocoa Avenue. When the Eagles left town, the Warriors arrived for their own preseason camp: Dipper Chamberlain, Pitchin' Paul Arizin, and Tommy Gola. Ryman watched Chamberlain play pool in the Community Club, awed at how he made shots by reaching his long arms to the far edge of the table and how he moved the scoring buttons along the wire near the ceiling with a simple reach and the flick of his fingers. (Ryman could only reach the wire with his pool cue.) The Dipper treated Ryman and his buddies like friends, nearly. He bought them ice cream cones and once, in a playful basketball game between the Warriors and local schoolboys, he'd lifted little Larry Wagner, a boy known as the Flea, and set him inside the basket, his legs dangling from the rim.

Ryman never had to leave Hershey to see or do any of this. Everyone and everything came to him. To a fourteen-year-old boy who loved basketball, it was all he could hope for: clean water, clean streets, clean parks, clean living . . . and the Dipper.

All thanks to Mr. Hershey.

Milton Snavely Hershey, a small man with a gray mustache, middle-aged paunch and, invariably, a cigar in hand, was a benevolent dictator, the wizard of his own chocolate Oz. It was his town, named for him, paid for by him, and populated by many of his workers. He christened the main boulevards Chocolate and Cocoa Avenues, and its side streets for brands of cocoa beans: Java, Granada, Areba, Caracas. He served as an early fire chief and mayor in town. In 1927, he said, "I am trying to build here a place where people can be happy and contented while they work, and live in pleasant surroundings." Of course, he had his own sensibilities, framed by his mother's strict Mennonite beliefs, and in return for his great civic gifts, he wanted his townspeople to act accordingly. Once, Hershey noticed a visiting salesman in the local department store, his arm draped around a young woman working the candy counter. This violated Hershey's own code of decorum. At once he found, and fired, the supervisor. As his driver, Roy Tice, chauffeured him through his town, M.S. Hershey jotted notes about which lawns and houses were not properly maintained; that was the least residents could do, he reasoned, given that he had made those homes available and affordable. He was known to hire private detectives to find out the source of the local liquor flow during Prohibition and even to learn who was dropping trash at his lovely Hershey Park. Long after Prohibition, a former chocolate factory worker named Ernie Accorsi opened a beer distributorship in a small shed in his backyard on Areba. Milton Hershey pulled up, Tice behind the wheel. Hershey had known Accorsi from the factory and liked him. He told Accorsi that day he would buy beer from him but with one caveat: "If this turns out to be a hangout for rummies, I'll run you out of business." Of course, when Milton Hershey became a regular customer, it did wonders for Accorsi's beer business.

After several early business misadventures, Milton Hershey had made his first big money in caramel. In 1898 he married Kitty Sweeney, daughter of an Irish immigrant ironworker, and when he sold his caramel business for $1 million two years later, he and Kitty intended to retire to a life of leisure and travel. He quickly bored of that. Hershey's father, Henry, was a nomadic dreamer, and his mother, Fanny, a humorless Mennonite with a Calvinist's love of labor. He took the best qualities of each—plus Henry Ford's genius for mass production—and built an empire. Better than anyone, Milton Hershey knew that if there was anything America loved as much as automobiles it was chocolate. On March 2, 1903—fifty-nine years to the day before Wilt Chamberlain's big night in town—the first spade dug into the valley's fertile soil at the spot where Hershey's chocolate factory would be built; his mother and father were there to see the symbolic moment. The Hershey milk chocolate bar was followed in 1907 by Hershey's Kisses and a year later by the Hershey Almond bar. The profits were staggering, and an American icon was born, although the Pennsylvania Dutch farmers nearby complained of *"da chockle shtink."*

In 1909 he and Kitty, with no children of their own, created a school in Hershey that was designed for white, orphaned boys, in keeping with the homogeneous tenor of their town (and with the language in the original mid-nineteenth-century deed for the Girard School in Philadelphia, which served as their model). "I have no heirs," Milton Hershey would say to *Fortune* magazine in 1934, "so I decided to make the orphan boys of the United States my heirs." He quietly endowed the school, where orphaned boys would learn thrift and how to work a farm, with his common corporation stock and other assets, totaling more than $60 million. Upon graduation, every boy received a handshake from Hershey and $100. When Kitty died in 1915 of a neurological disease at the age of forty-two, M.S. Hershey poured himself back into his business, back into his town, never to remarry.

M.S. Hershey had wizardlike powers in his town and that was never more apparent than during the 1930s: In a remarkable sleight of hand, he made the Great Depression disappear. He went on his own building boom and so kept his people employed. He built the $3 million Community Club (Secretary of Agriculture Henry A. Wallace dedicated its ornate theater in September 1933); he built the $1.5 million Hotel Hershey with its grandiose fountains and botanical gardens; he built an office building on Chocolate Avenue; he built the new Milton Hershey Industrial School for his white orphan boys; he built a football stadium seating 16,000 and the Hershey Sports Arena with its state-of-the-art concrete roof. Milton Hershey liked sports. He was seen at the stadium watching car races and once at a hockey game at the old Ice Palace where afterwards fans unknowingly jostled him as they headed for the exits.

In the 1930s, when he was in his seventies, Hershey still toyed with new chocolate concoctions. Out at the old homestead, where he had been born in 1857, he fiddled with recipes in the kitchen. He never knew the name of the teenaged boy working at the homestead—it was Brent Hancock—so each time he spotted him Hershey said, in his squeaky yet cheery voice, "Hi, boy!" Once, M.S. Hershey stepped from the kitchen at the homestead, wearing his apron and carrying a pail. He'd mixed onions and carrots into his chocolate. He wanted the boy to have a taste. Hancock did. It was dreadful, though he couldn't quite say that to Mr. Hershey. So Hancock nodded and, with the oniony paste still thick in his mouth, smiled bravely and said only, "Yes." When Mr. Hershey walked away, Hancock rushed into a bathroom. He needed water to wash away the taste.

Early 1930s: Joseph Nardi, an Old World man, approached the bank teller in Hershey. Like so many of the Italians in town, Nardi worked at the factory, in molding, where over the decades he had earned more respect than money. He spoke broken English—you could hear the Tuscan village of Pitigliano in his voice—and so, just to be sure everything went right, his son-in-law had written specific directions in English for him to give to the bank. Nardi, a meticulous saver, wanted to withdraw $5,000 to buy a house. He handed over the handwritten note. The man behind the counter gave him the money. Nardi counted it. He told the teller a mistake had been made, that he'd been given $6,000, too much. "Listen, you dumb Wop," the teller replied angrily, "I didn't make a mistake!" Nardi put the money in his pocket and went to work. There he waited for Mr. Hershey on his rounds. "I've got a problem," he said. Milton Hershey listened patiently as Nardi recounted his story and then found Nardi's boss and said, "I'm taking Joe Nardi with me for a while." Tice took them to the bank, Mr. Hershey sitting in the backseat, holding the straps. Nardi was nervous. Confrontation made him uncomfortable. "Point out the man to me," Hershey said. Nardi pointed across the room. Hershey approached the man. He told him Joe Nardi's version of the story and said, firmly, "Did this happen?" The teller blanched and said, "No, he's lying." Milton Hershey knew Joe Nardi as a loyal worker. Joe Nardi didn't lie. Hershey eyed the teller suspiciously. "You're fired," he told the teller. Back in the car, Joe Nardi, still trembling, asked about the extra thousand dollars. "Keep it, Joe," Mr. Hershey said. As he returned to molding, Joseph Nardi told himself that Milton Hershey took care of his people.

The Rymans set up home at 50 West Chocolate Avenue in a duplex. *Half a house,* they called it. On winter mornings, Reuel Ryman (a graduate of the

Hershey school for orphans, class of 1944) bundled up and walked a few blocks to the factory. For nearly fifteen years Reuel Ryman had been walking these same steps, just like so many other Hershey men. He kept working at the factory, in printing, making labels for the Hershey bar and Mister Goodbar, not because he enjoyed it but because it provided benefits, insurance for his family, and the opportunity to rent the duplex. He worked in the factory from 6:30 A.M. until 2:00 P.M. and then returned home to sleep a few hours. After dinner, he showered and drove to the 210 Club, a smoky bar in Harrisburg, where he performed at the Hammond organ until 2:00 A.M. as a member of the Charlie Morrison Trio. (His music was his joy; he performed once at a governor's conference at the Starlight Ballroom in Hershey. President Eisenhower walked by the stage and said cheerfully, "Hey, fellas, it sounds really good!" Then the dour vice president, Richard Nixon, walked past the musicians, head down, and said not a word.) Each night, Reuel Ryman returned home to sleep a few more hours, then bundled up in the darkness and retraced his steps to the factory. The Ryman's duplex only had one bathroom and sometimes, rather than wait for one of his younger siblings to vacate it, Kerry walked over to the Community Club to use the facilities. The local firehouse was in back, and when its fire bell sounded in the darkness, neighborhood volunteers were seen running, pulling on their shirts and pants as they went. In the row of six houses, five were duplexes, only one a single. Neighbors knew each other, and their homes swelled with children's laughter. Without fences, yards and lives converged. Through the wooden boards in their cellar, Kerry Ryman sometimes heard Mrs. Norman Smith, who lived in the adjoining half, calling to his mother: "Yoo-hoo, Looseal? Can I borrow a stick of butter?" Lucille Ryman passed the butter through the hole alongside the cellar steps. It was closely knit living, everyone family.

Ryman and his buddies usually could be found playing sandlot football in the meadow near the factory or basketball games on the macadam in Kenny Snyder's back alley on Areba. (Snyder was Ryman's town hero, a Hershey High sports star who, upon graduation, went on to excel in football at Gettysburg College.) Sometimes boredom set in, and the boys wandered to the abattoir. Passing time at the slaughterhouse, they watched workers shock squealing pigs or lift them with a chain only to slit their throats and cut off their heads. The workers stored the heads out back in fifty-five-gallon drums.

Other times the boys created their own unique thrills. They carried nicknames such as Sandman, Spammer, Big Al (for Capone), and Bugs (for gangster Bugsy Moran). Ryman's closest friends were the Damore brothers, Dave and Steve, a.k.a. Sandman and Bugs. They made quite a trio. Dave Damore, three years older than Ryman, was a smart-alecky, hard-nosed athlete, his younger brother, Steve, predictably unpredictable or, as the boys would say, "Bugs will do anything."

Years later, Kerry Ryman would say, "We raised a little hell, but we raised good hell."

From the rooftop of the Community Club, Kerry and Bugs once dropped a water balloon only slightly smaller than the Hindenburg. Five stories below, it struck a woman's umbrella with such force it inverted the umbrella, sucking it upwards. The boys hid on the rooftop, howling, "That's the biggest damned raindrop *she* ever saw!"

Tourists were their favorite prey. Standing on the bridge near the Acme grocery store across from the chocolate factory, they waited to see an out-of-town license plate. When a tourist's car passed, one of Ryman's buddies pushed another, who fell backward off the bridge, screaming. A watching tourist could not have known that the falling boy had landed only a few feet below the bridge—on top of an unseen freezer. Once, a tourist saw this, screeched his car to a stop, raced over to the bridge's edge, and looked down, only to hear the boys' laughter. The easiest marks, of course, were those picnic baskets left on Hershey Park tables by tourists who strolled off to the Tunnel of Love or Ferris wheel. Ryman and the scamps swept in and claimed a ham-and-cheese sandwich, a chicken leg, or maybe an apple.

To sneak into the Hershey Sports Arena and Hershey Stadium, the boys used their speed, ingenuity, and at least once, bolt cutters. No one saw them do it. In a hidden area at the football stadium, they snipped the chain-link fence, stepped through, tied back the fence so nothing appeared out of place, and merged with the crowd watching the Eagles play an exhibition game. If caught in the act, the consequences would be dire. The constables would turn them over to their fathers—and to their fathers' leather belts— a predicament that was, to the boys, every bit as grim as what the pigs faced at the abattoir.

．　　．　　．

According to the 1960 U.S. Federal Census, among the more than 12,000 people living in Derry Township, which included Hershey, there were but six African-Americans. The only black man in Hershey known to Kerry Ryman was Ollie, the Community Club janitor, who years earlier had chauffeured for Ryman's maternal grandfather, Leo Poorman, a Hershey butcher and local politician.

Being back in Hershey now reminded Timmy Brown and Clarence Peaks of the Philadelphia Eagles how uncomfortable and culturally isolated a black man could feel in the town. A night owl, once a nightclub singer with his own band, and friends with Philadelphia's Fabian and Chubby Checker, Timmy Brown lamented Hershey's social torpor. To him, that was even worse than the hardship of wearing eighteen pounds of football equipment in Hershey's ninety-five-degree summer heat and humidity. So bored was Brown during the Eagles training camp in the summer of 1961, he saw *El Cid* in the Hershey Theater eleven times. He loved the movie's end when the lifeless body of Charlton Heston's character was placed atop a horse and carried into battle, his image scaring off the enemy. (Brown had started to honor El Cid during games, emerging from huddles and holding up his arm, bent at the elbow, in an L-shape. "You supposed to be the indestructible El Cid or something?" Packers linebacker Maxie Baughan asked him during one game. "Yeah," Brown answered, "that's right. I am indestructible!") Hershey made Clarence Peaks uncomfortable, too, especially Martini's. Peaks had the sense that blacks weren't welcome at the bar, "kind of an unwritten rule." After several summers of discomfort, Peaks decided to prove a point. He walked into Martini's. There he saw Sonny Jurgensen and teammate Billy Barnes at a table, listening to a band. Peaks joined them and felt every eye in the room on him. But he wasn't leaving, not yet. He stayed about thirty minutes. He felt self-conscious but proud. When he finally left, he was relieved. Clarence Peaks told himself, "There. That's done."

Wilt Chamberlain had an immodest desire to the perfectible. It was a classically American impulse, an ambition to greatness. The business titan Milton Hershey had a similar impulse. Hershey attempted to create a utopian town from chocolate, seeking his own symbolic perfection.

And so here, in M.S. Hershey's neat, quiet, modest, well-run, paternalistic, virtually all-white company town, with its postwar vision of the good life and the American Dream, came a new vision of that Dream: Wilt Chamberlain blaring down Chocolate Avenue in a drop-top Cadillac, a black man flaunting his wealth in a way that fascinated and discomfited locals. The Dipper's hundred-point game would create that same fascination for fans in Hershey who would come to see the Dipper play basketball as no one else could—they would get their money's worth, and more—and create that same discomfort, distaste, and dissonance for Eddie Donovan and Richie Guerin and other custodians of the game's hard-earned traditions.

A brief notice appeared in the Hershey newspaper: "Star performer for the Warriors, Wilt 'the Stilt' Chamberlain will be among the host of top ranking basketeers to be seen at the National Basketball Association contest." As if Kerry Ryman didn't already know all about it.

As the fourth quarter dawned, Ryman and his scamps still were on the move. They had started in the cheapest seats in Peanut Heaven, where they played "Kick Hockey" near the concession stands, positioning a goalie at each end and using a crushed cup as their puck. Then, when the arena lights turned low for the playing of "The Star Spangled Banner," they'd slid beneath the railing and lowered themselves one level. *Jumping,* they called it. (Once, Bugs Damore had jumped and landed on the shoulders of an unseen constable, Clem Miller, who had just emerged from the men's room below—a bad night for Bugs.)

When they reached the lower level, they separated into smaller groups. As part of their earlier reconnaissance, they had scoped out vacant seats near the court. They went to them, breaking into groups of two or three. Ryman found his way near the front row.

On this night, with forty-six seconds to play, history moving him to audacious derring-do, Kerry Ryman would improve even on that front-row position. He felt certain Mr. Hershey would understand.

PART TWO

The Fourth Quarter

CHAPTER 12

Stirrings

THE HERSHEY SPORTS ARENA HAD AGED like Dorian Gray: not at all. Inside, it looked and felt like the year of its birth, 1936—severe. Here was the arena: half empty, cold, and gray, cement barrel shell roof, cement floors, and a metallic scoreboard at one end, up in Peanut Heaven, designed for hockey, reading HOME, VISITOR, FOUL, PENALTY. Beside it, a Canadian flag, limp. However drab, this was now the Zink's stage, the showman sensing the curtain drawing back, rising to meet the moment, his persona unleashed, no pretty *waitresses* to schmooze at courtside now, no Formost salamis to give away, his words on the p.a. echoing off so many empty wooden, hard-backed, fold-down seats in the arena's upper reaches.

It was 10:30 P.M. in Chocolate Town. The Hershey Department Store, open late on Fridays, was closed. At the Hershey Theater, *Sail a Crooked Ship* with Robert Wagner, Dolores Hart, and Frankie Avalon was over, the folks gone home. Mr. Hershey's factory was yet alive and thrumming, the late-night workers moving through miles of aisles of chocolate vats and machinery. At 50 West Chocolate Avenue, Lucille Ryman had watched the president, in a nationwide television address from the Oval Office, say that the nation would resume nuclear testing as a deterrent to Khrushchev's missiles. "Were we to stand still while the Soviets surpassed us—or even appeared to surpass us—the Free World's ability to deter, to survive, and to respond to an all-out attack would be seriously weakened," John Kennedy said. Four of Lucille Ryman's five kids were home, tucked in bed. She waited for Kerry to get back from the game. On the living room couch, she read and dozed.

Outside, only twenty degrees, wind chilled the streets of Hershey.

In Harrisburg, thirteen miles away, Reuel Ryman played the Hammond organ with the Charlie Morrison Trio at the 210 Club, a crowded downstairs place, thick with smoke, a favored spot for Pennsylvania legislators and conventioneers. A few blocks away, at the Hotel Penn Harris, lay Phil Jordon. The only other Knick who might've slowed the Dipper was in dire straits—hungover, the flu, vomiting. Eddie Donovan could've used Jordon, who had played the Dipper nearly even in an early-season game, scoring thirty-three points to the Dipper's thirty-four. For that matter, Donovan could've used the entire New York City skyline—the Chrysler Building, the Statue of Liberty, and the Empire State Building (with little Maurice Podoloff, NBA president, rising to Wilt's waist, on its eighty-second floor). In the fourth quarter, Donovan would use what he had, all of it. With Imhoff in foul trouble, Donovan had no player taller than the six-foot-eight Buckner. Naulls and Budd were six-foot-six, Green six-five, Guerin six-four, Butcher six-three, Butler six-two. If Donovan stood all seven players, one atop the next, he could build a wall forty-four feet, ten inches high, weighing more than 1,400 pounds. He then could raise it, like a prison wall, tall and turreted, around the Dipper. Only problem was, he could build no such wall; he could only order his undersized men to throw themselves against Chamberlain.

In New York City, at the sports desk of *The Herald-Tribune,* no one had penned the Knicks-Warriors game on the schedule. A wiseacre asked, "Hey, where are the Knicks tonight?" Sportswriter Jerry Izenberg, who often covered the team, said, "I don't know. Want me to go look for them?"

Entering the fourth quarter, the Warriors led by nineteen points, 125-106, the final outcome all but sealed. Yet Chamberlain was on a scoring spree. With sixty-nine points and twelve minutes yet to play, the Dipper stood ready to enter uncharted territory. This was not merely about a scoring record. He'd already exceeded Baylor's old mark of seventy-one points twice this season, with seventy-three and seventy-eight. It was about pushing the limits of curiosity and imagination, a notion that energized the Dipper.

For the Knicks, it was a train wreck. But for fans, in a more thrilling way, it was akin to watching the Friendship 7, which only ten days before, with John Glenn aboard, had rocketed into space and orbited the earth at 28,000 kilometers per hour. Upon his return to earth, Glenn said, "I don't know what you can say about a day when you see four beautiful sunsets." As no other American had seen what Glenn had, no other player in NBA history had gone where the Dipper would go on this night. The fans and Warriors players shared Chamberlain's passion for going into the unexplored, to see basketball's equivalent of four sunsets. The possibility piqued Meschery's curiosity, as it did to all the Warriors. They would have to subjugate themselves in the fourth quarter to become the Dipper's partners in exploration. The Knicks didn't know where this would end, though surely they didn't like where it was heading.

Richie Guerin, the gladiator, grew angrier by the moment. Chamberlain's rising total amounted to *rubbing it in,* an honor code broken. Guerin's face became a mask of tension and fury. Eddie Donovan, with his wife, Marge, in the crowd, had to wonder: *What is Frank McGuire thinking?*

In a few minutes, all these colliding thoughts and emotions would intensify.

In the crowd, a few NFL players had stayed after the prelim to watch the main event. Clarence Peaks, Timmy Brown, and Sonny Jurgensen were enthralled. Peaks, who knew Chamberlain's strength from watching him lift weights in his garage, now saw the Dipper overpower several Knicks defenders. Jurgensen, in near awe, marveled at Chamberlain's fade-away shots. Through the Zink's announcements, Jurgensen would track the rising point total. No awe for Timmy Brown. The way Brown figured, *Wilt was a dominant force and he was in his own zone, getting the ball and taking it at inferior players.* Besides, Timmy Brown never got too excited watching a game because he was used to *being gotten excited about.* The Colts' Gino Marchetti told teammate Bill Pellington that he'd never before watched a player that big who was so agile and strong. "Usually tall guys are sort of clumsy," Marchetti said. But, thirsty and thinking about beer, Marchetti and Pellington left the Hershey arena at the start of the fourth quarter and headed for Martini's.

Kerry Ryman and his buddies had dispersed. Dave Damore had pulled off a miniature coup. Even before the game started, the Sandman sat on a bench at courtside next to folding chairs for Warriors players. A team manager questioned Damore. The Sandman said he'd been told that kids from the Community Club could sit there. He stayed and soon looked back to his buddies and motioned for them to join him. None did.

Referees must keep their thoughts to themselves during games. Pete D'Ambrosio had officiated many of Chamberlain's games, though never one like this. Once, after working a Warriors game in Hershey, D'Ambrosio and referee Earl Strom stopped at a Howard Johnson's restaurant. Inside were the Warriors. In the parking lot, Chamberlain saw D'Ambrosio's 1956 Plymouth station wagon. "Yo, Pete," Wilt said, smiling broadly, "go get yourself a better car!" "If I had your money, Wilton," he replied, "I'd have a better car." D'Ambrosio liked Chamberlain. *A good kid.* Chamberlain had never caused him trouble on the court, not like Bill Russell, who sometimes muttered sarcastic jibes—nothing D'Ambrosio could whistle him for, but unsettling. Working this game on this night, D'Ambrosio watched Chamberlain's physical superiority and thought, *He's just eating them up.*

As Chamberlain and the Warriors came out onto the floor for the fourth quarter, some fans moved closer to the court. Ushers did not try to stop them, for they, too, were caught up in the excitement. A basketball arena, like a courtroom, can become a universe unto itself, drama unfolding with its own distinctive characters and truths. As the outside world fell away, Bill Campbell leaned into his microphone and told his listeners, "This is the big fourth quarter and everybody's thinking, 'How many is Wilt gonna get?'"

CHAPTER 13

Meschery

TOM MESCHERY WAS THINKING ONLY this: *Don't shoot.* An odd thought for the Mad Russian. His jumper was smooth, the dangerous dagger in his game. He was an eighty-two percent free-throw shooter, among the NBA's best. Usually searching for an opening, now he had one: The Knicks' Dave Budd and Naulls sloughed off to surround the Dipper, leaving Meschery open, more than just open, *We-dare-you-to-shoot, rookie* open. But Meschery knew his place. He heard the kids in the arena, screaming, "Give it to Wilt!" He didn't need to be reminded.

Meschery would shoot now only if he had no choice. In the fourth quarter's opening moments, the veteran Ed Conlin, wide open, had lobbed the ball inside to Chamberlain, who turned in, amid a crowd, and scored: seventy-one points.

Meschery was an analytical fellow, always thinking. *Frank clearly is absolutely awed by Wilt. But Frank's a con artist.* Meschery knew McGuire's strategy: Give the Dipper his space, let him think he's in full control, cajole him, play to his pride with the usual "Attaboy, Wiltie," and then quietly slide in Arizin and Gola and the rest, get them their numbers, put a little salve on their self-respect. Behind his cufflinks and presence, McGuire was a talker, a motivator, and a shrink. McGuire wanted the Dipper to score and, well, here was his night, Meschery figured. This night was the pinnacle, all right . . . for Frank McGuire and his stealth and guile. Not only was it the Dipper's big night, Meschery, Rodgers, and Attles all were scoring above their averages; only Arizin, who was resting now, was slightly below his scoring norm. Months before, Meschery's canceled double date with the stewardesses had brought him and the Dipper closer. Now he willingly submitted to his teammate's chase of history.

Attles dribbled above the circle, stalling, giving Chamberlain time to move through the Knick-thicket in the lane. Budd, Buckner, and Naulls bounced the Dipper around like an amusement park bumper car. Attles moved the ball across the perimeter to Meschery. The Dipper covered, no other options, Meschery shot and scored, 129-108. The Zink, matter-of-factly on the p.a.: "Meschery."

On WCAU, Bill Campbell said, "The Warriors are keeping the defense honest." The Knicks swept down the court quickly, Willie Naulls on the fly, hitting a jumper from the left corner, virtually uncontested, 129-110. The Warriors were hardly playing any defense. The Zink: "Nauuullllssss."

Meschery had felt for much of the year like most twenty-three-year-old rookies: alone, trying to fit in, staying with the other rookies, never overstepping with the veterans. Early on he attended a dance with Ted Luckenbill at a Polish-American club in Philadelphia. He had roomed on the cheap for a while with Frank Radovich in a small apartment, near a deli, in the Olney district—they'd bought a used TV for thirty bucks—but then Radovich got his own place. Over time Meschery's confidence and his game expanded, one feeding the other. His intensity on the court was, to Attles, *scary*, especially the way Meschery would lose himself in the moment, the way his eyes would roll back in his head. To Darrall Imhoff, Meschery played "like a cock-eyed wild man. It was like they'd turned somebody in Borneo loose." Meschery produced some big games, drew some big headlines, and even some high praise from St. Louis's Bob Pettit in *The Saturday Evening Post* ("That Meschery is going to be a real terrific player, one of the great ones"). He averaged twelve points and nine rebounds, solid numbers for a player aiming just to prove his *Americanness*. As the season wore on he became more talkative—he was, at heart, a noisy fellow, though not now. In this fourth quarter, he was quiet, submissive, hardly the Mad Russian. This was all about the Dipper.

Looking for Chamberlain, Attles instead passed to Guy Rodgers. Rodgers's jump shot missed. Chamberlain leaped for the rebound but misjudged its direction. The ball hit his wrist and went into the basket, the crowd erupting: seventy-three points. "Boy, what a tap he made that time!" Bill Campbell said. "He just tied the record, ladies and gentlemen, for a regulation game."

The Knicks countered quickly. The Warriors preferred it that way. They played defense like matadors, swooshing their capes and allowing the Knicks to pass. Cleveland Buckner, with that quirky over-the-head shooting style, hit yet another jump shot, 131-114.

Looking for Chamberlain, Rodgers passed inside to Attles, a little man in the big man's space. Attles's shovel pass found Chamberlain underneath, too close to the basket for the Knicks to stop. The Dipper turned and there came a roar from the Hershey crowd. The Warriors reserves reacted, leaping from their chairs and cheering as if they hadn't already seen the Dipper score 3,840 other points in the season, as if these seventy-five points were a newly minted first of their kind.

Ten minutes to play: Meschery sensed a seismic shift in the Warriors offense. The whole team concept had broken down. The usual passing and cutting and moving without the ball stopped. Meschery felt himself slowing down, stopping, literally stopping, becoming almost a spectator—a spectator wearing white Philadelphia jersey No. 14 and standing twenty feet from the basket. He had never performed this way before. He would get the ball to the Dipper and then . . . watch.

CHAPTER 14

Guerin

R ICHIE GUERIN, *SEMPER FIDELIS*, always faithful. Here's what he was thinking: *This is a travesty! I cannot wait to get out of here!* The madder he became, the better he played. It was one of Guerin's more unusual traits. Pent up anger or frustration ruined many players, but not Guerin. With a little rage, the Leatherneck could go a long way. It made him stronger, meaner, better. When the NBA players of the early Fifties retired, their rugged sensibilities and habits from the war years did not fade quickly from the game. Richie Guerin yet embodied their spirit, chin up, elbows out. He played like the old Marine he was. Meschery would see him in a New York bar late one night in less than peak condition. They had a game at the Garden the next night. Meschery thought, *Hell, Richie's not going to be able to play tomorrow.* But Guerin played and scored twenty-six points.

Now, furious with what he saw as a travesty in Hershey, Guerin played in a *semper fi* frenzy. *If they earn this the right way, more power to them. I could care less. But this is not right. This is outside the normal flow of the game.* Now, Guerin sank a two-hand set shot, a shooting style that connected him to a nearly faded era. In the 1920s, Kansas's Phog Allen, writing an article in *The*

Athletic Journal entitled "Anatomy of Basketball," had described the game's three fundamental shots: the free throw, the two-hand push shot, and the one-hand English shot from the standing position, though the latter, he noted, was not often used. Of the two-hand shot later favored by Guerin, Allen wrote, "The flexing pronators are attached to the internal condyle of the humerus [and] the supinators and extensors are attached to the external condyle." Now Guerin took a pass from Cleveland Buckner, drove to the tip of the circle, and fed Dave Budd nicely for an easy basket. Then he penetrated the lane, shoulder down, daring anyone—Attles? Meschery? The Dipper?—to stop his charge. He fooled them all. He pulled up and drained a jumper. It was as if Richie Guerin was making a statement: *You can embarrass my team but you cannot embarrass me.*

If only Guerin could have closed his eyes and made this game go away. There wasn't anything he could do about the Dipper—even rage wouldn't allow him to stop a player nine inches taller. But of course, he tried, anyway. Budd stood in front of Chamberlain, Buckner behind, and Guerin sometimes crept in to add an angry obstacle. Other than this, all Richie Guerin could do was get in his teammates' faces and scream at them and show them, yet one more time, how the game was played, alone, storming a hill into enemy gunfire, proving to the enemy and his shrinking comrades that he was fearless.

Now, in the Hershey arena, Guerin heard the fresh-faced kids: "Give it to Wilt!" He saw the Warriors on the bench yukking it up when Chamberlain reached seventy-three points. Guerin's red-faced rage grew. Then, driving hard to the Warriors basket, he hit another pull-up jumper, and Bill Campbell said, "And the shooting tonight is phenomenal!"

In his first game in the NBA in 1959, against the Knicks at the Garden, Chamberlain scored forty-three points and pulled down twenty-eight rebounds. That night, Guerin and the Knicks noticed the way Chamberlain set up for his fall-away, getting the ball on the left side, down low, sticking his posterior into the defensive man to knock him off balance, and then turning, leaping, and firing. "There's no way you can stop him from getting the ball. We tried to collapse around him, but it didn't do any good," Knicks Coach Fuzzy Levane said that night. "He might hit ninety points in some game sometime." That night Carl Braun said the Dipper already was better than George Mikan ever was. Here's what Richie Guerin said: "Wait until he learns his way around this league. Then watch out. Right now, he's still feeling his way. Boy, what power!"

Now, it was again Dave Budd's turn to battle the Dipper. Budd outraced Chamberlain down the floor. He arrived first to Wilt's intended destination, the left side, down low. Then again, it didn't matter who got there first. The Dipper, so powerful, leaned into Budd and forced him to give ground. Budd knew, *If Wilt wants to stand in my spot, he is going to stand in my spot.* Budd would have moved to Plan B except *there is no Plan B.* Conlin passed the ball inside to Chamberlain. He shot and missed, though Conlin rebounded. He put the ball back in the Dipper's hands: another miss. The Knicks took off on fast break, Willie Naulls to Al Butler, driving and then dishing to Guerin for a layup, 133-118. The Warriors mounted only a token defense.

There's a code of honor in sports, Guerin believed. *You do not deliberately embarrass your opponent or set records outside the normal flow of the game.* The Warriors were breaking a code. This was not *earning it.* Of course, Guerin knew what was required for a scorer to break records. On a night in December 1959 when he set a Knicks single-game mark by scoring fifty-seven points against Syracuse, Guerin had screamed at teammate Cal Ramsey, who would last just seven games with the team, for daring to shoot with two minutes left. Ramsey knew that Guerin wanted the ball but screamed back, "Hey, you're trying to set a record. I'm just trying to get a job!"

Now, Frank McGuire, leading by fifteen points with nine minutes, twenty-four seconds remaining, called a timeout. Campbell said, "History is being written here tonight in Hershey. The big man has broken the record and he is going for more!" *Boy, what a travesty!*

What Guerin would not accept was a deeper truth: If this game was devolving now into a *travesty,* it was doing so under the massive force of the Dipper's talent. It was Chamberlain's talent that broke the dam, and the Knicks could not keep it from breaking. Guerin considered the game a farce as a way to protect his own dignity. It was as if the past was mad at the future because the future no longer involved him. Richie Guerin got madder and more aggressive as his rage infused his game, his own point total rising. What else could he do now but score?

CHAPTER 15

Attles

DURING THE TIMEOUT, tugging on his cufflinks, Frank McGuire did not tell Rodgers and Attles, Conlin and Meschery, "Get the ball to Wilt." Standing beside his coach, Attles was thinking, *You don't have to say it, Frank. It's like the nose on my face: right there, obvious. I will get the ball to the Big Fella. We all will.* Attles never worried about getting his name in the paper. He put the ball in the hottest hand, that's the way he played the game, every game. He was a team guy, understated, without ego. In summer 1960, Attles had no expectations of ever playing in the NBA. In fact, he'd accepted a teaching job at a junior high school back home in Newark—he even took possession of the keys to his new classroom—when, in a series of personal twists, he found himself in the Warriors training camp in Hershey. Once he made the team, the Dipper looked after him. In a small town in Missouri once for an exhibition game that year, Attles saw his white teammates step off the bus and walk into a café. He followed until the Dipper and Andy Johnson shook their heads and told him, "We're going to Dutch it." The two old Globetrotters took Attles to a grocery store across the street for a loaf of bread, bologna, and cheese. Rather than risk the embarrassment of Jim Crow rejection, they ate their sandwiches on the bus.

Now a rising fascination crept into Bill Campbell's voice: "We're just conjecturing here how many can he make. He's got nine minutes and twenty-four seconds, and the guesses are running as high as one hundred." Just saying it—*one hundred*—titillated Campbell. He added, "Wouldn't *that* be something?"

Conlin pulled up his dribble, momentarily stuck. Seeing Chamberlain surrounded by too many Knicks, Conlin took a long set shot that missed. Attles snuck through the lane and tipped it in, 135-118, his eighth basket in eight attempts.

Back came Guerin, Attles's man to cover. The Knicks had scored their last four times down the court, and Guerin had been in the middle of all four possessions. Together, Guerin and Attles made for a dynamic matchup: the Leatherneck and the Destroyer, players as different in style and persona as their hometowns, Gotham and Newark. Attles had first seen Guerin play years before on Channel 9 in Newark, which featured games of New York area colleges such as Guerin's Iona. On the small screen, in black and white, Guerin had seemed formidable. In person, he was even more than that: all swagger. But Attles already was making his name as a ferocious defender by confounding the league's best young guards, including Robertson and West.

Guerin took the ball to the middle, Attles on his hip, and passed to Willie Naulls on the left side. Naulls drove the baseline and scored on a one-hander, 135-120. The Zink: "Naauuuuuulllllssss."

The ball came to Meschery. He looked for Chamberlain. Suddenly . . . an opening! Not for the Dipper but for Meschery. He had a wide-open fifteen-foot jump shot, but the Mad Russian hesitated. He didn't want to shoot. He looked for Chamberlain again. He still wasn't in the clear so Meschery shot a jumper and made it, 137-120. *These baskets are like sewers,* Attles thought as he ran down the court. *Nobody's missing.* The Warriors would score a record ninety points in the second half.

There had been a play earlier on this night that fully captured the Dipper's dominance and majesty. Attles saw it years later in freeze-frame: a photograph of the Dipper at the left baseline, swinging past the flat-footed Imhoff and rising, his head above the rim, for an easy finger-roll basket. Seeing Imhoff in that frozen image, Attles would feel nearly sympathetic for the young Knicks center: *He's got no chance. He knows it. We know it. They know it.*

Wilt Chamberlain could do that to almost anyone. Attles had seen it, over and over. That's why when he heard Chamberlain complain about Red Auerbach repeatedly saying, "All Wilt can do is dunk," Attles waved off the comment. He told the Dipper what the Dipper already knew: This was Red playing another head game, reverse psychology, Red encouraging you to keep shooting that fall-away to pull you further from the basket because Red does not want you to dunk. Attles told him, "Big Fella, just take it and turn in," the same advice given to him by every coach he'd ever had, dating to Coach Cecil Mosenson at Overbrook High School. But Attles knew that you didn't tell the Dipper what to do because the Dipper would only smile and brag about his fall-away jumper, saying, "It's the best shot in basketball!" The Dipper knew no one could block it, unless some guard caught him from the blind side. Some teams screened him after he shot his fall-away, then sent their own center sprinting down the court. If Chamberlain followed time after time, he would fatigue; if he didn't follow, the opposing center had an easy basket. As a rookie, Attles heard his roommate, Andy Johnson, tell the Dipper how to respond to criticism that he *only* scored points. Johnson put it succinctly. He looked the Dipper in the eye and said, "Big Fella, score every point you can get."

Naulls's jumper missed, Chamberlain rebounded but dropped the ball. Attles dove for it—vintage Attles—and so did Cleveland Buckner. The referees called a jump ball.

Buckner won the jump easily, as Bill Campbell rhapsodized: "Imagine a guy getting seventy-five points and you still have eight and a half minutes to play?" Again, Naulls drove the baseline and scored, 137-122.

On any other night, it would be ludicrous to think an NBA player might score twenty-five points in these final eight minutes—a rate that would produce 150 points in a full game. Oddly, on this night, it seemed possible.

Calling for the ball at the baseline, Chamberlain took a pass from Rodgers. He scored from close in and was fouled by Naulls. The Zink: "Dipper Dunk, Chaaaam-ber-lain! Goooooood!" He had seventy-seven points. Now, the Dipper positioned himself for his underhanded free throw, the shooting style that made him feel silly, like a sissy. His free throw missed, circling the rim and spinning out, the Hershey crowd, spinning with the ball: "Ohhhhhhhh."

Campbell marveled over the Dipper: "Tremendous performer. This guy is just a magnificent athlete. There's no question about it. He's quite a runner. He's a good high jumper. He handles the weights. He takes excellent care of himself. And it pays off here."

The Knicks moved, fast forward, the other way. Butcher to Naulls to Guerin, who drove underneath. As Guerin shot, Attles fouled him.

With Guerin at the free-throw line, Campbell filled the moment: "Jimmy Brown of the Cleveland Browns was telling me just yesterday that he is a great friend of Wilt's and he was saying how Wilt really works at physical conditioning. He said, 'It's no surprise that he's so great. He works so hard to attain it.' "

Guerin made the first free throw, 139-123.

Campbell: "Jimmy Brown says he has one distinction. He says he's the only guy who has ever beaten Wilt Chamberlain at hand wrestling."

Guerin made the second free throw, 139-124.

Campbell: "And Jimmy Brown says it took him twenty-three minutes to get his arm down. . . ."

CHAPTER 16

Imhoff

BACK INTO THE CRUCIBLE CAME DARRALL IMHOFF. He returned to face the Dipper with these thoughts: *Stay with him. Pin him in. Body him. Keep him from turning in. Watch your fouls. Whatever it takes.* The game was in its fortieth minute. Imhoff had watched twenty-six of those minutes from the New York bench, wearing his warm-up jacket against the arena's chill. In time Imhoff would become known as the Axe because if he didn't block your shot, he would chop you to pieces: You might get your two free throws against the Axe but not a three-point play. In this game, Imhoff had succeeded only in collecting fouls, four in fourteen minutes, a rate that would have fouled him out before halftime had Eddie Donovan not benched him. Chamberlain had overwhelmed Imhoff in the first quarter.

Still learning the pro game, Imhoff was a quick study on how to defend the league's centers. Each had his traits and tricks. Ray Felix and Swede Halbrook and Walter Dukes were no trouble; Imhoff believed he could handle them. Syracuse's Johnny "Red" Kerr was more difficult, a finesse passer who once embarrassed Imhoff by passing a ball between his own legs *and Imhoff's*. So Imhoff made a tactical shift when guarding him, always keeping one foot between Kerr's legs. Kerr was sly, tricky. He slathered Firm Grip, a sticky solvent that helped him hold the basketball, on his sneakers and snuck in quick dips to cover his fingers until the NBA banned its use, threatening offenders with a $25 fine. So Kerr then hid the Firm Grip, in small globs, in new places around the court: at the scorer's table, under the bench, behind the backboard. Against Bill Russell, Imhoff didn't have to play tight defense. Russell would catch a pass and then step back so that Imhoff couldn't *feel* where he was. Not to worry, Russell wasn't a shooter (a left-handed hook was his best shot) though he was sneaky around the basket and had to be watched. Russell often scored by tipping in missed shots. Chicago rookie Walt Bellamy, heralding a new generation of quicker and more athletic NBA centers, would lean and push. He was essentially a jump shooter though he also liked to drive. Bellamy played even bigger than six-foot-eleven and was difficult to defend. To Imhoff, Cincinnati's Wayne Embry was like a tree, a very wide tree, and set the meanest picks in the league. *You've got to pack a lunch to get around him,* Imhoff thought. Though just six-foot-eight, Embry weighed two hundred fifty-five pounds, and as Oscar Robertson passed alongside his picks, Embry usually took out a couple of defenders, clearing a path for the Big O. St. Louis's Clyde Lovellette was an especially scary prospect for opposing young centers, not only for his shooting skill but his deception. Imhoff knew, *Lovellette will pat you on the ass and say, "Way to go," and then smack you in the mouth with an elbow.*

Chamberlain was an altogether different proposition. The Dipper didn't talk or deceive. He came right at you. You knew his shots—the finger-roll from the right side, the fall-away from the left side—and he knew that you knew them. He rarely deviated, figuring you couldn't stop him anyway. Imhoff knew it was important to let Chamberlain feel his defensive presence, whatever it took, pinning him in place with his feet (much as he did with Kerr), putting a well-placed knee in the Dipper's upper thigh or buttock or the point of his elbow into the rhomboids between his shoulder blades. Imhoff knew there were no defensive tricks or ploys that Chamberlain hadn't already experienced.

Now here came Chamberlain down the court with a surprise, a jumper from the circle. It shocked Imhoff, as it did Bill Campbell, who saw the ball cut through the nets and shouted, *"Good!!"* Imhoff was incredulous. *Wilt taking a twenty-foot jumper? What's that about?* He hoped the Dipper would continue taking twenty-foot jumpers; that would be a gift, pennies from heaven. The record now was Wilt's—that is, still Wilt's, seventy-nine points. "He's broke the all-time . . ." Campbell's thoughts outraced his words. He amended ". . . all kinds of records now." The Warriors led 141-124.

At the other end, Naulls missed a jumper. Attles rebounded and cleared the ball to Rodgers for a fast break. Rodgers swept down the left side. Chamberlain stormed the middle, a portrait of athletic grace, the huff-and-puff cadence of his breath so familiar to Attles. The Dipper wanted the ball. From Rodgers, as ever, he got it. Chamberlain charged toward the basket and tried to shoot but was fouled. At the courtside table, Harvey Pollack notified Zinkoff that Chamberlain had broken the all-time scoring record. Zink, the showman, nodded. Breathing heavily at the free-throw line, Chamberlain squatted down low and shot his free throw underhanded as he heard the Zink say, "Ladies and gentlemen, a new scoring record has been created by Wilt Chamberlain." Four thousand voices rose as one. The Zink broke his syllables into small bits and stretched them like taffy. "He has seven-teee niiiiine pooooooinnttts!" The Dipper made his first free throw to reach eighty. He bent low again—his sweat-soaked face revealing total focus and intensity—and made the second, too. He'd missed only two of twenty-six free-throw attempts thus far, for him unprecedented. The Zink caught up: "He now has eight-teee onnnnne poiiiiinnttttssss!!" A roar passed like a wave through the Hershey Sports Arena.

Until this announcement, Imhoff had had no idea how many points Chamberlain had scored. Few of the Knicks or Warriors had known. Neither had the Dipper. The impact of Zink's announcement was instant. It intensified everything, the crowd's excitement, the Knicks' dread, the Warriors' curiosity, Chamberlain's scoring impulse and desire. *How high could this go?* Reputations were at stake. The game had a new urgency, purpose, and meaning.

His fury ratcheted up a notch by the Zink's announcement, Guerin knifed through the lane for a layup, 143-126. That gave the Leatherneck thirty-five points, twenty-two in the second half. No one noticed.

On the trip back up the court, Attles spotted Chamberlain open. The Dipper took the pass, too eagerly, and dropped the ball. Meschery dove for it. So did Darrall Imhoff. A tie-up, jump ball, seven minutes to play.

CHAPTER 17

The Dipper

FOR ALL THE ELBOWS, MINOR daily media slights, and humiliations of persistent segregation, this was the Dipper's revenge. The single-game scoring record, already his, was not enough. He wanted more, triple digits. Following his big scoring nights in the NBA he had typically passed along modest comments to sportswriters, such as "Winning is more important," and "Luck plays a big part in scoring streaks like this," and "I believe I've just about reached my limit." He made these comments without conviction, as if they'd been rehearsed, and now that the opportunity showed itself in Hershey, the humble routine vanished. He wanted one hundred. It was only a number, of course, but there was much in it: proof of his own outsized greatness, satisfaction for his ego, and a prophecy fulfilled. Only a month before, even Bill Russell had said, "The only way to stop Wilt and his dunk shot is to lock him in the dressing room or use a shotgun. He has the size, strength, and stamina to score one hundred some night."

A tradition runs deep in black culture and athletics to respond to the challenge of humiliation with just this kind of gorgeous, awe-inspiring *overkill* as proof of value in a world that would devalue black life and performance: Willie Mays's basket catch in baseball, an unnecessary and showy display of virtuosity; the young Cassius Clay's big-mouthed showmanship in boxing; Malcolm X's overheated rhetoric on street corners in Harlem; James Baldwin's snaking, furious sentences. The Dipper's climb to one hundred had those same qualities: a gorgeous, showy, overheated, snaking, furious display of overkill and virtuosity. He played now with relentlessness, as if working alone in a single white-hot spotlight, one against five, his body punished by opponents whose size, talent, and ambition couldn't match his own. In his dominance, he revealed the magnitude of his skill, and even more so, the magnitude of his will. It was colossal. He felt the game becoming a one-man show; a team concept no more. He set up on the left side, down low ("We couldn't put our hands around that spot and say, 'You can't come here,' " Johnny Green would say), and held his right hand high, calling for the ball.

Philosophically, the Dipper's only concern was that he might be perceived as a *gunner.* That was the term he'd heard playing at the Haddington Recreation Center in west Philadelphia, a code from the streets: If you took too many shots, you were a glory-hound, a *gunner.* Averaging forty shots per game, he'd heard that criticism all season, anyway. The Hershey kids, with different ideas, screamed, "We want one hundred!"

The Dipper had heard these screams seven years before, in February 1955, at Overbrook High School's cramped gymnasium in west Philly. As a gangly eighteen-year-old tagged "Wilt the Stilt" by a local sportswriter, the Dipper had toyed with the overmatched Roxborough High Indians as fans stood against the walls of the gym and chanted, "We want one hundred! We want one hundred!" Chamberlain had scored seventy-four points against the hapless Roxborough team a few weeks earlier, and this time he threatened to go higher. Overbrook's gym looked like someone's garage: Poorly lit and with steam radiators along the walls, it featured a tile floor, wooden backboards, and metal girders at the ceiling that reduced shots to low line drives. The Overbrook court measured just sixty-eight feet in length, twenty-six feet shy of regulation. Dippy Chamberlain covered it, baseline-to-baseline, in about nine strides.

Chamberlain tore into Roxborough for twenty-six points in the first half, at which point Mosenson told him, "Okay, Wilt, we're going for the record"; in Philadelphia, the high school record then was seventy-eight points. By the end of the third quarter, Roxborough had scored only thirteen points, and Chamberlain fifty-seven. Teammate Dave Shapiro had scored a season-high fourteen points largely because the undersized Roxborough players fully surrounded Chamberlain, leaving Shapiro alone beneath the basket to rebound and put back missed shots easily. In the third quarter, though, Shapiro got the message from his teammates: "Don't shoot anymore. Give it to Wilt. He's got a chance to get one hundred." All passes went to the Dipper. His teammates lobbed the ball to him or simply threw it against the backboard, allowing him to catch and dunk it, over and over. As Overbrook's lead grew to more than eighty points, the Dipper himself reached seventy points. Mosenson felt conflicted about running up the score without mercy. He'd earlier asked the school's athletic director: "We could run up the scores. What should we do?" The athletic director, who also served as the school's track coach, replied, "I never tell my runners to slow down because they might beat another runner by ten yards or twenty yards. We're out to break records." *Okay, then,* Mosenson decided, *as long as records are kept, Wilt Chamberlain is entitled to them.* He knew that one day Chamberlain would become the greatest player in the history of the game. That much already was obvious. *Who better deserves to set records than Wilt Chamberlain?* He heard the several hundred fans lining the walls inside the Overbrook gym calling for blood: "We want one hundred! We want one hundred!" But with two minutes, fifteen seconds remaining, Overbrook leading by nearly one hundred points, Mosenson couldn't bear to watch anymore. He removed Chamberlain from the game. Overbrook won, 123-21.

Chamberlain finished with ninety points, a local record, even though he sat out four minutes, forty-five seconds. He had converted thirty-six of forty-one shots and eighteen of twenty-six free throws. Remarkably, playing eleven minutes and fifteen seconds of the second half, he scored sixty-four points. The next morning *The Philadelphia Inquirer* theorized, "Chamberlain might have hit 100 if he had played the entire 32 minutes." In the Overbrook locker room after the game, the celebration was muted. Dave Shapiro would say, "We were disappointed that he didn't get one hundred."

Now, at home in Philadelphia, Cecil Mosenson was listening to the game in Hershey on WCAU on his bedroom radio. All those points and the crowd's chants reminded him of Roxborough. Intrigued, Mosenson waited to hear how Frank McGuire would handle it.

Of course, McGuire was not about to pull Chamberlain from the game. He never pulled the Dipper, not in any game all season, no matter the score. (When replaced by Russell during the second quarter of January's All-Star Game in St. Louis, Chamberlain had hesitated for a moment, and a writer cracked, "See there, Wilt doesn't know where to go. He thinks it's half-time.")

A night such as this had been on Chamberlain's mind from the beginning. Only twenty games into his NBA career, he had talked of one day breaking Baylor's NBA scoring record, then sixty-four points. The way defenses ganged up on him, though, would make that a supreme challenge, he admitted. On some plays, he said, "I start a play in the pivot, end up in the corner, and never know how I got there." To reach sixty-five points, the rookie Dipper had calculated he would have to average fifteen points for three quarters and then bust out for a twenty-point fourth quarter. Given the way teams collapsed around him, "I would have to set such a record on three shots: the jump, rebound tap-in, and foul. If I could move around more to add the hook and the dunk, I'd have a better shot at records." He said he would have to play the full forty-eight minutes to surpass Baylor's mark, aggressively run with Rodgers on fast breaks, and his team would, like Baylor's, have to give him the ball. He understood early on that the way to react to a collapsing defense was to pass the ball to an unguarded teammate, but Gola and Rodgers (and now Attles) did not excel as outside shooters. He could pass to them as they cut to the basket, but the lane was too cluttered with defenders for them to pass through. His best alternative was to pass to Arizin in the corner.

His Warriors teammates had spoon-fed him the ball all season, McGuire's orders. The Dipper knew about their resentments on and off the court. It would be only logical for him to wonder: If he had the opportunity to score one hundred points, how would his teammates react? He did not know the answer—until now. They would acquiesce. His talent would bend them to his will, too.

CHAPTER 18

Ruklick

FROM THE BENCH, ALWAYS FROM THE BENCH, Joe Ruklick watched the Dipper's point total rise. Much like Edgar Allan Poe's famous raven—*"And the raven, never flitting, still is sitting, still is sitting . . ."*—Ruklick sat for three years, watching Chamberlain score nearly 10,000 points. As the games, the cigarettes, and his life passed by, Ruklick scarcely played, scoring just 398 points during those three seasons. He was a hundred-point guy, too—he scored about a hundred points *per season*. For a living . . . he sat. Not that he had expected anything more as a six-foot-nine backup to Chamberlain. Each year he entered games for a few minutes, typically at forward, made a basket or two, and heard people ask, "Why doesn't he play more?" The simple answer: the Dipper. "Joe Ruklick's beautiful hook shot apparently is doomed to bench rust again," Jack Kiser wrote at the season's start. Later, nearly taunting, Kiser typed, "Whatever happened to the Joe Ruklick fan club?"

What Ruklick did best was pay attention, not only to the team but the world: to race, politics, literature. Now, sitting at his usual spot at the end of the bench next to Frank Radovich, Ruklick thought the Dipper's performance seemed a replay of so many other games, a mighty and swollen example of what the Dipper could do, only more so. Forty-three times this season, he had watched the Dipper score fifty points or more. The way he scored most of those points—forcing himself toward the basket, lunging, finger-rolling the ball downward, Dipper Dunking, falling away with his jumper, returning rebounds as if he were plucking bird eggs from a tree limb and gently putting them back, pushing himself ahead on fast breaks, catching so many lob passes from Rodgers and Attles and Gola and dropping them in—had ceased to amaze Ruklick. Oh, he would appreciate an isolated play revealing a new twist on the Dipper's athletic elegance, but the Dipper's performances, viewed in full, didn't raise in him the visceral thrill of a Mickey Mantle homer or, in years past, a Joe Louis haymaker. Then again, if on each night he'd seen Mantle hit twenty-five homers and Louis throw twenty-five haymakers, they might have bored him as well.

Ruklick watched Woozie Smith toss the ball, Meschery and Imhoff leaping, Meschery winning, tapping the ball back to Attles. The Dipper missed his fall-away, Imhoff well positioned on defense. Buckner's outlet down the court to a streaking Guerin sailed over his head and into the crowd.

The Dipper wanted this; you could see it in his taut expression. From Ruklick's view, Chamberlain nearly always hustled. As long and lean as the Dipper was, Ruklick thought, *If Wilt ever shut down, he would look like a marionette out there.* From the bench now Ruklick saw Guerin's rage. He figured that if the Knicks were angry, truly angry, at the Dipper and the Warriors for what was happening, they had no one to blame but themselves. *If a guy goofs off at work and his boss screams at him, why would he be mad at the boss?* That was confusing the messenger with the message. Same here. *If Wilt scores one hundred points, whose fault is it?*

Conlin missed a layup. Chamberlain scored on a put-back and was fouled. He had eighty-three. "What a night!" Bill Campbell said. "Mark this day down!" The Dipper made his free throw for eighty-four. The Warriors led by twenty points, 146-126. "If you know anybody not listening, call them up," Campbell said. "A little history you are sitting in on tonight."

Once, Ruklick asked the Dipper about the rubber bands he wore at his wrists. "You wear them all of the time, don't you?" Ruklick asked. Typically, the Dipper said he wore rubber bands to warmly remind him of childhood friendships. This time, though, for whatever reason, perhaps to impress

Ruklick, the team's social justice intellectual, Chamberlain replied, "Yeah. When I feel like I'm doggin' it, I snap them to remind me of when my people were under the lash." That was the thing about Wilt Chamberlain, Ruklick understood: There was so much more to him than most people knew.

Ruklick was earning $8,000. He knew that if Gotty had really wanted an NBA title, he would've spent a few thousand dollars more and signed a frontline forward such as Rudy LaRusso or Ray Scott. Instead, Gotty chose to save a little money with Ruklick and Radovich as backups to the Dipper.

Already Ruklick had played five minutes in the game, more than usual. With six and a half minutes to play, Chamberlain's eighty-four points demonstrated not only a scoring machine's efficiency but mastery over an entire sport. Entranced, his teammates moved to the front edge of their seats. They sat up a little straighter. Ruklick wondered if the Dipper would hit one hundred. He wondered, too, if Frank McGuire might put him back in the game. If he had to guess, it was more likely the Dipper would hit one hundred.

CHAPTER 19

One Hundred

SENSORY OVERLOAD NOW in the dimly lit arena: squeaking Converse high-tops and the echoing of a leather basketball against a clicked-together maple hardwood floor designed for roller skating; the olfactory sensations of chocolate, hot dogs, and popcorn mixing together, the smell of a small-town carnival. Nearer the court, the gym smell—sweat—Chamberlain bathed in it and Eddie Donovan, too, his neckline saturated. And smoke, cigarette smoke, filling the pores of this arena: Parliaments, Marlboros, Lucky Strikes. The ham-it-up calls of the Zink on the p.a. and the prepubescent cheers for the Dipper coming from the chocolate factory workers' kids pressed close to the court, "C'mon, Wilt!" The scoreboard clock high up in Peanut Heaven—everyone's looking at it now, after every basket, after every foul—cold, boxy, and metallic. Wilt Chamberlain's own sense of touch on high alert: Imhoff's elbow in his back, the stilettoish Buckner sticking into his ribs, Guerin and Butcher adhering to the front of his jersey, all but replacing the "1" and the "3" stitched into it. At such tense moments, the telltale tics of rookie coaches emerge: Donovan biting his lower lip, McGuire tugging at his cufflinks, as if to remind himself of his gentleman's reputation even as he allowed the Dipper to embarrass the visitors.

Earl Whitmore, the man in the crowd because he'd purchased a refrigerator, pointed to the Dipper. "Look!" he said to his friend. "Four men are on Wilt." Whitmore ticked them off: "One on his left hip, one on his right hip, one standing on his foot, one yanking on him." A part-time local high school and college referee, Whitmore knew his basketball. He also knew the ushers at the arena. They let him and his friend move to prime seats, down low. To one usher now, Whitmore said, motioning toward a five-foot wall, "You won't care if I hop over this at the end of the game, will you?" Not a problem, said the usher. Whitmore noted how Chamberlain planted himself inside a swarm of Knicks, immovable.

Naulls converted two free throws, 146-128. Now, as Rodgers dribbled at the circle, Guerin rushed out to foul him. Watching, Donovan admired Guerin's intensity and his pride. The game stretched out, another foul stopping the clock. This gave Harvey Pollack time to type on his Olivetti, his son waiting for the next sheet to run to Western Union, to send to *The Philadelphia Inquirer* for the early edition. The newspaper beat men, Jack Kiser of *The Daily News*, Poison Pen himself, and Jim Heffernan of *The Evening Bulletin*, had half-suspected this day might come. Watching now, Heffernan thought, *This might be the best chance anyone ever has to reach a hundred points in an NBA game.* On the court, Al Attles had the same number in mind.

Rodgers made one free throw. Imhoff missed a jumper from the right side. Running now, Chamberlain took a fast break pass from Attles only to drop the ball. Butcher recovered it. The Dipper sensed the magnitude of the moment. His nerves began to show.

Guerin's attitude was defined by a sneer. From the crowd, the two Harrisburg weightlifters taunted him. "You're a bum, Richie!" Guerin threw a fancy pass behind his back. The ball sailed into the crowd. "Nice pass, Richie!" a weightlifter shouted. "NICE PASS!!"

Again the Knicks quickly fouled Guy Rodgers near half-court. Their strategy was clear: To keep the ball from Wilt, they would foul the Warriors guards and let them shoot all the free throws they wanted. Imhoff, meanwhile, seemed nearly attached to Chamberlain, trying to deny him the ball.

Buckner, with his cockeyed over-the-head shooting style, scored again from the high post, 148-130.

The Axe sensed the Dipper's growing impatience. With time slipping, the Dipper became more restless and aggressive. He leaned back into

Imhoff, taking the offensive, making him recoil. Rodgers, the Dipper's sup-ply line, got the ball to him down low. Imhoff, arms raised, held his ground, but it didn't matter. Chamberlain scored, reaching eighty-six, and Willie Smith's whistle signaled Imhoff's fifth foul. Another Chamberlain free throw gave him eighty-seven points, still with five and a half minutes to play.

Imhoff missed another jumper down court, and the Warriors thorough-breds were loosed: a three-on-one fast break, Chamberlain with Attles and Rodgers. Rodgers pulled up and passed to Attles, who sent a lob pass to Chamberlain. Leaping with arms fully extended, at a height of nearly twelve feet, the Dipper caught the pass, turned toward the basket with a fury and stuffed it, the crowd erupting: eighty-nine points.

Trailing by twenty-three points, the Knicks ran a backcourt weave now, Guerin and Butcher dribbling and passing, moving the ball slowly in a Z-pattern, to drain a few more seconds from the clock. Loud, cascading boos, kids calling Eddie Donovan's team *chicken*. The Knicks aimed to use as much of the twenty-four second clock as possible on each possession, leav-ing less time for Chamberlain to reach a hundred. Finally, Naulls missed a jumper. Conlin rebounded and threw a long outlet pass to Attles, the Dip-per's closest friend on the team. *"Guess how many people live in Toledo?"* No such silly games now. Attles passed to Chamberlain. But Wilt fumbled the ball, off his fingertips, losing it out of bounds.

The Dipper's nerves again.

McGuire tugged at his cufflinks and called a timeout.

Guard Sam Stith hadn't taken off his Knicks warm-up jacket all night. He stood now and joined Donovan's courtside huddle. What Stith saw and heard, he had seen and heard many times before—Richie Guerin screaming in a *semper fi* frenzy. "Will somebody hit him! Hit him in the nuts! Do some-thing!" Stith heard Guerin say. Spit flew from Guerin's mouth: "Don't just let him go in!" Guerin looked—glared, really—at Imhoff. Stith looked at Imhoff, too, and heard Imhoff reply, "But I've got five fouls . . ." Now Stith looked at Richie Guerin. Incredulous over what he'd just heard Imhoff say, Guerin dropped his hands in disgust and turned away.

The Knicks returned to the court, moving the ball deliberately, Buckner to Guerin to Butcher to Naulls. The fans and the Warriors looked nervously to the boxy metallic scoreboard clock, ticking, ticking. As the twenty-four second clock at courtside neared expiration, Naulls misfired again and

Chamberlain rebounded. For Meschery, the game now seemed nearly an out-of-body experience. The Warriors simply passed the ball to Chamberlain and watched him work, one against five. Nothing strategic, no screens, just get the ball to Wilt. No other Warrior had scored a basket in nearly four minutes. Now Chamberlain, with the ball, hemmed in on all sides, flipped it back to Attles, who passed to Meschery. The Mad Russian drilled a jumper, 155-130 with four minutes, fifteen seconds to play.

Two Hershey constables, in their chocolate brown uniforms, ambled in on their usual patrol of the arena. Gabe Basti and Bud Miller had performed the constables' nightly check out at the farms where the orphan boys of the Hershey Industrial School lived. Basti and Miller had made certain the doors there were properly locked. They had searched for signs of vandalism, finding none. The constables' primary role was to keep peace between the orphan schoolboys and the public school kids of the township; that wasn't always easy. The public school kids at Hershey High often taunted the industrial school students, calling them "cows" because, as part of their daily farm chores, they milked them. There had been more than a few Friday night fights over the years between boys at the two schools, usually over girls. Miller once found a runaway Hershey Industrial School boy, bound for New York, frightened and hiding in the bushes near the chocolate factory; he talked calmly to him, then returned him to the farm. Basti and Miller had been assigned guns, as all constables were, but had never had cause to use them. The only incidents at the Hershey arena stemmed from kids sneaking into games without paying—the usual suspects. Basti and Miller knew them all, and their families.

Such an odd game now: the Warriors hardly playing defense, the Knicks hardly playing offense. Reluctantly, Buckner shot and made a one-hander from the free-throw line, Mississippi lightning striking again, a personal high, thirty-three points. As soon as Rodgers dribbled into the forecourt, Guerin fouled him, serenaded by boos. Among those booing loudly was Kerry Ryman, sitting with his rascal friends, several rows from the court. Moments later, Rodgers fouled Guerin. A chess match played by the pawns.

Down low, the vise tightened around the Dipper.

Jumpin' Johnny Green used his wiry frame against the Dipper, banging against him, hardly his style. Johnny Green felt, mostly, embarrassment. Covering Chamberlain, he was reduced to supplication and silently he beseeched the Dipper: *Don't put up any more crazy numbers out here, big man. Enough!*

On consecutive possessions, the Warriors committed turnovers, making wild passes to Chamberlain, the first too long, the second too high. "If," Bill Campbell told his listeners, "you can picture a pass being too high for Wilt." The Warriors determined to foul the Knicks as quickly as possible, merely reciprocating the strategy, as they saw it. Conlin fouled Butcher, stopping the clock, and then Rodgers fouled Butcher, stopping the clock again. Among those looking up at the scoreboard clock now was referee Pete D'Ambrosio. *This is going to take forever,* he thought.

From the bench, Arizin was thinking, *If someone walked into the arena right now, they'd be confused. They'd wonder, "Why are the Knicks freezing the ball? They're behind."*

Three minutes, twenty-three seconds to go, Wilt Chamberlain stuck for six possessions at eighty-nine points. Eddie Donovan thought the scoreboard clock was stuck, too. Donnie Butcher saw his coach pound a fist on the scorer's table and complain that the game clock wasn't starting, per regulation. It was as if the official timer was attempting to give the Dipper extra time to reach one hundred, or so Donovan thought.

The Axe shadowed the Dipper.

"Boy, they are belting Wilt around!" Campbell said.

Breaking out of his game, searching for an open space, searching for points, Chamberlain moved to the outside and shot a long one-hander, missing. The Knicks rebounded and moved . . . so slowly. Johnny Green passed behind his back to Naulls. He passed to Imhoff, still in the backcourt. More loud booing. Meschery intentionally fouled Naulls with two minutes, fifty-one seconds left. At courtside, Pollack typed another quick paragraph and then, with the ball back in play, focused on game statistics. Each time the Warriors took possession, the arena crowd percolated, a murmur becoming a rumble. Anticipation. Expectation.

Attles lobbed a pass into Chamberlain. Playing from behind, the Axe could only hack. The sound of Willie Smith's whistle: Imhoff was done, fouled out.

In twenty minutes Imhoff had committed six fouls. Buckner, given a brief rest, came back into the game. Frank McGuire, meanwhile, turned to the eighth, ninth, and tenth players on his eleven-man roster. He tapped

York Larese, Ted Luckenbill, and Joe Ruklick on their shoulders to replace Meschery, Conlin, and Attles. The Dipper made one free throw and missed another. He had ninety.

Earlier in the game, Larese had made four of five shots. A pure shooter, he now had the shooter's can't-miss feeling. But there was no chance he would take another shot this night. Neither would the lefty Luckenbill nor Ruklick. They knew their roles. McGuire hadn't told them to quickly foul the Knicks. Didn't have to.

Guerin rebounded the Dipper's missed free throw and passed to Naulls. Ruklick fouled him instantly and not delicately. For a moment it seemed Naulls and Ruklick might come to blows, but the moment passed, Bill Campbell leaning into the microphone and saying, "Of course you can understand the Knickerbockers, trailing, and they don't want to have it rubbed in a little bit like this with a guy on a scoring rampage." With Naulls at the free-throw line, the mathematical possibilities could be explored: less than three minutes to play, Chamberlain at ninety, a finite number of Philadelphia possessions remaining, perhaps a half dozen or so in the flow of a normal game. But this game was not, in any way, normal. It had its own stilted flow, moving from free throw to free throw. Here was the Knicks lineup: Buckner, Naulls, Green, Guerin, and Butcher, measuring six-eight, six-six, six-five, six-four, six-three. The Dipper had the height advantage, but he was surrounded on all sides. Facing ridicule and basketball infamy, the Knicks positioned defenders without any pretense of covering the other four Warriors. Only the Dipper mattered. Could the Warriors even get the ball to him?

That, of course, was Guy Rodgers's great skill. Already on this night Rodgers had eighteen assists, nearly all to Chamberlain. Now seeing the Dipper flashing free in the lane like the sun emerging momentarily from behind clouds, Rodgers whipped the ball inside.

Donnie Butcher sensed impending doom.

As Chamberlain rose to shoot, Butcher grabbed him around his waist, so the Dipper couldn't dunk it . . . that is, unless he dunked the ball and Butcher together. Butcher gladly absorbed the foul as Chamberlain went to the free-throw line once more, energized by the pursuit, if physically exhausted.

Bending low, knees flared out wide, Chamberlain made the first underhanded free throw, then missed the second. With the Knicks over the limit of six teams fouls, the Dipper received a penalty free throw and made it. Remarkably, he had made twenty-eight of thirty-two foul shots, unprecedented.

With two minutes, twenty-eight seconds to play the Dipper had ninety-two points.

Some Hershey adults did now what they never had done before: They pressed closer to the floor, same as the kids. To reach a hundred, the Dipper needed eight points in one hundred forty-eight seconds—roughly the rate of one hundred fifty-two points for a game.

"Anything is possible," Campbell said.

Larese fouled Guerin almost at once. Guerin made both free throws, 159-140.

Chamberlain stationed himself at his preferred spot, surrounded by Knicks. Rodgers fed him the ball anyway. With his five-inch height advantage, the Dipper set up for his fade-away. *The best shot in the league!* He stepped from the basket, turned, and shot over his right shoulder. The ball banked off the glass and into the basket, 161-140, the most points the Warriors had ever scored, a dozen shy of the NBA mark of 173 by Boston. The Dipper had ninety-four, his fierce focus melting now into a smile as he ran down court. Bill Campbell said, "Wilt laughs as if to say, 'What am I doing out here?' " Campbell answered the question for him and for his listeners. "He knows what he's doing out here—he's going for one-zero-zero."

Beneath the Warriors basket, the off-duty Associated Press photographer, suddenly on duty, snapped a few action photos. He had twenty photos to a roll. He thought about the postgame. He needed to save a few photos for that, just in case. Paul Vathis locked his camera sights on Wilt Chamberlain, waiting to capture that one moment.

The Warriors' twenty-two-year-old equipment manager tried to think ahead, too. Larry Jacobs always wore a coat and tie, to let people know he took his job seriously. Now, in the heat and the excitement over the Dipper, Jacobs, perspiring, removed his jacket. When Chamberlain hit ninety-four, off came Jacobs's vest. As a nine-year-old ball boy for Gotty in 1949, Jacobs had watched Joe Fulks set an NBA record with a then-astonishing sixty-three points against the Indianapolis Jets. The Dipper's performance now made Fulks's sixty-three seem like mere pennies. Jacobs repositioned his ball boys at the corners of the court. He wanted two ball boys close by, nearer the Warriors bench, to protect the team's equipment, namely the basketballs, in case the Dipper hit a hundred and all hell broke loose.

From the bench, an unusual place for him, Arizin took in the fourth quarter much as a fan would. The Knicks were giving Chamberlain nothing. They battled him at every step. *Wilt hasn't gotten one cheap basket tonight,* Arizin thought. *Every last one he's earned.*

Two more quick fouls: the Warriors sent Donnie Butcher to the line. Butcher immediately returned the favor, fouling Rodgers. Two minutes to play. The Dipper needed six more points.

A familiar voice rang out: "When are you going to stop him, Richie?" Richie Guerin looked to the voice. It came from the Warriors bench—Paul Arizin. Arizin was riding his old friend, teasing him about the Dipper, a very un-Arizin-like bit of heckling. Guerin sneered, then smiled in a failed attempt to rise above it. Guerin called out to Frank McGuire, apparently in jest, though still with a sneer. McGuire leaped from his chair, as if offended. He shouted back at Guerin. Paul Arizin had been a Marine once, too. He was at Quantico, Virginia, a few years before Guerin arrived there. Now he called out again: "Hey, Richie, when are you going to stop him?" Guerin shook his head and then laughed.

From the Knicks bench, Imhoff watched the exchange. He shared Guerin's view. *Why would the Warriors be a part of this?* Imhoff knew that Eddie Donovan, a gentleman, never would embarrass a team, not like Frank McGuire was now. Donovan would've pulled Chamberlain once he'd hit seventy-five or eighty points. Imhoff could tell that Donovan was incredulous. So was Guerin. The only difference was that Guerin gave voice to the emotion.

A minute fifty to play, the scoreboard clock up in Peanut Heaven ticking, the Knicks running a weave, Naulls and Butcher stalling. The ball moved to Guerin in the right corner. He passed back out to Johnny Green.

Guy Rodgers stole the ball.

Rodgers pressed up court, quickly, to avoid getting fouled again. He flipped a pass to Chamberlain underneath, before the defense could set up. The Dipper laid it in; Rodgers had his twentieth assist, the Dipper ninety-six points.

At the other end, the ball came to Naulls. He had an open layup but didn't take it. Instead he let a few more grains of sand fall through the hourglass. Luckenbill fouled him.

There came more jeers for Richie Guerin—this time not from Paul Arizin but from the two Harrisburg weightlifters: "YOU'RE A BUM, GUERIN!!!!!" Richie Guerin was fed up with it, all of it—Chamberlain, the chase for a hundred, Arizin, and now this. Sitting in the front row thanks to a small fib, Jim Hayney, a junior college student masquerading as a salesman in his fine suit and signing autographs for kids before the game as if he were the Dipper himself, saw Guerin move up court, then divert toward the hecklers. Other fans saw it, too. The Leatherneck looked ready to wage war. He glared at the two hecklers and said, biting off each syllable, "What . . . did . . . you . . . say?" Hayney looked at the weightlifters sitting a few rows back. Their moxie and their biceps shrunk. They cowered, not to utter another heckling word, as Guerin returned to the action.

Among the league's finest free-throw shooters, Naulls made two, 165-145.

And so with a minute twenty-five to play in the chocolate town with the flimsy rims, here came Larese, the tinsmith's son, leading the Warriors fast break. With teammates angling toward the basket from his right and left, Larese thought only of the Dipper. He didn't see him, but he felt his presence, in the thrum of the crowd and the vibration of the floor. He knew the Dipper was closing ground from behind. Driving into a wall of sound he heard the chorus, "Give it to Wilt!" Nearing the Knicks basket now, Larese maneuvered to his right and lifted a lob pass that the trailing Dipper caught and, in one fluid motion, dunked with a vengeance rare to his game. So close to achieving his goal now, Chamberlain was beyond finesse, beyond the usual Dipper Dunk, a considerably less emphatic basket stuff, like a rock that barely ripples the pond. The Zink playing to the crowd, cut loose: "That's nine-tee-eigghhhttt!"

The Dipper took several steps, then turned around. Tricking the unsuspecting Knicks, he intercepted the inbounds pass and put up a shot from near the free-throw line. The ball went into the cylinder, rolled around one of the friendliest rims in Pennsylvania, and spun out: a miss. The crowd became a perfectly synchronized chorus: "Ohhhhhhhh!"

Johnny Green pulled down the rebound. He passed to Guerin, who passed to Buckner. He returned the ball to Guerin. The chorus: "Booooooooooo!" A minute ten seconds to play.

"They are not taking the shot," Campbell said. "They are eating up time."

Luckenbill fouled Guerin. One minute one second to play, Chamberlain at ninety-eight. With twenty-nine points in the fourth quarter, the Dipper already had shattered the NBA record for points in a twelve-minute quarter, breaking by one a record he had established (against Buckner and the Knicks) five days before and then tied a half hour earlier, in the third quarter.

A conversation broke out in the lane now between the referee Smith, Ruklick, and Guerin. Campbell attempted to describe it for his listeners: "Guerin, who is really jabbering, I don't know what he is arguing about." Guerin would not go down without a fight or at least an argument, not now, not ever. He missed his first free throw and the crowd cheered.

At courtside a dam was about to burst, a wall of humanity, mostly kids, surging, awaiting the moment.

From his table near the court, Campbell mused, "He has ninety-eight points . . . *in professional basketball!*" Then he said, "I'll tell you, that's a lot of points if you are playing grammar school kids, isn't it?"

Guerin missed his second free throw, too. More cheers. Since the Warriors had exceeded the limit of six team fouls per quarter, Guerin was awarded a penalty third free throw and made it, 167-146.

Campbell: "Now let's see if they foul somebody quick."

Guy Rodgers didn't give the Knicks that chance. He threw a length-of-the-court pass. The Dipper rose to the heavens to grab it. Surrounded by Knicks, too short, but still scrapping and battling, Chamberlain shot and missed. With all attention on the Dipper, Luckenbill, the earnest rookie, snuck in for the rebound. He caught a glimpse of the Dipper, pointing toward the basket, as if to say, "Let's get this over with."

Luckenbill passed back to Chamberlain. Another short shot by the Dipper, his third try for one hundred . . . in and out! The Hershey chorus: "Awwwwww!" Luckenbill grabbed this rebound, too.

He passed to Ruklick.

Fifty seconds to play.

Now, with the ball in the hands of Joe Ruklick, the Kennedy liberal, the Knicks had their opportunity—their man to foul. Guerin knew it. Ruklick saw Guerin bearing down on him, like a football linebacker. He saw something else—the Dipper, down low, bumping away from Cleveland Buckner. Ruklick heard the Dipper call out, "Woo!" a short barking sound, a signal that he was in the open. Ruklick flipped the pass perfectly, high and into the middle. The Dipper caught it in front of the basket, only inches away, and rose high above the Knicks, high above the rim. Bill Campbell, energized, made his own loud barking sound, husky yet clear, "He made it! He made it! He made it! A Dipper Dunk!"

CHAPTER 20

Celebration

A DAM BURST. Kids poured onto the court, a flash flood in Chocolate Town. Whooping it up, they bore down on Chamberlain, wanting only to touch him. The shutter on Paul Vathis's Mamiya Flex 2¼-inch camera blinked and caught the Dipper in the act of one hundred: his feet returning to the floor, his right arm still vertical and fully extended, Zeus-like, as if releasing lightning bolts, the basketball snapping through the net, Cleveland Buckner's left-handed swipe too small and too late to matter, an opponent and his team fading into nothingness. A transcendent moment: The congregation in the arena stood as one. Even the Knicks rose from their chairs next to Donovan, brought to their feet by shock, awe, disgust, and embarrassment. This hundredth point, Sam Stith knew, was the final indignity for his Knicks: *ass-whupping time.* Warriors players, who thought themselves no longer capable of being impressed by Chamberlain, rushed in to congratulate the Dipper, the only time in three record-breaking seasons that *that* had happened.

Ruklick was not among them. He made a beeline to the scorer's table. There, official scorer Dave Richter, wearing his red cap and whistle, stood and cheered lustily, same as Pollack and the others beside him. Ruklick waited, patiently. For three years in the NBA, no one had noticed Joe Ruklick. Even referee Woozie Smith once said to him at a bar, playfully, "Who are you, Ruklick? And why are you even wearing a uniform?" Yet now, in a remarkably clear-headed act of self-interest that others might have been too embarrassed to carry out, Ruklick made certain that he would not be overlooked or forgotten. The assist on Wilt Chamberlain's ninety-ninth and one-hundredth points was his. He wanted it duly recorded; and it was. Bill Campbell couldn't stand—his microphone was on a tabletop, down low. Neither could he whisper as Ted Husing had during that legendary Budge–von Cramm tennis match in the Thirties, the moment that had convinced Campbell to become a sportscaster. Instead, he shouted, to be heard over the crowd: "He made! He made it! He made it! A Dipper Dunk! He made it! The fans are all over the floor. They've stopped the game. People are running out on the court. One hundred points for Wilt Chamberlain! They've stopped the game. People are crowding, hounding him, banging him. The Warrior players are all over him. Fans are coming out of the stands. Forty-six seconds left. The most amazing scoring performance of all time! One hundred points for the Big Dipper!"

Here was what the hundred-point Dipper looked like at this moment: utterly fatigued, out of breath, his upper body slightly bent, carrying the air not of a conqueror but a laborer. He had wanted this, worked hard for it, and now was surrounded by Hershey kids. Kids long have rushed to the center of thrilling sports moments. When Babe Ruth hit his five hundredth home run in Cleveland in 1929, a small Italian boy saw the baseball rolling in an alley behind League Park, outran the bigger kids, and got it. A policeman approached him minutes later and said, "Come with me." Scared, naturally, the kid replied, "I aint' done nuthin'. I aint' done nuthin'." The cop told him, "Babe Ruth wants to see you," which terrified the boy. They brought him to the Yankee dugout whereupon the Babe asked for the ball as a keepsake and in return gave the trembling boy five dollars and a new ball.

Among the first to reach the Dipper on the court, fast filling with fans, was fourteen-year-old Kerry Ryman. He had seen Wilt playing pool at the Community Club and driving his convertible past his house on Chocolate Avenue. Out on the floor, amid a growing mass of people, were Ryman's rascals: Bugs, the Sandman, Spammer, and others. But to Ryman it was as if he and the Dipper stood alone. What an image they made: Rising to the level of Chamberlain's thigh, the small-town boy stared up, up, up.

Ryman stuck out his hand.

The Dipper shook it.

Ryman saw Willie Smith throw the hundred-point ball to Wilt. He saw Chamberlain bounce it once. Then, on impulse, Ryman did an adventurous, unplanned Huck Finn thing: He grabbed the ball . . . and ran with it. Across the court, he zig-zagged between fans, clutching the ball to his chest, feeling leather, the moment, the adrenal thrill of it all. The constables, Basti and Miller, saw it happen. They gave chase, part-time rent-a-cops, all in a night's work. When Spammer noticed a man on the court move toward his friend Ryman, he casually stepped in front of that man, blocking his path. The Sandman saw Ryman with the ball, but figured he would simply take a shot at the basket . . . until Ryman did an about-face and charged up the steps. *Go, Kerry!* Small and fast, Kerry Ryman hit the steps running. He bounded up thirty cement steps two at a time with springing lunges. He had snuck into the Hershey Sports Arena so many times over the years that he knew its every passage. He reached the concourse, clutching the ball to his breast, fans pointing at him and shouting, "That kid's got the ball!" He passed Earl Whitmore, the man in the arena because he bought a refrigerator. Whitmore worked at the chocolate factory with Ryman's father. He said, "That's Kerry Ryman!" And told a friend beside him, "They'll never catch him." The constables, a two-man posse in brown uniforms, lagged far behind. Ryman turned left and ran past a sign that read REFRESHMENTS CANDY SOU-VENIRS and past restrooms he and his friends had used as hiding posts on many occasions. He burst out of the arena, ran along the catwalk, his every warm breath in the cold air puffing like smoke then dissipating. Kerry Ryman knew only one place to go—home. The Hershey amusement park spread out before him: cold and wind-blown in the darkness, desolate, not a person in sight. He ran past Kiddyland and down the hill. He passed the carousel, The Comet roller coaster, The Bug and The Whip, The Skooters bumper cars. The Ferris wheel loomed up ahead.

Breaking outside along the catwalk at last, the constables knew the boy they were chasing. Kerry Ryman was one of the usual suspects. They saw him with the ball. They knew him. They followed him into the park. One of

Ryman's friends had run out of a different arena exit and now, deep into the park, yelled, laughing, "Run, Kerry, run!" The Sandman stepped out into the cold, too—he could not see them, but in the distance he heard the echoing laughter. Ryman ran three-quarters of a mile and more, the fear of God propelling him, climbing the far hill and running toward Chocolate Avenue. By the time the constables reached that same hill, they'd lost sight of him. Didn't matter. Constable Gabe Basti could barely breathe; driving a delivery truck for Sears Roebuck full-time was hardly training for this. Besides, he knew where Ryman lived. He would talk to the chief constable. He would see what the chief wanted to do. If need be, Basti could go by the Ryman house in the morning, take the ball back, and bring the kid in.

Back in the arena, Earl Whitmore's friend said, "Wouldn't it be something if they don't have another ball to finish this game with?"

Forty-six seconds remained. The Zink pleaded with fans to return to their seats; it took several minutes to clear the court. As a matter of course, a replacement basketball was kept at courtside near Harvey Pollack's feet, in case the game ball met with calamity, mysteriously losing air or perhaps flying into the crowd where someone spilled a drink on it. (And also to adhere to a rule on page 216 of the 1961–62 NBA Guide: "A new or nearly new ball shall be kept at the scorer's table.") A new ball was brought into play. Even now, with the Dipper at a hundred, Frank McGuire did not remove him from the lineup.

The pace of the game did not change. Ruklick fouled Naulls, whose two free throws made the score 169-148, the most points ever scored in an NBA game. Butcher stole a pass, drove the length of the court for a basket with twelve seconds left, then immediately fouled Ruklick, grabbing him before he could get the ball to Chamberlain. Only eight seconds remained but Ruklick, as ever, had a plan. As the Dipper lined up for Ruklick's free throws, he heard Ruklick say, in a low voice, "Wilt, I'm dumping." Ruklick planned to intentionally miss the second free throw in hopes that Chamberlain might rebound and score once more for 102 points. But Willie Smith heard what Ruklick said. *"What?"* the referee said, the word sounding like an angry slash. As lead referee, he approached Ruklick. "Ruklick," Smith said, "you're trying to influence the outcome of a regularly scheduled game." Smith threatened to forfeit the game, take the scoring record from Chamberlain, and see to it that

Joe Ruklick never played another minute in the NBA. Never mind that no such rule or penalties existed. Ruklick felt intimidated.

Chamberlain, thinking about posterity, pointed at the ball and said, "Ruh-da-lick, after the game you take this ball to the locker room." Ruklick nodded. He missed both free throws. The Dipper couldn't reach the second. The final seconds ticked away as Guerin took a wild hook shot that missed. The game ended, 169-150, and now adults joined their kids, flooding the court, surrounding Chamberlain, reverential, ten-deep, glad-handing him, slapping his back as he trudged wearily, head down, toward the locker room. Ruklick saw a basketball rolling on the court, away from the masses. He scooped it up, carried it into the locker room, and placed it in the Dipper's gear bag. Ushers pried open the crowd enough to allow Chamberlain to make his slow way to the locker room, exhausted but finished for the night. Head bowed, he pressed through a crush of smiling Hershey boys, wearing their winter coats and loafers, their hair slicked back with gel. A few carried pens and game programs, no doubt hoping for autographs. A camera flashbulb popped. The boys slapped the Dipper on his back, touched his arms, grabbed for his hands, caught their fingers in the rubber bands at his wrists. It was pure hero worship, and the Dipper, though trudging, felt the satisfaction of a prophecy fulfilled. He attempted to shake each small hand within reach.

Harvey Pollack typed a quick lead for *The Philadelphia Inquirer* and then typed "Pick-up X copy," a reference to material he'd sent earlier. His son Ron dashed the new page over to Western Union. Now Pollack and Richter tabulated statistics, cross-checking their numbers. Pollack had a frightening thought, *What if Wilt only scored ninety-eight points?* The Dipper's hundred checked out. Richter filled out the official scorer's report in a cursive scrawl, listing players in alphabetical order, and scribbling over the names of those who didn't play: Tom Gola, Frank Radovich, Phil Jordon, Whitey Martin, Sam Stith. Somehow, perhaps in the confusion that began with the Dipper's hundredth point, the Knicks lost three points in the final calculation, the 169-150 final reported several times on the radio postgame show becoming permanently, 169-147. (Decades later, no one could explain this.) Pollack's ditto machine was put to use, and soon stat sheets circulated through the locker rooms. Not that the Knicks wanted to see them. A game such as this, Stith believed, "makes your teammates enemies." The less said about it the better. The Knicks dressed quietly, Imhoff answering questions from a Harrisburg newspaperman. He answered honestly, respectfully. "We tried everything we could. We tried fouling him because he usually misses the foul shots. But he was making them. We collapsed three men around him and tried to keep our hands in front of him. But he was making that fall-away jump shot or rattling them off the backboard. It seemed like everything he threw up went in but that mustn't be right"—he had read the stat sheet—"because he missed almost thirty shots. He's a great offensive machine, just a machine." Imhoff estimated that Chamberlain had scored about forty points against him. "I didn't play too long," he said, adding, "Everybody had a shot at guarding him, but no one could do anything."

Pollack entered the buoyant Warriors locker room where he found the AP photographer, Paul Vathis, struggling to create a photo opportunity with the Dipper. A ball passed around the room was being signed by players, ball boys, Gotty. Pollack proposed an idea to Vathis: "How about if we write '100' on a sheet of paper and have Wilt hold it?" Vathis nodded and asked, "You think Wilt will do it?" Pollack said, "Heff, give me a piece of paper." The sportswriter Heffernan gave Pollack a sheet of copy paper on which he sometimes kept play-by-play notes. Pollack wrote on it with a pen, "100," and handed the paper to the Dipper, who sat on a low-slung wooden bench, his knees in his chest. Behind him, his slacks, shirt, and overcoat hung from wall hooks. Chamberlain held up the paper with both hands and smiled sheepishly for Vathis. His face glistened with sweat, one bead clinging to the beard stubble on his chin. It was nearly 11:15 P.M. Vathis left to process his photos. Pollack rushed off to phone the wires. He would dictate his stories, compiling the paragraphs in his head, first to United Press International and then the Associated Press, conjuring different leads.

From across the locker room, Meschery noted the crowd pressed around Chamberlain. *It's always this way,* he thought. The postgame was the same as the game itself. The Dipper always got the ball . . . the Dipper always drew the light. Now Meschery watched Wilt and McGuire talk with reporters. The other Warriors dressed quietly in the corners.

McGuire beamed. "It was a wonderful tribute to the team. Remember when he got the 78 [points] against Los Angeles? I told them that Wilt would score 100 some day, even if five men played him." McGuire reveled in the magnitude of the accomplishment. "You know, I remember the thrill I got the first time *a team* of mine scored one hundred points. Now this. Why, it would take anyone alone in a gym about 20 minutes to score that many." The coach's eyes sparkled.

Paul Arizin had entered the NBA in 1950. In the Hershey locker room, Arizin admitted, "I never thought I would ever see it happen when I broke into this league. But when Wilt came along I knew he'd do it some day. It's a fantastic thing. I'm very happy for him." The chatterbox Guy Rodgers said, "That's the easiest way I know how to get an assist. Just give the ball to the Big Fella." Teammates kidded Chamberlain: Since he'd been called for defensive goaltending twice against the Knicks, he'd really scored 104 points.

The Dipper deferred to his teammates. "It wouldn't even have been close to possible without them. They wanted me to get it as much as I did." These were respectful, if predictable, comments, but Chamberlain felt a genuine gratitude for what they had done. They did not share a deep kinship with him. He knew they had submitted to his ambition in Hershey and he was grateful for it. To the reporters he said with pride, "I'd hate to try to break it myself." Later, when Attles sidled up to him, the few reporters having left, the Dipper stared at the stat sheet, his eyes tight at the corners. "Big Fella, what's the matter?" Attles asked. All season, Chamberlain had heard criticism that he took too many shots; he averaged forty shots per game. Now he replied, "I never thought that I would take sixty-three shots in a game." "Yeah," Attles replied, "but you made thirty-six of them." Attles smiled and said, "Hey, we'll take that any day of the week."

In Philadelphia, two reactions: Listening to WCAU at a neighbor's house, Tom Gola, bad back, beer in hand, hung on Bill Campbell's every word. Amazed, Gola only wished the game had been televised. It would have been good for the league.

Listening on his bedroom radio, Cecil Mosenson heard Campbell shouting, "He made it! He made it! He made it!" and Mosenson thought, *Yes, he did!* Mosenson had gotten answers to his questions: Frank McGuire would allow it to happen and his players would willingly become Wilt's accomplices. Beyond that there was no mystery. Mosenson always knew that Wilt Chamberlain would become the greatest scorer in basketball history.

· · ·

At *The New York Herald-Tribune,* where sports editor Stanley Woodward considered basketball unworthy of manly attention, no one knew that the Knicks had even played. When sportswriter Jerry Izenberg walked to the row of telex machines—AP, UPI, Reuters among them—he tore off a page of the latest news. Earlier in the night, Izenberg had said he had no idea where the Knicks were. Now, reading Pollack's UPI account, Izenberg announced to his colleagues, "Hey, look at this! I found the Knicks. They did play tonight against Philadelphia, and Chamberlain scored a hundred points."

Not one head turned.

His radio equipment packed up, Bill Campbell bundled up and stepped out into the cold night air. What he saw outside the arena startled him: Wilt Chamberlain climbing into the driver's seat of a new Cadillac with the Knicks' Willie Naulls sitting beside him. *Am I seeing things?* Campbell thought. *The guy scores a hundred points against the Knicks and they ride together back to New York?* Campbell thought this just one more happy peculiarity of the NBA. It was deeper than that, of course, a racial solidarity that transcended team affiliation.

In Raleigh, North Carolina, six Wake Forest University students left the Atlantic Coast Conference basketball tournament and crowded into a powder blue '52 Chevy known to its owner as "The Blue '52 That Runs Like New." Scrunched in the front seat was Ernie Accorsi, a native of Hershey whose grandfather and father had worked in the chocolate factory and had known Mr. Hershey personally. (Accorsi himself would become a Philadelphia sportswriter and, in a distant day, general manager of the NFL's New York Giants.) Now, on a rock and roll radio station, Accorsi heard the nightly news headlines: "The biggest news tonight comes out of Hershey, Pennsylvania." Instinctively, Accorsi had a sinking feeling. *Something bad has happened.* "Shhhhhhh!" Accorsi pleaded with his buddies, but their banter continued. "Shuddup!" Accorsi shouted. They quieted. Accorsi's worst fear bubbled up. *The chocolate factory has blown up!* Then he heard disconnected words floating

through space: "Wilt Chamberlain" . . . "100 points" . . . "Hershey Sports
Arena" . . . and he knew at once—this was even worse than he had feared.
The greatest moment in the history of Hershey! "I can't believe it," Accorsi said,
"and I missed it!" Accorsi had worked several years as an usher at the Hershey arena, proudly wearing his burgundy blazer. There he had watched
hockey games. He had watched Wilt Chamberlain with the Globetrotters.
He'd watched far too many ice shows. *How could I miss this?* From his fraternity house in Winston-Salem, Accorsi phoned home to Hershey. His mother
answered. He didn't even say hello, only, *"Was Dad there?"* His mother understood. Her pause was long enough to break it to her son gently. Ernie Accorsi
knew: *Dad was there.* Finally, his mother said, "I'll let you talk to him."

At Martini's bar in Hershey, the NFL players congregated after the game
for beer earned from their work in the prelim. Everyone in the place knew
Sonny Jurgensen. The all-pro quarterback talked with the Colts' Gino Marchetti, Bill Pellington, and others about the Dipper, marveling over the accomplishment of scoring one hundred points. Marchetti couldn't get one
thought out of his head: A hundred points yes, but, *God, Chamberlain would
make a terrific football player!* The fan Jim Hayney, wearing his fine suit,
showed up at Martini's, too, with his two "clients"—the milkman and
the bartender from Harrisburg. They also toasted Wilt Chamberlain.

At Castiglia's, an Italian restaurant in Harrisburg, a few blocks from the
Hotel Penn Harris, a sixteen-year-old fan, Eliot Goldstein, dined after
the game with a William Penn High School classmate and his classmate's
father. They, too, talked about the Dipper's hundred and their great luck
in having seen it happen. Goldstein remarked about the boy he saw run
onto the court and steal the basketball—so bold! Now, at Castiglia's, Goldstein noticed a familiar man enter the room and sit at a nearby table. Goldstein asked his classmate quietly, "Isn't that the guy on the Knicks, Richie
Guerin?" It was. The two teens summoned the courage to approach
Guerin's table. As Guerin signed autographs for them, Goldstein blurted,
"Wasn't that amazing and unbelievable what happened tonight?" Goldstein
got the impression that Guerin didn't want to talk about it. He only heard
Guerin make a passing remark that he'd scored thirty-nine points but no
one would ever know it.

• • •

It was as if Wilt Chamberlain and Willie Naulls were on the same side now, alone, in the midnight darkness, driving through the open spaces of Pennsylvania, heading for the New Jersey Turnpike. Their car was a beauty, a new Cadillac that belonged to attorney Ike Richman, Gotty's friend, who had fast become the Dipper's friend after negotiating his first NBA contract covertly on the streets of Philadelphia three years earlier. Now Richman was the Dipper's business manager of sorts, suggesting deals and investments, looking out for his finances. Naulls knew that Wilt loved cars and that what most mattered was not how plush or streamlined a car was, but how fast it could be driven. As the Dipper talked now, casually moving his hand in wide arcs for emphasis, Naulls glanced at the speedometer. It raced past eighty-five toward ninety. Naulls felt the engine's exhilarating thrum beneath them.

They were headed to Big Wilt's Smalls Paradise in Harlem where there would no doubt be revelry and celebration about the hundred-point game. Naulls was glad to get out of Pennsylvania, away from the embarrassment of the game. Naulls told the Dipper that the Knicks would have *beaten the Warriors' butts* if not for a few teammates becoming more preoccupied with slowing Chamberlain than with winning the game. The Dipper smiled and took it in. In truth, Naulls was happy for him. He liked and admired Chamberlain, especially the way he seemed so totally in command, not only on the court but also in life. Naulls had heard that the Dipper demanded half the gross from any summer league game in which he played; the word on the streets was that the Dipper counted receipts at halftime with the promoter, then put his percentage in the trunk of his car, which was, naturally, guarded. Naulls seized the moment now and asked Chamberlain about investments and how he handled contract negotiations. Chamberlain talked freely about tax shelters and real estate holdings that Ike Richman had helped him put together; his racehorse, Spooky Cadet (which rarely won); the Bentley being custom-made in England; and the nightclub to which they were headed.

Their conversation returned, invariably, to the hundred-point game, the back and forth nature of it, the way fouls had been committed intentionally at the end. They talked about the NBA. So many talented African-American players—including more than a few of their friends—had been left behind, losing their primes to games in the ghettos. Naulls believed a truly open competition would seek its highest level of expression: Only the best would play. The NBA, Naulls believed, was strangling itself with a racial quota, constricting the talent flow. There was humiliation in it for so many black players. Of course, Wilt Chamberlain had just dished out his own humiliation to the Knicks, the NBA, and to a system that would diminish him.

The Dipper and Naulls also talked about the nicknames they loathed— Wilt the Stilt and Willie the Whale—and the way sportswriters applied to black athletes nicknames or descriptions that condescended and lacked sensitivity. The hour grew late, past 1:00 A.M. Naulls grew tired. He really didn't need to hear the hundred-point huzzahs in Harlem. The Dipper drove him home to Montclair, New Jersey, and turned off the engine in front of Naulls's place. There they talked a bit longer. Chamberlain spoke about how sportswriters harped on him for taking too many shots and for failing to win a championship in his first two seasons. This criticism always found its way back, he said, to Bill Russell. Sportswriters had overdrawn and oversimplified the comparison—the great player (Chamberlain) versus the player who makes his team great (Russell). He was tired of hearing it. In the darkness, Chamberlain vowed to Naulls that he would win his NBA championships but said that when he retired he would be known only for his individualism, for his scoring and rebounding. He would be remembered for nights such as this. At last Chamberlain said his goodbye. In Harlem, a nightclub crowd awaited him.

In the darkness of Friday night, Kerry Ryman threw open the front door at 50 West Chocolate Avenue. His mother reclined on the living room couch, waiting for him. She noticed that he was short of breath, excited. "I just got a basketball, mom," he said. His chest heaved. "Wilt Chamberlain just scored a hundred points over at the arena." He didn't say how he got the ball. He did not mention his dash through the amusement park or the constables giving chase. Lucille Ryman eyed him. "You can't keep it," she said. "You've got to give it back." Her son nodded and said, "All right." He went upstairs, put the basketball in his closet, and listened for the constables, but their knock at the front door never came. Reuel Ryman returned from the 210 Club in Harrisburg several hours later. His wife told him about the basketball. They agreed it had to be returned. Besides, if Kerry had stolen it, they might have to pay a fine. In a company town, the neighbors would talk. Reuel Ryman would tell his boy, "The ball goes back where it belongs," and his boy wouldn't argue. He told his wife that he would call the people at the arena in the morning.

Long before Reuel Ryman awoke, though, his boy already was in Kenny Snyder's macadam driveway in the alley behind Caracas Avenue, where a basket was nailed to the garage. Kerry Ryman took his NBA leather basketball with him. In his hands it felt sweet.

In Harlem, as the 4:00 A.M. closing time approached, the Dipper luxuriated in the neon light, caught up in the moment, caressed by jazz and by a crowd that, much like the kids in Hershey, simply wanted to touch him because of who he was and what he had just done. The Dipper would finally fall asleep at 8:00 A.M., and then wake at 10:30, still energized by the sensation of Hershey.

When Chamberlain awoke, no New York City newsboy was heard hawking "Extra! Extra! The Big Dipper scores a hundred!! Read all about it!" The New York City newspapers, absent in Hershey, had only the barest coverage of the hundred-point game on the morning after, same as most other major American newspapers. *The New York Times* and *The New York Herald-Tribune* ran Pollack's AP account on pages fourteen and eleven; *The Times* merged the story with staff coverage of the forty-third annual Knights of Columbus track meet at Madison Square Garden. *The New York Daily News* buried its five-paragraph UPI story (also Pollack's) from Hershey on the bottom of page twenty-six. *The New York Post,* the paper in town that most valued professional basketball, on Sunday gave prominent back-page coverage to Chamberlain's performance; on that day *The Post* playfully interspersed italicized gee-whiz laugh lines in unrelated columns about the Yankees and high school sports such as *"Did you hear about Wilt?"* and *"Wilt got 100 points!"* and *"100 points? That's crazy!"* and *"Wilt really went crazy."*

Not one New York sports columnist thought enough of the Dipper's performance in Hershey to write about it, though Jimmy Powers of *The*

New York Daily News would write that, generally, he was not impressed by "praying-mantis types 'goal tending' or merely dunking the ball for astronomical totals." Two days after Hershey, Powers wrote: "Basketball is not prospering because most normal sized American youngsters or adults cannot identify themselves with the freakish stars. A boy can imagine he is a Babe Ruth, a Jack Dempsey or a Bob Cousy, for example, but he finds his imagination stretched to the breaking point trying to visualize himself as one of the giraffe types on display today. You just can't sell a seven-foot basket stuffing monster to even the most gullible adolescent." If Powers wasn't impressed by the Dipper, at least one Associated Press feature writer was. A brief profile of the Dipper written by the AP in Philadelphia found its way onto the front page of *The New York Times* two days after Hershey, in which it was stated that Chamberlain "speaks four languages (French, Spanish, Italian and German), plays the guitar and bass fiddle, sings folk and popular music." This was not true. It was true, however, that the source of the information was Wilt Chamberlain himself.

The newsboys weren't shrieking in Philadelphia, either. The Dipper's big night barely rippled the front pages of any of the city's three dailies on the day after. Both Pollack and Heffernan, working for mainstream broadsheets, wrote straight news stories in *The Inquirer* and *The Bulletin* about how Chamberlain had fulfilled prophecy by scoring one hundred points. Jack Kiser, in his own inimitable, tabloidian fashion, gushed: "Impossible? Sure it was impossible. But Wilt Chamberlain did it. One hundred points in one game. One oh! oh! Writing the most fantastic chapter to an already unbelievable career, the 7-2 center made a complete shambles of the NBA record books here last night as the Warriors defeated New York, 169-147." When Jack Kiser wasn't covertly stirring small controversies for his own benefit, he served publicly and at times defiantly as the Dipper's shield, defending him against charges that he took too many shots and cared only about his own statistics. Now, Kiser wrote: "Not one of them was tainted. No basket hanging, no 'gimme' layups, no cooperation from the Knicks in any shape or form. Just the most devastating offensive show ever staged by a basketball player. . . . The Knicks did their best to stop him, or at least slow him down. They played five men on him at times, not even attempting to cover anyone else in the last four minutes." Kiser added, "True, overanxiousness caused Wilt to miss some shots he'd ordinarily make. But he made some he wouldn't have dared taken under ordinary circumstances. Long jumpers from 25–30 feet out with two and three men clinging onto his wiry, 260-pound frame. Power-packed dunk shots when he had to bull through, around and over a tight knot of defenders. Blazing speed that carried him downcourt for layups after he had launched the fast break with a rebound himself. He earned every point."

Around the NBA the reaction to Chamberlain's hundred-point night was mixed. The Lakers' Tom Hawkins heard teammate Frank Selvy recall his own hundred-point game for Furman against little Newberry College and say, "Well, I had one hundred points with no dunks." To which Hawkins replied, "Yeah, Pops, but look at the competition you were facing." Syracuse's Dolph Schayes and Red Kerr stared at the Warriors-Knicks box score with disbelief. Kerr said, "How about this: He's the world's worst free-throw shooter and he's twenty-eight out of thirty-two!" Boston's Bob Cousy heard about it and dismissed it as a game that must have raged out of control, just like when Cousy had recorded a record twenty-eight assists in a 1959 shoot 'em up game in which his team scored the record 173 points against Minneapolis. Boston Coach Red Auerbach, whose praise for the Dipper came reluctantly if it came at all, heard about the hundred-point game and laughed. "He's playing against nobody," Auerbach would say much later. "Imhoff, yeah. That's like me playing against a guy that's five-foot-three. All you have to do is give me the ball, I'll turn around and put it in." Auerbach's own center had a different reaction. In St. Louis on the morning after the Dipper's hundred, Satch Sanders saw Bill Russell smile and heard him say, "The Big Fella finally did it."

PART THREE

Aftermath

CHAPTER 21

The Legend Grows

WHEN BRITISH MEDICAL STUDENT Roger Bannister ran the first sub-four-minute mile in 1954, he attained instant celebrity. The previous record of 4:01.4, set nine years earlier, had seemed the outer limit of human possibility. Bannister stretched that limit and was knighted for it years later by the Queen of England.

No one awaited pro basketball's first hundred-point scorer. The game in Hershey disappeared from conversation quickly. It became like a sunken galleon, resting on the ocean floor, riches in its hold waiting to be recovered. There were references to the hundred-point game over the years, usually with a mixture of awe and curiosity, no one certain how it had happened. Despite newspapers' fondness for stories that commemorate anniversaries of memorable events, no retrospective on the hundred-point game appeared on its first anniversary in March 1963 nor on its fifth or tenth anniversaries nor the twentieth in 1982. Not even the cantankerous Jack Kiser wrote one during these years, having long since turned to his first love, harness racing. (Kiser had been living in Nevada and writing about stamp collecting when in 1993 he died of cancer.) Not until 1987, the silver anniversary of the Dipper's big night in Hershey, did the media attempt to

reclaim an important piece of the NBA past. By that time, the NBA had
grown truly into a major league sport with a network television contract,
star players such as Magic Johnson, Larry Bird, and Michael Jordan, and an
average of more than 13,000 fans per game. That no television videotape of
the hundred-point game existed only added to its mystique. The Dipper told
the Associated Press in 1987 that his teammates had gone "way beyond the
call of duty" in Hershey. "They were so clever finding ways to get me the
ball. They had to do more than just give up open shots. They had to avoid
fouls and pass me the ball in traffic," he said. Of Hershey, he added, "That's
my tag, whether I like it or not."

Once the anniversary stories began, there was no end to them. The
game's legend grew. Whenever his phone rang at home in Oregon in early
March, Darrall Imhoff thought, *Must be Wilt Chamberlain time.* On the fortieth anniversary, Richie Guerin still was angry about it. In March 2002, the
Leatherneck told ESPN Radio, "In all honesty I was annoyed at the way the
second half proceeded. I could care less if somebody scored one hundred
points against us or eighty-five or ninety points against us. If they earn it
and they get it, more power to them. But I just didn't think that the second
half was played the way it should be played." Marge Donovan felt that same
pent-up emotion over the decades. She sat in distress in the Hershey Sports
Arena that night. Forty years later, Coach Eddie Donovan's widow would
say only, "They passed Wilt Chamberlain the ball every time. It wasn't like
he did some great thing." Willie Naulls slid his wire-rim glasses down the
bridge of his nose as he examined the statistics from that long-ago night.
Still handsome, his white hair electric in the afternoon light of north
Florida, he said, "Wilt Chamberlain was thirty-six for sixty-three!!!! I didn't
realize he took that many shots. *Thir-tee-six for six-tee-threeee!*" Naulls said,
"The game was not a fluke . . . I thought it was absolutely authentic."

Darrall Imhoff has been unfairly labeled "the man who gave up Wilt's
hundred," given that Imhoff played only twenty of forty-eight minutes.
Still, he endures with good humor. "Every March first," he said, "I break out
into a rash." And: "When I fouled out in Hershey, I told Wilt, 'You know, Big
Fella, just remember my name and carry me into the Hall of Fame with
you.'" And: "It was an honor to spend twelve years in Wilt's armpits."
Imhoff once cohosted a celebrity golf tournament at Lake Tahoe with former Lakers guard Rod Hundley, who introduced Imhoff to an audience as

"the man who held Wilt Chamberlain to one hundred points." Imhoff took the microphone and said, "That's a bad rap. Look, I didn't play the whole game." He raised a brow, then deadpanned: "Wilt only got eighty-five off me." Imhoff labored to elevate his game and once made the NBA all-star team. Decades later, as a vice president for the U.S. Basketball Academy near Eugene, Oregon, he would say, "I wasn't a great player, and feel privileged to have played then. I was a part of the transition of the game that was to the game that is." He would recall that Chamberlain had scored sixty-seven, sixty-five, and sixty-one points in games leading up to Hershey. "So I mean, in four games that week he averaged about seventy-three points. He was un-believable." Only deep in conversation, the memory of the hundred-point night rekindling, would Imhoff say, "The game was a farce. They poured it on. . . . It was because of the way they were feeding him the ball. . . . When you go beyond seventy [points] and now they are fouling in the backcourt to get the ball back to you, that's when it became a farce. And the announcer said, 'And he just broke the record!' And 'He just broke the record again!' Their announcer, Zinkoff, didn't help us much."

A telegram for Darrall Imhoff arrived two days after Hershey. Signed by two of Imhoff's college teammates on Coach Pete Newell's team, it read: *"D—Congratulations on a fine defensive effort. Pete would be proud of you."* Imhoff smiled and that afternoon in Madison Square Garden, he limited the Dipper to fifty-eight points. When he fouled out near the end of a tight game (won by the Warriors on Arizin's late basket), Imhoff couldn't believe what happened: He got a standing ovation.

Consider the scale of the Dipper's accomplishment in Hershey: Denver's David Thompson rates next highest in NBA history with seventy-three points in the final game of the 1978 season when he fell just six-hundredths of a point short of wresting the scoring title from George Gervin who, in re-sponse, scored sixty-three later that same night. Chamberlain's hundred rates a startling thirty-seven percent higher than the next best single-game performance in NBA history.

Furthermore, no other player has ever averaged as many as forty points per game in a full NBA season. The second best—Michael Jordan's 37.1-point average in 1986–87—would need to be pumped up 36 percent to equal Wilt's

50.4. By comparison, to rise 36 percent above Ted Williams's revered .406 batting average in 1941, a batter would need to hit .552.

Chamberlain's hundred-point game and his fifty-point seasonal average are statistical outliers—so far beyond the norm as to be considered something entirely different.

In his 1973 book, *Wilt: Just Like Any Other 7-foot Black Millionaire Who Lives Next Door,* the Dipper added to the myth of the hundred-point game, though not much to the truth. He wrote of how Frank McGuire, in the Hershey locker room before the game, had shown him two New York newspapers quoting the Knicks as saying they were going to run the Dipper ragged because they knew he was slow and lacked stamina. Chamberlain said that McGuire had grinned and said, "Let's run 'em tonight, Wilt." This tale nicely transformed Goliath into David but why would the Knicks say such a thing? Why would they call a player averaging fifty points per game *slow*? Why would they say that a player who only five days earlier had scored twenty-eight of his sixty-seven points against them in the fourth quarter was *lacking in stamina?* In his book, the Dipper also suggested he rode the team bus to Hershey (he did not), that he napped in his hotel room before the game (the team did not stay in a hotel), and that he played in an arcade shooting gallery before the game with Ike Richman (he played against Ken Berman).

Only in his final years did the Dipper publicly embrace the hundred-point game. On a radio show in San Francisco in March 1993 commemorating the game's thirty-first anniversary, he said, "As the time goes by, I feel more and more a part of that hundred-point game. When it first happened—you must understand, I'm from the streets and when you throw up sixty-three shots in a game you are considered to be a gunner, understand? I always looked at that as me having my best day gunning, not really performing. But it has become my handle and I have begun to realize just how and what I did. . . . People who know nothing about basketball or nothing about sports will see me and they will point to their little kid and say, 'See that guy right there: He scored one hundred in a game.' I know that it has been my tag. I am definitely proud of it. But it was definitely a team effort. You had to see some of the things my teammates did to get me the ball. . . . It was almost like a circus out there for a while." His words had the feeling of a fifty-seven-year-old father professing devotion to his long-lost thirty-one-year-old son. But he was still the Dipper, after all. That night on radio, he also said, "If the New York Knicks had decided to play basketball and not tried to concentrate on me scoring one hundred points, I might have had one hundred-forty or one hundred-fifty."

Al Attles remains proud of his role in the hundred-point game: six assists, five rebounds, seventeen points. Speaking to a group of high school and college basketball players in Holyoke, Massachusetts, Attles said, "How many of you would want to play in a game where a guy on your team scores one hundred points?" Fewer than ten percent of the players raised a hand. One said, "I wouldn't want to play in a game like that because you don't get a chance to do what you do." Attles posed a different question: "Okay, how many of you would like to play in a game where *you* score one hundred points?" About ninety percent raised a hand. "Wait a minute, something is wrong," Attles said. "You don't want to play the game when someone else on your team scores one hundred points, but you do want to play in a game where you score one hundred points." Attles zeroed in on the larger point: "The single most important thing that you play for in a team sport—there's only one reason you play—to try to win. You need to do whatever is necessary to win. If you win, that means you *all* share in it."

As if in fear of Fitzgerald's dark view, "There are no second acts in American lives," the Dipper never wanted his first act to end. He invested well enough to become the rarest of NBA players from his generation, never working a day job. Upon his death, his estate would bequeath more than $6 million, the lion's share to children's causes, and $650,000 to his alma mater, Kansas University, according to the Dipper's attorney, Sy Goldberg. After the 1961–62 season, the Dipper remained on the periphery of the civil rights movement and politics. A chauffeur driving Chamberlain's new Bentley would drive him and his friend Cal Ramsey to LaGuardia Airport in August 1963. They flew to Washington, D.C., to attend the March on Washington where the Dipper stepped into the crowd of 200,000 gathered near the Lincoln Memorial and drew stares as Dr. King delivered his "I Have a Dream" address. In the middle Sixties, Harry Edwards, a black sociologist at San Jose State University, would counsel with many black athletes as he led his human rights protests on college campuses across the nation. Edwards's movement reached its zenith when American track stars John Carlos and Tommie Smith bowed their heads and held up black-gloved fists at the 1968 Summer Olympics in Mexico City in protest of racism in America. Edwards spoke with Bill Russell, Arthur Ashe, O.J. Simpson, and dozens of others, but not the Dipper. He thought Wilt Chamberlain too far removed from the civil rights struggle. "Wilt wasn't a guy that existed at a level where you went up and got in his face and got into an argument and discussion with him about his politics," Edwards would say. "You simply looked at him, saw him for what he was, and moved on." The Dipper would move on, too, engaged momentarily by politics in 1968, announcing his endorsement of Richard Nixon's presidential candidacy, a move that prompted some of his black friends to charge he was letting down his race. (Chastened by events, the Dipper would later say that Nixon cynically exploited him to get black votes.) "I'm just as aware of the injustices done to the black man as anyone," the Dipper would explain years after. "I just don't believe you help things by running around, saying how evil Whitey is. I figure I've done my share—the restaurants I integrated in Kansas, the busloads of black kids I used to take to summer camp from Harlem, the contributions I make, in name and money, to various black causes and programs. Just because I don't call a press conference every time I do something like that doesn't mean I'm insensitive to the black man's plight." Much later, his friend Lynda Huey would say, "Wilt would vacillate between feeling exempt from being black and seriously taking to heart the hardships of black America. I saw him waver between the two depending on what was going on and what mood he was in."

The players of the hundred-point game necessarily moved on in their lives: Tom Gola as a Republican state legislator and city of Philadelphia comptroller (and unsuccessful mayoral candidate); Paul Arizin of IBM; Richie Guerin running with the bulls on Wall Street; the Rev. Willie Naulls; the poet Tom Meschery; and Joe Ruklick as editorial page editor of the historic black newspaper, *The Chicago Defender*. The hundred-point game's more obscure players still keep, close at hand, reminders of their participation in the famous game. In Texas, businessman Ted Luckenbill keeps folded in his wallet a yellowed newspaper clipping of a photograph, shot by AP's Paul Vathis at game's end, of Luckenbill and two young fans congratulating the Dipper. Many people don't believe Indiana Pacers scout York

Larese when he says he played as the Dipper's teammate that night, let
alone assisted on the basket that gave Chamberlain ninety-eight points. In
his wallet, Larese keeps the game's box score. He pulled it out so often he
had it laminated. Meanwhile, Harvey Pollack donated his old Olivetti typewriter—one of several he used while becoming the only man to work for
the NBA during all of its first fifty-eight seasons—to the Naismith Basketball Hall of Fame in Springfield, Massachusetts. Bill Campbell's voice, still
heard on Philly sports radio more than forty years later, was also heard for a
while on NBA Commissioner David Stern's office phone; when a caller was
put on hold by Stern, he heard, among other famous NBA moments, Campbell's call of Chamberlain's hundred-point basket: "He made it! He made it!
He made it! A Dipper Dunk!"

The Dipper himself did not boast of the hundred-point game, not ever.
He spoke little of it as the decades spun past. When asked about it, typically
he replied that he was prouder of his NBA record fifty-five rebounds in a
game against Russell. He understood that the hundred-point game fed criticism that he was more interested in stardom than in winning—even though
his teams did win two championships in his fourteen seasons. He never
again came close to scoring one hundred points in a game, nor did he try to
(he reached seventy-three and seventy-two a year later). He already had
proven that he could do it. In the two seasons that followed his remarkable
1961–62 campaign, by which time the Warriors had moved to San Francisco,
Chamberlain averaged 44.8 points and 36.9 points per game.

In an attempt to rein in the Dipper, the NBA in 1964 widened the lane
by four feet, to sixteen feet, moving him further from the basket. Yet his
style of play already was evolving. Traded back to Philadelphia in 1964, he
would lead the 76ers to a world title in 1967, beating Russell's Celtics in the
playoffs and exploding one myth (that he couldn't win a championship). A
year later, he set out to prove his passing skill and led the league in assists,
thereby exploding another myth (that he couldn't, and wouldn't, pass). Of
winning the NBA's assists title, the Dipper crowed, "It's like Babe Ruth leading the league in sacrifice bunts."

He left Philadelphia in 1968, returning again in a trade to California, this
time to the Lakers. Los Angeles appealed to him for a few reasons: He
wanted to get into the movie business; his parents and several siblings lived
there; and as Nate Thurmond, his former San Francisco teammate, would

say, "The West Coast was more Wilt's style: faster, more liberal. It ain't no secret about Wilt liking white girls. It was an accepted thing out here. When he got to L.A., he was bigger than life and he's got a whole new playground." The Dipper spent his last five seasons with the Lakers and helped the team win a record thirty-three consecutive games en route to the 1971–72 world championship. During his two championship seasons (1967 and 1972), he led the league in rebounding but also produced two of his smallest scoring outputs, averaging twenty-four points and nearly fifteen points per game. Whereas he had averaged forty shots per game in 1961–62, he took only nine shots a game when he won his second title a decade later, at age thirty-five. By then his body had changed—his chest, shoulders, and arms were bulked up from weightlifting, and he no longer ran the floor well—and his role on the team had changed, too. The transformation of his game was complete.

When he retired in 1973, his records glittered like Ursa Major itself. He led the NBA in scoring seven times, in field goal percentage nine times, in minutes played eight times, in rebounding eleven times, and in assists once. He never fouled out—never—in more than 1,200 games, including playoffs. He produced five of the six highest scoring games in history and fifteen of the top twenty. He scored more than 31,000 points (a thirty-points-per-game career average), the highest ever at that time (double the total of Bill Russell).

The Dipper and Russell met 142 times over ten seasons, an average of fourteen games per year. Russell's team won eighty-five, the Dipper's team fifty-seven; in playoff series, Russell's teams won all four seventh games against the Dipper, the total margin in those games only nine points. A question was put forth: If Russell and Chamberlain had been traded, straight up, could the Celtics have won all of those titles with Wilt? Cousy said, "We might've won one with Wilt. We certainly wouldn't have won eleven. . . . We had eight Hall of Famers on that unit [during the Sixties]— or seven surrounding Russ—and we lived and died with the transition game. There was no way we were going to put the brakes on and wait for the Big Fella to amble down and set up and run an offense." Puffing on a cigar early one morning, the eighty-five-year-old Red Auerbach pondered the question and shrugged as if to say, *Maybe.* "If Wilt would have given in," Auerbach said. "I mean I had the big ego, too." But Chamberlain in his career had already proven that he could and would alter his game: Gotty wanted him to score big and he did. 76ers Coach Alex Hannum wanted him to pass and play stopper on defense and he did. The Dipper annihilated Russell in every statistical category but one—NBA titles captured. Russell won eleven, Chamberlain two: the Dipper's cross to bear.

At the end of the 1961–62 season, the Dipper surpassed 4,000 points, an average of fifty per game. The Warriors finished at 49-31, three victories more than the year before but still eleven games behind Boston. The playoffs brought disappointment again. The Warriors struggled past Syracuse and then lost to the Celtics in a conference final series so tense that at one moment Guy Rodgers punched the Celtics' Carl Braun and at another Boston's Sam Jones defended himself against an angry Dipper by picking up a photographer's wooden stool. Boston won a controversial seventh game, 109-107, as Jones converted a jump shot with four seconds to play. Frank McGuire exploded at referees Mendy Rudolph and Sid Borgia who, he said, had been intimidated by Red Auerbach's courtside shouts. McGuire was heard in the locker room afterward, muttering, "Mendy threw the game. . . ." The Celtics went on to defeat the Lakers in seven games to win their fourth consecutive NBA title. And Bill Russell again was named by players the NBA's first-team all-star center, outpolling the Dipper.

Gotty sold the Warriors to a San Francisco syndicate a few months later. Wilt Chamberlain, of course, was the most valuable piece in the transaction. Gotty received $850,000, a neat return on his $25,000 investment made a decade earlier. At long last, the Mogul truly was a mogul.

The players of the hundred-point game scattered. Along with Chamberlain, five more Warriors went west—Gola, Attles, Meschery, Rodgers, and Luckenbill. Gotty went briefly, too, to help get the team on its feet, proudly telling his friends at home he was "going to S.F." Arizin and Conlin retired; Ruklick, Larese, and Radovich never again played in the NBA. For a time, Ruklick played in a recreational league in Northbrook, Illinois. He wrote a letter to Gotty, by then an NBA consultant, asking for an official NBA leather basketball for his team and, just in case, enclosed a signed, blank check. Sure enough, the Mogul charged him $25. (The last little laugh went to Ruklick, though: he and Ed Conlin had taken their home uniforms from the 1961–62 season; Ruklick wore his "Phila 17" jersey in recreation league games for years.) Frank McGuire spent a year away from coaching and then took his Irish charm and good looks back to college. He spent sixteen seasons at the University of South Carolina.

The last-place Knicks shuffled their deck over the next year, too. Imhoff was traded to Detroit. Willie Naulls was dealt to the San Francisco Warriors where he briefly played, and lived with, the Dipper. Guerin's all-star days were nearly done; the Knicks traded him to St. Louis in October 1963. The Leatherneck spent six seasons with the Hawks, becoming head coach of the team and winning NBA coach-of-the-year honors in 1967–68. Phil Jordon, the center who spent the night at the Hotel Penn Harris, played one more NBA season, in St. Louis, his dedication to late night frivolity driving him from the game prematurely. Jordon died in 1965 in a river rafting accident, drowned in the swollen night waters of the Puyallup River in the state of Washington; his three raft mates swam to safety. Jordon, employed on a county road crew at the time, was thirty-one years old. The Knicks finished each of the next four years in last place, though Eddie Donovan would make his mark later, as the team's general manager, drafting Willis Reed, Bill Bradley, and Walt Frazier, and trading for Dave DeBusschere, a cadre of stars that Coach Red Holzman forged into the 1969–70 NBA champions.

When Gotty died in 1979 at the age of eighty-one, Dave Zinkoff felt like a star that had lost its sky. "You're asking 'How close is close?' " the Zink said. "Well, we'd kind of eat together and go to a movie together. I was his driver for a long time. Year in and year out, I was at the wheel of the car that took us to Springfield, Mass., for those Hall of Fame games. We'd make our annual chocolate-bar haul up to Hershey where he'd buy cases and cases. How much closer can guys get when, if there was a vacation, a ten-day break in the schedule, the two of us would go to Florida? Except for spending most of my waking minutes with him, day in and day out, for so many years of my life, I don't know how to say how close Gotty and the Zink were." The Mogul was inducted into the Basketball Hall of Fame in 1971. The NBA also honors him by calling its annual rookie of the year award the Eddie Gottlieb Trophy. When the Zink died on Christmas day six years after Gotty, more than a thousand people came to mourn, including three Philadelphia mayors. The 76ers ceremoniously retired the Zink's microphone the following

spring and later dedicated Dave Zinkoff Boulevard. The team also recognized the Zink with a banner hung from the rafters of its arena, joined later
by one honoring the Dipper.

A piece of the hundred-point game was uncovered by the NBA in 1988: a
Philadelphian, using a Dictaphone, had taped part of Bill Campbell's fourth
quarter play-by-play call on WCAU, but only the Warriors possessions. His
tape ended with the hundred-point basket. It wasn't much, but it was something, a few pieces of gold pulled from the sunken galleon.

Two years later, an educational consultant arrived at the Hershey area to
deliver a talk about reading aloud to children. His name was Jim Trelease.
Meeting a member of the Hershey community archives, a repository of local
history, Trelease asked, "What's the single greatest historical sports moment
in Hershey history?" Without hesitation, the man from the archives, Paul
Serff, replied, "The Wilt Chamberlain hundred-point game." Trelease smiled
and said, "I've got a tape of that game." In fact, Trelease had a reel-to-reel
tape that was to become to the hundred-point game much like what the
Zapruder film was to the Kennedy assassination. On the night of March 2,
1962, Trelease had been in his dormitory room at the University of Massachusetts at Amherst. An avid Knicks fan and broadcaster of UMass basketball
games on the student radio station, Trelease propped a radio in the corner of
his room against a five-story drainpipe that made a splendid antenna on a
clear night. Borrowing his girlfriend's reel-to-reel tape machine, he recorded
Campbell's call of the entire fourth quarter—the biggest haul of treasures
yet lifted from the galleon. The NBA learned of the Trelease tape and made
a copy; through studio wizardry, technicians removed distracting sounds and
merged this tape with the earlier Dictaphone tape (which included a brief
postgame show), creating a new master version. Trelease was astonished to
learn that the NBA did not have a copy of the WCAU coverage after so many
years. NBA archivist Todd Caso had no doubts about the authenticity of the
Trelease tape. "You can hear Dave Zinkoff's voice [on the Hershey Sports
Arena p.a.] in the background," Caso said. "People might try to imitate
Zinkoff, but who would really know how to do that?"

At the Dipper's death in October 1999, the poet Tom Meschery thought of
the sports axiom, "The game's not over until the fat lady sings." By then he

was a high school English teacher in Reno, Nevada, who had published a second book of poetry, *Nothing We Lose Can Be Replaced,* about his family's Russian past, the NBA, and his years of teaching. Now, in "Mourning Wilt the Day After His Death," Meschery wrote, in part:

> Remember, if I can,
> Aquinas' five proofs for God's existence:
> The Uncaused Cause or was it The Divine Plan
> that toppled Wilt? It might help reading
> about the Prime Mover, but I doubt it.
> Words alone are never enough. Today,
> I need opera—Wagner's Ring—a blonde soprano
> with big bosoms belting out her last aria.

In Gainesville, Florida, the Rev. Willie Naulls would recall the hundred-point night as a statement about race and freedom. Naulls had spent his last three NBA seasons with the Celtics, winning three championship rings, and then had prospered over the decades as a businessman. He turned to the ministry in the early 1990s. Just two months before Chamberlain's death, Naulls had been thinking of his old friend. In his church newsletter that August, he wrote extensively of the NBA and of the hundred-point game: "Wilt had rung the bell of freedom loud and clear, shouting, 'Let my people be free to express themselves.' For we were and will be for all time those who withstood the humiliation of racial quotas even to the point of the NBA's facing extinction because of retarded expression and stagnating growth."

Remembering their shared car ride home from Hershey, Naulls wrote, "The ride and the fellowship on the night of the 100 point explosion is exclusively ours; and in that regard, we are Brothers, in the Night of His Flight, Forever."

At a fishing store in Portland, where he went to buy waders, Imhoff learned of the Dipper's death. He heard a voice in the store say, "Wilt Chamberlain just died." Imhoff turned and said, "Whaaaat?" He had been carrying a game photo for the Dipper to sign—the Sixers' Wilt Chamberlain going up for a dunk against the Lakers' Imhoff, the Axe chopping the Dipper's right forearm. Stunned now, Imhoff returned to his car where he heard a radio news report confirming the death. He sat for a while in silence.

In the newsroom of *The Chicago Defender*, Ruklick got word from a CNN news flash. A year before, at the Dipper's invitation, Ruklick went to Lawrence, Kansas, to see Wilt's college jersey retired. "Always glad to see you, Ruh-da-lick," the Dipper had said, remembering his first college game, "because I scored fifty-two against you." Ruklick noticed the Dipper perspiring and how his confident walk had become an old man's shuffle, the result of an ailing hip. The Dipper looked old, vulnerable. Chamberlain would later send his college jersey as a gift for Ruklick's son. But when they shook hands late that night in Lawrence, they parted forever. After leaving the NBA, Ruklick had followed his intellectual curiosity back to Northwestern where he earned a master's in literature. For many years an investment manager, he decided at the age of fifty, divorced and with three children, to earn another master's, in journalism. An intellectual renegade still, he took a reporter's job at *The Defender*, becoming the only white on the newspaper's twenty-two member staff. He had long been thinking about race. Ruklick looked back at the NBA with a jaundiced eye, seeing everything more clearly, he believed, and more objectively. He saw how the Dipper was treated as an oddity, exploited by Gotty and the league ("Eddie put on a circus, and Wilt was his sideshow"), and how the NBA's white players had rejected Chamberlain. "When Wilt came along, the attitude [among white players] was, in my opinion, 'This is a freak who will come and go. There will never be a black guy doing this again.' " To have told the NBA's white players in 1962 what the league would become . . . why, it was enough to make Ruklick laugh. "Oooooh!" he said. "To say to Conlin or Gola or Arizin, 'There's going to be a time when a guy named Shaquille O'Neal—*Whaaaaat?!! What do they call him?*—he's going to make untold millions of dollars and have white girls on his arms in television commercials. And he and eighty percent of the guys in the league are going to be black and earning millions.' " Ruklick shook his head. "Gola would have gone to Gottlieb and said, 'Cut this guy. He's crazy.' " To Ruklick, the hundred-point game was "part of the mythology. It's part of the dream world, the field of dreams counterpart in basketball, that the NBA grew into this marvelous thing that it is with pioneers like Bob Cousy and Wilt Chamberlain . . . and to see it extend inevitably to Wilt's mythological 20,000 [women] is part of the whole tawdry history of those early days." In summer 2004, a massive eighteen-foot, three-ton bronze sculpture of the Dipper was unveiled outside the Wachovia Center in Philadelphia, and Ruklick, Attles, and Arizin attended the dedication. There they saw a bronzed avant-garde, multifaceted likeness of Wilt Chamberlain, including the Dipper slam-dunking at a forty-five-degree angle, with an accompanying plaque that read: "The worth of a man is measured by the size of his heart." Earlier, Ruklick had seen the work in progress and casually mentioned to the sculptor that the Dipper wore a rubber band at his wrist. The artist added that touch to the final product and Ruklick, recalling his role in the hundred-point night, would note proudly, "So I give Wilt another assist—this one eternal, forever memorialized as art."

Attles was the only player from the hundred-point game who attended the Chamberlain memorial service in a Los Angeles church. He was among many notable sports figures that day: Jim Brown, Elgin Baylor, Bill Walton, Nate Thurmond, and the old Globetrotter, Meadowlark Lemon. Bill Russell delivered a tribute to the Dipper, saying, "As we got older, the more we liked each other because we knew basically that we were joined at the hips. . . . We were both important to each other. . . . The only person who knew what we were doing was the other guy. I knew how good he was"—here, the Dipper's fiercest rival smiled—"and he knew that I knew how good he was." A slow, rolling laughter filled the church. Russell concluded by saying, "And so I'll just say, as far as I'm concerned, he and I will be friends through eternity." The Dipper's death was hard on Attles. They'd stayed in touch over the years. Attles once said, "People would never be happy with what he did, and beneath that veneer, I knew how much it was hurting him. He was so misunderstood. So few people took the time to try and appreciate Wilt. Most everybody just assumed that a great player couldn't possibly also be a great person." The miracle of Al Attles was that nearly forty years later he remained with the team now known as the Golden State Warriors. He had played eleven years, coached fourteen (winning the 1974–75 NBA title), and now served as a vice president. In the church, Attles saw the picture of the Dipper from the hundred-point game. Attles had made all eight of his shots in Hershey, and years later the Dipper presented him with a basketball and a plaque for Attles's perfect shooting night: *To Al: Who Did All the Right Things at the Wrong Time.*

Gola and Arizin attended a memorial church service for the Dipper in west Philadelphia, not far from Overbrook. Gola spoke of his enduring appreciation for Chamberlain. He pointed to the crook at the bridge of his nose, the product of a Dipper elbow nearly a half-century before. An emotional Arizin told of how Chamberlain had befriended his sixteen-year-old granddaughter, Stephanie, as she was dying of an inoperable brain tumor. The Dipper corresponded with her for months and phoned her regularly; when the NBA in 1997 honored its greatest fifty players at the all-star game in Cleveland (including Arizin and the Dipper), Stephanie came with her grandfather, hoping to collect autographs. The Dipper embraced her and pushed her wheelchair around the room, getting all fifty NBA legends to sign her book, including Russell, long notorious for refusing to sign autographs. "Wilt, I'm in your debt," Arizin told him in Cleveland. "I owe you." Five months later, Stephanie Arizin died and Chamberlain sent a Dipper-sized floral arrangement. Paul Arizin had hardly known him in 1962. There was the age difference, the racial separation, Arizin was married, the Dipper single. Wilt was hard to know. What Paul Arizin felt, but struggled to say, was that only now did it feel like they truly were teammates.

CHAPTER 22

The Ball

ON THE DAY THE DIPPER DIED, in a town called Annville, eight miles from Hershey, Kerry Ryman worked a fifteen-ton remote control crane, its movements directed from a small box strapped to his stomach. At fifty-one, plumped up and with his thick wavy hair gone gray, Ryman unloaded steel just arrived to the factory, plate steel and coiled steel, used in prefabricated buildings. He had twenty-three years on this job. Divorced, with his grown daughter married and moved away, Ryman lived alone in a rented place; in his spare time he watched TV, old shows from the Sixties, *Mayberry RFD* and the like, and played a little golf. He didn't own a computer or a VCR. He preferred the quieter, simpler days of his boyhood when everyone in town was like family. Since the hundred-point game, Hershey had changed more than Kerry Ryman. For one thing, HersheyPark had been fenced-in so that cars could be charged entrance fees to an amusement park that seemed to have Disneyland-like aspirations. The Penn State Milton S. Hershey Medical Center, meanwhile, grown since 1970 to more than 5,000 employees, had brought in a new, more diverse population. According to the 2000 Federal Census, among Derry Township's more than 21,000 residents were 843 Asian-Americans, 297 Latino-Americans, 355 African-

Americans, and fifteen American Indians. While this didn't exactly make the township *diverse* in a big-city way—it was still more than 92 percent white, after all—Kerry Ryman felt Hershey growing less familiar, more complicated. To him, Hershey seemed more determined to connect with the world than with its old families—that is, with the people who knew and loved Milton S. Hershey. Now, what began as just another day for the $30,000-a-year crane operator changed dramatically when a worker named Mike Blouch said excitedly, "D'ya hear? Wilt Chamberlain just died."

Blouch wasted no time: "Kerry, I want that ball."

"Aww, Mike—"

"Just give me that ball now!"

"Let it alone. Just forget about it."

This conversation had been going on for years, ever since Blouch first learned that Ryman had, in a big plastic bag in his closet, Wilt Chamberlain's hundred-point basketball. *Wow, what a treasure,* Blouch thought. "Give you five hundred dollars for it," he'd told Ryman. Ryman had taken the ball on that long-ago night for one reason—to play with it—and he had done just that, for years, in the school gym, outside in the back alley. The ball had turned black, its texture rubbed raw. The printed words, including the NBA insignia, were gone by the middle Sixties. The ball had literally and figuratively deflated. It looked as if it had spent the last thirty-seven years in a vat of Hershey's chocolate.

Ryman's stock reply: "Mike, that ball's not worth a damn thing. Look at it." But Blouch was persistent. Scrappy and resourceful, Blouch would describe his modest upbringing as "upper-lower class." He would say, "I have that used-car salesman mentality at times." He was forty, had a wife and kids, and forever searched for new ways to make a buck. He said, "Kerry, we're working-class people. We don't get opportunities like this very often in life." With the Dipper's death, Blouch saw an opportunity. He told himself, *When things happen . . . that's when things happen.*

Kerry Ryman gave in. He gave Blouch the ball. Soon, it was being sold on eBay, with a $1 million reserve; a $2 million bid surfaced, but the bidder couldn't be found and Blouch considered it all a hoax. Horrified, Ryman told Blouch, "I want that ball back." Ryman thought about giving the ball to charity. He had another passing thought: *It would be nice to bury the ball with Wilt.* Shortly after the hundred-point game, Ryman's father had contacted the Hershey arena to explain about the ball. Word came back: the Dipper didn't want it. Kerry Ryman kept it.

The sports memorabilia market had barely been born. A nineteen-year-old fan sitting in the Yankee Stadium bleachers five months before Hershey had caught Roger Maris's sixty-first home run of the season that broke Babe Ruth's famed record. Maris told the teen to keep the ball, make some money on it. A restaurateur gave the teenager $5,000 for the ball and then presented it to Maris, who then gave it to baseball's Hall of Fame in Cooperstown, New York. Kerry Ryman hadn't heard a word about any of that. Besides, that was the New York Yankees and Babe Ruth. Cooperstown had been collecting baseball relics since the Thirties. Basketball hadn't even established its own Hall of Fame yet. Decades later, in 1991, a Philadelphia 76ers official would contact Ryman as the team prepared to honor the Dipper, asking if Ryman would give the ball back to Wilt. Sure, Ryman said. The official called back, though, and said never mind, the Dipper doesn't want it.

After the eBay debacle, Blouch had bigger ideas. He contacted auction houses in Chicago and New York. Agents agreed his story was unusual, odd, remarkable, though one New York dealer advised, "Don't say the ball was 'stolen.' Just say that it was 'borrowed.' " Blouch struck a deal with Leland's, a New York house specializing in sports memorabilia. He hired a local attorney who drew up papers for his agreement with Ryman: Since Blouch was putting out his own time and money (mostly, attorney's fees), Blouch would get three-eighths of the proceeds from the sale of the ball and Ryman five-eighths. Ryman signed the papers even as his father told him that selling the ball was a bad idea. "You ought to just put that thing in a burn barrel," Reuel Ryman said. As Christmas 1999 approached, Leland's president Mike Heffner sat in Blouch's living room and looked at the ball. It wasn't what he had expected. *Is this it?* Heffner had authenticated sports memorabilia worth tens of millions of dollars and consulted with the FBI on fakes and frauds. The hundred-point ball didn't have a hologram on it or any special tagging like Mark McGwire's seventieth home run baseball. It wasn't an autograph that could be substantiated by exemplars. The authenticity of the hundred-point ball would be based entirely on someone's word. Heffner met Kerry Ryman and listened to his story. He found Ryman credible; his story had an essential integrity. Local newspaper articles from the past decade quoted fans at the game who saw him take the ball. Mike Heffner decided, *It doesn't matter what this ball looks like, this is it.* Heffner thought the ball might sell for as much as $100,000.

As Leland's publicity machine kicked in, Blouch grew increasingly nervous. He didn't get the cover of the Leland's catalog for the April 2000 auction. Charlie Sheen did. The actor was selling his private baseball memorabilia collection, which featured some remarkable items, including Babe Ruth's white mink overcoat, a piece of Joe DiMaggio's wedding cake (from his 1941 marriage to actress Dorothy Arnold), and the ball hit by the New York Mets' Mookie Wilson that went through the legs of Boston first baseman Bill Buckner helping the Mets win the 1986 World Series. Besides, Heffner told Blouch he couldn't put the hundred-point ball on the cover: "People would look at it and say, 'What the hell is that?'" In its catalog, though, Leland's described the ball as "the most important piece of basketball memorabilia on the face of the earth." That, Blouch liked.

Blouch rented a big car and drove Ryman to New York. Leland's put them up near Central Park, not far from the Dipper's old place. Ryman appeared at a press conference at Mickey Mantle's restaurant. Early the next morning, a limousine picked him up and took him to *The Today Show,* where a woman applied makeup for him. Blouch paced nearby; he knew *The Today Show* was huge exposure. Just then, an assistant to the Leland's publicist showed up with the ball. Blouch nearly had a seizure. The ball was concave! He'd told everyone to make certain the ball was kept in a warm place overnight. Otherwise, it would collapse and look like . . . this. The hundred-point ball looked like it had been stored in an igloo.

Blouch needed to do something, and fast. Beneath a desk in the guests' waiting room, beside a table brimming with bagels, fruit, and coffee, Blouch spotted a room heater. "Can we use this?" he asked. He plugged it in and held the hundred-point ball in front of the blowing heat. Five minutes passed and the ball began to fill out. After ten minutes, to Blouch's great relief, the ball looked beautiful.

He looked up on the TV monitor and saw Kerry Ryman sitting with Tom Brokaw. After his lead-in, Brokaw said, "Kerry Ryman joins us this morning. He's obviously no longer a teenager." Ryman smiled wanly. "Exactly," he said.

Ryman told of how he'd taken the ball at the arena. "And what did you do with it?" Brokaw asked. "I played with it," Ryman said. "We played with it for years in the alley, at the playgrounds."

Then Ryman, enjoying his moment, said, "Wilt scored one hundred points with that ball, and I scored a couple hundred thousand with that ball." If Ryman loved his own line, Brokaw didn't seem to like it much. He said, "You think that's going to add to the value, Kerry, the fact that you scored a couple hundred thousand points?"

Ryman: "Probably not."

Ryman returned to the waiting room after the interview. He had another scheduled at CNN. Blouch was thinking about the appearance of the ball. "Can we borrow that?" he said, pointing to the room heater. A woman there said no. Blouch offered her $500 for the heater. "Can't," she said. "Union property."

En route to CNN, Blouch and Ryman stopped at a drug store and purchased a hair dryer. As a makeup artist worked on Ryman, Blouch plugged in the blow dryer and heated the ball. He turned the dryer to high. Slowly, the ball began to rise . . . until a fuse blew and the CNN rooms lost all power. Two technicians appeared, one shouting, "WHO DID THAT?" Blouch raised a brow.

The controversy erupted later that afternoon. As Ryman and Blouch decompressed over a few beers in the hotel bar, they heard that people in Philadelphia said their basketball wasn't *the* hundred-point basketball. Harvey Pollack, the old Warriors publicist who still worked as a statistician for the 76ers, contended that after the Dipper had scored the hundredth point, referee Willie Smith took the historic ball out of play and gave it to the Warriors for posterity. The Warriors ball boy at the time, Jeff Millman, now the 76ers equipment manager, confirmed the sequence. Millman said he took that hundred-point ball to the locker room when the game stopped with forty-six seconds to play, placed it in the Dipper's bag, and covered it with towels. Further, Millman recalled returning to the court, the crowd still congratulating the Dipper, whereupon he noticed a giddy Guy Rodgers joyfully heaving basketballs into the air. He said Wilt asked him in the locker room after the game to have Warriors players and team officials sign the hundred-point ball, and he did.

Pollack said Ryman must've grabbed a replacement ball and run off with it. Millman remembered that when the Warriors left the Hershey Sports Arena on the team bus, he had only six of the twelve balls—a costly loss that must have enraged the Mogul.

Now Harvey Pollack appeared on national television saying Ryman's basketball was a hoax, a fraud. The real hundred-point ball, Pollack said, was brought to the team offices. On the morning after the game in Hershey, Pollack said, the Zink had used liquid white-out to paint a single panel of the signed ball—apparently there were no signatures on that panel. The Zink then wrote over the white-out the basic game information, namely that Wilt Chamberlain had used this ball to score one hundred points against the Knicks in Hershey. Gotty then placed this signed ball in a window for passersby to see in the few months before the team was sold. Pollack wasn't certain what became of that ball, though he assumed it had gone with Wilt Chamberlain to San Francisco. Some suggested that, given Gotty's promoter's instincts, he might have put any signed ball in the window for a little extra publicity, authentic or not. The Dipper himself said years later that he had given his hundred-point game ball to Al Attles; that was what he told Ruklick, who asked Attles about it when the Ryman controversy broke out. Ruklick remembered Attles saying, "Don't tell that I've got it. I don't want people climbing into my bedroom." Publicly, Attles steadfastly maintained the Dipper gave him a different ball.

Kerry Ryman was incredulous, angry, hurt, and confused. Stealing that basketball, silly as it was, had been a life-defining moment for the small-town crane operator. He wasn't proud of what he'd done, but nearly everyone in Hershey knew that he had done it. He had not taken the ball for its memorabilia value: There was virtually no such thing as sports memorabilia then. To Ryman, this wasn't about money; it was about a different currency—telling the truth. How could Harvey Pollack, or anyone else, doubt him thirty-seven years later?

Even more stunning was the news that came the next morning. Back home from New York, wishing he'd never allowed Mike Blouch to convince him to sell that ball, Ryman received a phone call from his barber, asking if he'd seen the morning paper. He hadn't. "You're on the front page. That ball of yours sold for $551,000!" Kerry Ryman felt light-headed. Was he ecstatic or sick? He was both. Only two sports memorabilia items had ever sold for more at auction: McGwire's seventieth home run ball in 1998 for $3 million and a rare 1910 Honus Wagner tobacco card for more than $640,000. The personal mathematics overwhelmed Ryman: his five-eighths share of $551,000 computed to more than $340,000—the equivalent of roughly eleven years' salary for him. Ryman left work early and went home. He took a call from ESPN Radio. He told the same story he'd been telling for nearly four decades: I shook Wilt's hand. The referee threw him the ball. Wilt bounced it once. I grabbed it . . .

An irate caller phoned from Chicago. *"This guy is building a hot dog stand on Wilt's grave!"* It was Joe Ruklick, from the newsroom of *The Chicago Defender.* Ruklick told his own story, how the Dipper had asked him at the free-throw line near game's end to get the ball for him, and how he'd picked up the ball and put it in the Dipper's gear bag. Ruklick didn't even know that Kerry Ryman was on the line. Once he realized it, he called Ryman a liar. Ryman told his version again—or tried to. "Well, I'll bet my house against yours," Ruklick said testily. He demanded that Ryman take a lie detector test. Kerry Ryman couldn't stand it anymore. He hung up.

Facing a high-profile controversy over authenticity, Leland's suspended the sale, pending further study. In the months that followed, Blouch went to work, gathering signed affidavits from locals who saw Ryman take the ball that night, the Sandman and Spammer among them. Around Hershey, there came whispered criticism of Kerry Ryman. Some suggested the sale of the ball proved only that crime paid.

Six months later, Leland's auctioned the ball a second time. The new Leland's catalog laid out the controversy and concluded: "If anything, the conflicting tales create even more lore behind the ball. Leland's feels that Ryman's story holds greater credibility, particularly with no counter version ball having been produced. Still, bidders can make up their own minds having been presented with all known facts. And, in the end, the ball remains the only ball from the historic game known to exist."

This time, the basketball sold for $67,791. Crestfallen, Mike Blouch did the math: almost $484,000 less than last time. Leland's announced that the bidder who won the ball in the first auction hadn't bid this time. Ryman was glad it was over. His share, minus taxes and small expenses, was about $25,000. With that money, he bought his daughter a used Dodge Arrow to replace her 1987 Ford Tempo (which he took for himself, even though its heater didn't work). Ryman also paid a few bills for his daughter. At a friend's urging, he invested the remaining $10,000 in video company stock, $4 a share. That stock rose to $16 a share and then, like his hundred-point game ball, collapsed. The stock was worth pennies. Ryman did not fret. He figured that money didn't belong to him, anyway, same as the hundred-point ball. His father was right: He should've put that thing in the burn barrel.

What mattered was the memory of the Dipper's extraordinary moment. Chamberlain had created a storm and then stood in the middle of it. Kerry Ryman only did what any right-thinking boy would have done. He ran out to meet the great man, same as the French had done once in a field when the Spirit of St. Louis dropped from the sky and out stepped Lindbergh. A unique moment in sports history—instantly identifiable—Ryman and the other Hershey kids wanted to share in it. Rising to the level of the great man's thigh, Ryman had looked up at Chamberlain. The Dipper was sweating, weary, famous, miraculous. Camera flashbulbs went off. A cresting wave of young fans about to crash down upon them, Kerry Ryman reached out his hand. Wilt Chamberlain accepted it. It was like a gift from a god.

EPILOGUE

T HE DAY AFTER CHAMBERLAIN'S DEATH, obituaries in newspapers across the nation made it clear that two numbers—100 and 20,000—would be the shorthand summary of his life. He had created the numbers, and if one could be verified and the other couldn't, they both were real in that they fit a unique man's idea of who he needed to be. If he was seven-foot-one and one-sixteenth, he could not hide it, so through such outsized numbers he made himself bigger, a lifelong pattern that fused reality and myth. "Yes, that's correct, twenty thousand different ladies," Chamberlain wrote in *A View from Above*, a memoir published by Villard in 1991, eight years before his death. "At my age, that equals out to having sex with 1.2 women a day, every day since I was fifteen years old." His literary agent had asked, "Are you sure you want to do this? That's all that people will talk about." But Chamberlain replied, "Any publicity is good publicity."

His editor at Villard, Peter Gethers, had sought a frank, intelligent book about a star athlete's life and times. In early conversations, Chamberlain had told Gethers about his many women. "You have to understand what it was like in those days. That's what an athlete did," Chamberlain said. To help flesh out a narrative, Gethers created a list of one hundred questions for the Dipper, starting with his childhood, and including this one: "Wilt, you've talked about this a lot—how many women do you think you've had sex with?" Chamberlain patiently answered each question in writing, including the one about his sexual encounters. From Gethers's question, the figure of 20,000 emerged.

"How can you possibly do *that?*" Gethers asked.

Chamberlain responded by telling stories: Once he was invited by a woman to another woman's birthday party only to discover that *he* was the birthday present. There were nine women at the party, and he told Gethers, he had sex with each of them. "That's nine in one night," Chamberlain said. Gethers would note that in all of the Dipper's stories there was no boasting, that he was "weirdly matter-of-fact. He definitely took glee in it. He obviously was a little pathological about pursuing women." Gethers added, "When he was obsessed with something, he went all out, as he did as an athlete. You can't separate that sexual voraciousness . . . with the fact he was capable of scoring one hundred points in a game."

The Dipper's book earned strong early sales, but while he was on an author tour, Magic Johnson disclosed he was HIV-positive. "Wilt became the poster boy for everything wrong with athletes," Gethers said, and the book sales died. The boast of 20,000 also cost Chamberlain commercial endorsements. The head of an advertising agency said as much to the attorney, Sy Goldberg. The problem, he said, was women. "The idea [of using Chamberlain in an advertisement] goes up to a certain level until it hits a female executive somewhere up the line—and then it's killed. As soon as a female has a kibosh position," the advertising man said, "it's dead."

Maybe the number 20,000 mattered in real estate, as well. Wilt's famous house in Bel Air remained on the market for more than two years, vacant, unloved, asking price plummeting, and occasionally featured on TV shows about odd or extreme places. In life, the house personified the Dipper, his genius and his excesses, his vision and self-absorption, his manliness. In death, the house became the anti-Dipper, the hundred-point scorer transformed to what he had never been in life, an underdog. Small wonder, then, that when Ursa Major finally sold, it was to a Hollywood couple, George Meyer and Maria Semple, comedy writers in their forties, self-described environmentalists, social contrarians, and devotees of underdogs.

Meyer served as co-executive producer and lead writer for *The Simpsons*. He once was described by *The New Yorker* as "the funniest man behind the funniest show on TV." He wore a beard and wire-rim glasses, drove a beat-up Honda Civic without air conditioning, and collected memorabilia from the Soviet space program in part because it, like the Dipper's home, seemed an undervalued underdog. Semple, the daughter of a screenwriter, counted among her writing credits *Mad About You, Beverly Hills, 90210,* and *Ellen.* Smart, edgy, quick-witted, Semple saw the Dipper's house first and told Meyer that she loved it. "If you're woman enough to live in Wilt Chamberlain's house," Meyer told her, "I'll buy it for you." Their purchase of the Chamberlain house lit up conversation in the room where writers for *The Simpsons* gathered. "Any guy who seems to be beating the system, like Hugh Hefner or Robert Evans or Wilt," Meyer would say, "obviously is a kind of patron saint of male comedy writers."

Meyer and Semple quickly developed an appreciation and respect for the Dipper. A year after living in his home, they still called it "Wilt's house." As in, "What do you want to do for dinner, honey? Should we just go back to Wilt's house?"

At a local restaurant, Semple saw a friend, comedian Mike Myers, and told him about buying the Dipper's house, which she described to him as a "very James Bond-villain house" and "this big Seventies sex palace." In the restaurant Myers broke into his Austin Powers act. Semple thought, *He's doing Austin Powers for me. God, I know you're famous, but . . .* Not until she was driving home did she realize, *Oh, yeah, that's what Austin Powers was all about.* James Bond, hedonism, sex.

Semple: "A lot of people, because we are comedy writers, will say, 'Oh, you guys *get* the house. You are perfect for the house because you are so ironic.' That is so *not* what this is about. . . . I'm not into the Seventies. I'm not going to live in a pet rock just for joke appeal. I mean, this is my home, and we are having children in this home. I think this is a beautiful house. . . . Since I've been here, I've learned to love Wilt so much. I feel so sad that he is dead. Sometimes I get so emotional and I say to George, 'I would just trade this house in if he were still alive so I could talk to him and get to know him.' It's just how he went out on a limb with this house and how much he loved it. He obviously loved it so much.

"I feel how misunderstood he is," she said.

Meyer: "We are always running into people who had some brush with him—obviously this is L.A.—but it's amazing how they almost always break into a smile when they recall their encounter with him. . . . You respect Wilt's individuality and his nerve. If he wanted a room in an odd shape, 'Who is going to stop me? You?' "

Semple: "You get into these weird corners in the house; instead of doing right angles so that you can live in an inhabitable space, he started making these parallelogram rooms with no windows, just these horrible little spaces. . . . It just got weird. Weird is the enemy of architecture. You want it to be cool. It has also been proven very difficult to kind of unweird the house because it's not the kind of house where you go rip a wall out or gut this. It is what it is. At some point you cry, 'Uncle!' You are like, 'You win, I give up. You get to stay the way you are. You are bigger than me.' "

Throughout the house, Meyer and Semple made changes. They put glass over the ornate marble bathtub in the master bedroom, as if it were a museum piece, to be seen and not touched. They removed the purple shag carpeting, added airy light and bookshelves. "There was just one bookshelf in the house," Semple said, "with crappy torn paperbacks. . . . For someone who was allegedly just constantly reading books, you would think he would have had more bookshelves.

"I feel like we are living in Wilt's arms," Semple said, "like he is cradling us. I feel very honored." Semple wondered, "Do you think Wilt was happy the last ten or twenty years of his life?" She added, "I hope he was."

About his boast of bedding 20,000 women, the Dipper told Lynda Huey, "What's a zero between friends?" Huey would later say, "He just wanted to see if people would believe something ridiculous and they did."

"I believe the 2,000 number," Huey said. "That makes sense."

The Dipper was, at the very least, complicated. Huey noticed how he could be garrulous and delightful while dazzling a dinner party with his witticisms and charm, but then, upon returning to Ursa Major, he would descend into silence and then meanness. "And that's when I'd have to go," Huey would say. Once, in 1977, Chamberlain had phoned her late at night, after they'd shared dinner, to say, "Don't you ever just wish that you could go home with the same person every night and just know that that person was going to be there?" Huey, only thirty and still caught up in the thrill of her independence, said, "Hell, no. I'm loving this." She'd seen the Dipper once open his gold leather pouch and out tumbled phone numbers of women, penned on envelopes, scraps of newspaper, matchbooks, cocktail napkins. There were fifty or so such numbers, perhaps more. "Lorna?" the

Dipper said, reading one. The name tested his memory. He asked himself, aloud, "Who is Lorna?" Huey saw him become jaded with women from "the sheer volume in number and repetition, the same-old, same-old, same-old thing. . . . He had sort of worn it all out and couldn't choose anymore, nothing looked interesting to him anymore." Huey would say, "Most normal people want a close, intimate relationship with someone, but neither of us did. I think that's why we sort of ended up with each other at the end—by default." The Dipper's oversized bed seemed the center of his universe. Huey saw him happiest in quiet moments there, watching a movie on television or reading his travel magazines. As the Eighties neared an end, the Dipper had looked back at his own life of leisure during the decade and saw "far too much nothingness." He vowed to be more productive, saying, "Why did I ever think that I could fool myself into believing that doing nothing could ever have any redeeming value? I lived this lie for a lot longer than I care to remember."

On the last Saturday night in Wilt Chamberlain's life, Huey saw him leaning against his kitchen sink, pressing a hand to his ailing teeth, as if to release pressure, rocking back and forth, and groaning in pain. She'd phoned him earlier in the day, then reconsidered and hung up before he answered. The Dipper had caller identification, and a moment later, Huey's phone rang, and she heard his typically gruff one-word greeting: "Yeaahh!" Their most intimate conversations always were on the telephone, where his physical presence couldn't dominate. The Dipper told her his sister and her husband were coming by that night, and Huey agreed to join them.

Huey had long noticed how the Dipper was wary of people. He feared they wanted his fame or his money. It was as if he made them pass a credibility test, and Huey believes it took her ten years to pass that test. At times, even when they were no longer lovers, he could seem possessive: Once Huey and her boyfriend dined with the Dipper and his lovely young date. Chamberlain ignored his date all night, kept his hand on Huey's knee, told fond stories about "us" and "we," and the next day Huey's boyfriend said, "That old man still loves you." A few days later the boyfriend disappeared from Huey's life, apparently chased off by Wilt. In 1997, on Huey's fiftieth birthday, the Dipper phoned her and sang "Happy Birthday." When he finished, he told her, "You better keep that tape. It's going to be worth something when I'm gone." She believed that he became a victim of his own celebrity: "And he was trapped there until the end of his life. He didn't know how to get out of it." Huey sensed the Dipper would rather stay at home alone on a Saturday night than admit he didn't have a date, "to propagate the legend." "He refused to be loved or to love," Huey said. "He could allow it only marginally or intermittently. He could never love one woman."

But their friendship endured. For the mental stimulation of it, they debated social issues. He noticed how Los Angeles had resegregated in the 1990s and how at most of the parties they attended either all of the guests were white (plus Chamberlain) or they were all black (plus Huey), unlike the more integrated parties of the Seventies. Huey thought the Dipper no longer identified himself as black, often referring to black Americans as "they" or "them." She asked him, "Why do you say *they?*" He didn't like the question and only grunted: "Huh-huh-huh-huh." He loved talking about his mother, whom he worshipped, and also about the old days of the NBA, including the hundred-point game. Not that he had to bring up the hundred-point game. Too many times Huey and the Dipper stood in an elevator and heard someone say, "I was at the hundred-point game, Wilt." Huey heard it in Miami, Rome, Helsinki, and the Dipper would only nod each time, saying nothing, and then later would tell her how the claim proved how silly people were. "They weren't there," he would say to Huey. "Why do they tell me that they came to that hundred-point game?" It never occurred to him, apparently, that people wanted to please him with the reference.

They had been vacationing with friends on the Amalfi coast in 1993 when Huey first noticed Chamberlain's physical decline. Hiking down mountains to the sea, the Dipper, his hip in pain, admitted, "I can't make it," and the admission stunned Huey. His world grew smaller at the end. No longer exchanging quips with James Baldwin or Redd Foxx at Smalls Paradise, now he was spotted alone at a serene spot overlooking the Pacific studying books on Spanish, while continually searching for friends to play with at night, often settling on his beach volleyball cronies for games of backgammon, cards, or dominoes. The Dipper slept little. His bedroom television always was turned on. In his final few months, when his virility was drained, Huey sensed he no longer knew what to do with himself.

In their last hours together, on the Dipper's bed, they watched *Shakespeare in Love*. With Ursa Major's ceiling open, a warm and lovely Santa Ana breeze moved through the room. He asked her to stay. Another movie, he said. But Huey had to leave, and as she did, she said, "Feel better, Wiltie."

Three days later, the Dipper died alone. On a table by his bed was a picture of his mother. Huey believed he would have chosen to die alone, that as he had held life to himself, so, too, would he make death his and his alone. Rushing back to Ursa Major one last time, Huey saw the reporters at the front gate and the helicopters in the sky.

NOTES

PREFACE

PAGE

xvii **sassing him by calling him "Globetrotter":** Wilt Chamberlain as told to Tim Cohane, "Pro Basketball Has Ganged Up on Me," *Look* (March 1, 1960): 52–53.

xviii **"a first sight of the New York skyline":** *Philadelphia Daily News* (December 15, 1957). The writer was Sandy Grady.

xviii **"The most perfect instrument ever made by God . . .":** Sandy Grady, "The Master Plan to Change Wilt Chamberlain," *Sport* (March 1, 1962): 67.

xviii **hide scars from thousands of mosquito bites:** Wilt Chamberlain and David Shaw, *Wilt: Just Like Any Other 7-foot Black Millionaire Who Lives Next Door* (New York: Warner, 1975), 29.

xviii **stories about a great-grandfather six-foot-ten:** Ibid., 33.

xviii **big crane standing in a pool of water:** *Philadelphia Daily News* (February 2, 1960).

xviii **Philadelphia had its share of guys named Dippy:** Ray (Chink) Scott interview.

xviii **wearing his three-piece suit, necktie:** Bill Kashatus. *Connie Mack's '29 Triumph* (Jefferson, NC: MacFarland & Company, Inc., Publishers, 1999), 12.

xix **some NBA dressing rooms kept boxes:** Terry Pluto, *Tall Tales: The Glory Years of the NBA, in the Words of the Men Who Played, Coached, and Built Pro Basketball* (New York: Simon & Schuster, 1992), 55.

xix **Players smoked cigarettes:** Joe Ruklick and Al Attles interviews.

xix **"Ladies and gentlemen . . .":** Marty Blake interview.

xix **up to 500 semipro baseball games:** Gaston J. Funzi, "The Warriors' Bouncy Boss," *Greater Philadelphia* (November 1960): 51.

xx *Incredible,* **he thought:** "How Do You Stop Him?" *Time* (January 25, 1963): 40.

xx **Larese lifted the ball high:** York Larese interview.

INTRODUCTION

PAGE

1 **The gardener found his body:** *Los Angeles Times* (October 20, 1999).

1 **first call went to Chamberlain's attorney:** Seymour (Sy) Goldberg interview. The detailed description of the Chamberlain death scene is drawn from Goldberg.

2 **"It was the first time . . .":** Ibid.

2 **every word of the Haggadah:** Ibid.

2 **The Dipper looked peaceful in bed:** Ibid.

2 **Built on a World War II Nike missile:** Maria Semple and George Meyer interviews.

2 **200 tons of stone and enough redwoods:** Chamberlain and Shaw, *Wilt,* 290–91.

3 **fur of 17,000 Arctic wolves' noses:** Ibid., 293–94.

3 **the "X-rated room," with mirrors:** Ibid.

3 **sharing chicken and dumplings and watching:** Lynda Huey interview.

4 **"Come on, baby! Come on . . .":** Ibid.

4 **They slept together in his trailer:** Ibid.

4 **"a lot of fun, just silly, playful . . .":** Ibid.

5 **"Almost by himself, he made the league . . .":** Oscar Robertson, *The Big O: My Life, My Times, My Game* (Emmaus, PA: Rodale, 2003), 150.

5 **"I believe Wilt Chamberlain single-handedly saved . . .":** Ibid., 151.

5 **only the second among the fifty:** Nate Thurmond interview.

6 **"We think it may have been a heart attack":** *Los Angeles Times* (October 13, 1999).

6 **"a Herculean figure on the basketball . . .":** *Washington Post* (October 13, 1999).

6 **"size, strength and intimidation . . .":** *New York Times* (October 13, 1999).

6 **"If Wilt Chamberlain can die . . .":** *Philadelphia Inquirer* (October 13, 1999).

7 **the Dipper cheated at cards:** Cal Ramsey interview.

7 **"I killed him with my bare hands":** Ibid.

7 **no statistical equal of the Dipper's hundred:** Frank Selvy, Clarence "Bevo" Francis, and Newt Oliver interviews. In the collegiate ranks (where games last forty minutes), the hundred-point level was reached in the 1950s by two stars playing for obscure schools in games against even more obscure opponents: Clarence "Bevo" Francis of Rio Grande (Oh.) College against Hillsdale (Mich.) College and Frank Selvy of Furman College against Newberry (S.C.) College. These games occurred eleven days apart in February 1954, one in rural Ohio, the other in a South Carolina textile town. A fluid six-foot-nine jump shooter named for his father (who had assumed the nickname "Bevo" from his favorite near-beer made by Anheuser-Busch), Francis played in southeastern Ohio for a college on the brink of bankruptcy; Rio Grande (pronounced *Rye-Oh Grand*) had only ninety-two students, including thirty-nine boys. Playing against Bible seminaries, military bases, and assorted junior colleges, Rio Grande swept to an unbeaten season in 1953. In a thirty-two minute game against Ashland (Ky.) Junior College, Francis scored 116 points, but the NCAA refused to recognize his performance as a Division II record because Ashland was not a degree-granting four-year institution. The next season, in a game against Hillsdale, played in a high school gym in Jackson, Ohio, Francis scored 113 points; he took seventy shots against Hillsdale (a degree-granting, four-year school) and was rewarded with his record. Selvy, a six-foot-three guard at Furman, converted a shot from nearly half-court at the final buzzer to reach one hundred points against winless Newberry College. A Newberry player was so aggressively inept in covering Selvy, he fouled out two minutes, forty-three seconds into the game. With his mother, Iva, watching him play in college for the first time, Selvy took seventy-two shots, including an array of hooks from the pivot and longer-range shots. "The only way we could've stopped him," the Newberry coach said afterward, "was to slow it down and we weren't going to do that." It was the first time a college basketball game had ever been televised live in South Carolina. On black-and-white TV screens, both teams' jerseys looked the same, prompting viewers to complain to local stations. Furman responded by changing at halftime into its purple road jerseys to provide more contrast.

9 **"You can start only one black . . .":** Neil Isaacs interview.

9 **standing reach was nine feet, seven:** "Wilt the Stilt Chamberlain," *Look* (February 19, 1957): 118.

10 **Malcolm X had served as a teenaged waiter:** Malcolm X, as told to Alex Haley, *The Autobiography of Malcolm X* (New York: Grove Press, 1964), 80–83.

10 **Gotty rented the Dipper a gorgeous:** Vince Miller interview.

10 **at least fifty players from twenty-seven schools:** Stanley Cohen, *The Game They Played* (New York: Carroll & Graf Publishers, Inc., 1977), 226–27.

10 **The team dispatched players in sound trucks:** Tom Hawkins interview.

11 ***"We're going to be at the Sports Arena . . .":*** Ibid.

11 **fought with the White Russians:** Tom Meschery interview.

11 **He was in a new Cadillac:** Willie Naulls interview.

12 **cremated, per his family's wishes:** Seymour (Sy) Goldberg interview.

CHAPTER 1: THE DIPPER IN HARLEM

PAGE

15 **"God, Satan, and Mississippi notwithstanding . . .":** James Baldwin, *Collected Essays* (New York: The Library of America, 1998), 136.

16 **six times the average yearly salary:** Scott Derks, ed., *The Value of a Dollar, 1860–1999.* Millennium Edition (Millerton, NY: Grey House Publishing, 1999). The average income of an American worker in 1962 (including farm laborers) was $5,155 per year. The book cites the average income for a public school teacher as $5,291, a federal civil employee $6,643, and a manufacturer $6,291.

16 **twenty fine suits, thirteen pairs:** Wilt Chamberlain as told to Tim Cohane. "Pro Basketball Has Ganged Up on Me," *Look* (March 1, 1960): 57.

16 **Oriental-motif apartment:** Kareem Abdul-Jabbar and Peter Knobler, *Giant Steps* (New York: Bantam Books, 1983), 82–83.

16 **two, three, or four kids in each:** Chamberlain and Shaw, *Wilt*, 19.

16 **each morning they felt the trolleys rumble:** Ibid.

16 **"No, mama, this seat right here is open":** Ibid., 57–58.

16 **"Sit down, relax . . .":** Tom "Satch" Sanders interview.

16 **Big Pete, Little Pete:** Vince Miller interview.

17 **his shirts picked up at the cleaners:** Ibid.

17 **stuttered slightly, he was a riotous emcee:** Lloyd Williams interview.

17 **"Lincoln got his head on all the pennies":** Redd Foxx, *Laff of the Party, Volume 1* (Los Angeles: Dootone Records, 1956).

17 **his first New York nightclub date in a decade:** *Amsterdam News* (November 25, 1961).

17 **"Preacher's wife had the biggest ass . . .":** Redd Foxx, *Laff of the Party, Volume 2* (Los Angeles: Dootone Records, 1957).

18 **a laid-back, Miles Davis, be-bop cool:** Ray "Chink" Scott interview.

18 **tried to pick up Chamberlain's suitcase:** Cal Ramsey interview.

18 **the Abyssinian Baptist Church crowd:** Bob McCollough interview.

18 **"Meeting again at Smalls Paradise . . .":** "Café Society Rediscovers Harlem," *Ebony* (June 1962): 35–42.

19 **overwhelmed by the magnitude:** K.C. Jones interview.

19 **"the Black World Beyond the Veil":** W.E.B. Du Bois, *The Souls of Black Folks* (New York: Avon Books, 1965), 265. This book was first published in 1903.

19 **Red Rooster, where Willie Mays had held:** Sam Stith interview.

19 **"I'll be back in an hour":** Ibid.

19 **"Will this thing never end?":** *Amsterdam News* (December 30, 1961).

19 **Jackie Robinson co-hosted a cocktail party:** *Amsterdam News* (April 8, 1961).

19 **dark suit and shined black shoes, made his rounds:** Malcolm X, as told to Alex Haley, *The Autobiography of Malcolm X* (New York: Grove Press, 1964), 402–404.

20 **"Anybody can sit. An old woman can sit":** Taylor Branch, *Pillar of Fire: America in the King Years, 1963–65* (New York: Simon & Schuster, 1998), 13.

20 **dropped off his date at her home in Queens at 6:00:** Chamberlain and Shaw, *Wilt*, 152.

21 **sending a ballboy to get him two hot dogs:** Pluto, *Tall Tales*, 334.

21 **"You should have seen this dame . . .":** Robert W. Creamer, *Babe: The Legend Comes to Life* (New York: Fireside, 1992), 185.

21 **"The blonde sitting underneath the basket":** Ken Berman interview.

CHAPTER 2: THE SHOOTING GALLERY

PAGE

22 **He showed the jeweler a ten-carat diamond:** Ken Berman interview.

22 **"I'll have you a match":** Ibid.

23 **Brown had attended the same parties:** Tim Brown interview.

23 **Chamberlain walked into his garage and lifted:** Clarence Peaks interview.

23 **his hand had disappeared entirely:** Tommy McDonald interview.

23 **Marchetti would spend about forty-five on beer:** Gino Marchetti interview.

23 *God, he would make a good tight end!:* Ibid.

23 **"Few people ever score four thousand . . .":** *Philadelphia Daily News* (March 3, 1962).

24 **the Dipper yowling, "Man, look at this":** Dave Budd interview.

24 *That's Wilt:* Darrall Imhoff interview.

24 **"The visitors saw what looked . . .":** *HersheyPark Arena: 50-Year Birthday Celebration, 1936/1937–1986/1987,* a commemorative souvenir program. Hershey Community Archives, Hershey, PA.

24 **manure carted in from the farmlands:** Ibid.

24 **briefcase full of one hundred dollar bills:** Donnie Butcher interview.

24 **reminded him of a coal mining camp:** Ibid.

25 **initially a kid disc jockey at the Steel Pier:** Bill Campbell interview.

25 **gargled before each broadcast with Turtle Wax:** Pat Williams interview.

26 **General Electric refrigerator with a freezer:** Earl Whitmore interview.

26 **"You're a sportsman, Mr. Whitmore . . .":** Ibid.

26 **"Okay, boys, that's it":** Paul Vathis interview.

26 **"I told you, 'No more . . .' ":** Ibid.

26 **"They can't even skate":** Bill Pavone interview.

27 **"I'm in ladies' panties":** Bern Sharfman interview.

27 **"that the two places you didn't try to live . . .":** Ibid.

27 **met Chamberlain once at the High Hat:** Ted Russ interview.

27 **"I've got two salesmen with me":** James Hayney interview.

28 **"Evo, how'd you like to see the Yankees . . .":** Evo Ianni interview.

28 **unpatrolled room where the Zamboni:** Michael Larkin and Woody Slaybaugh interviews.

28 **boy with the ticket would have propped open:** Kerry Ryman interview.

28 **keep sneakered feet out of sight, clambered atop:** Kerry Ryman and Michael Larkin interviews.

28 **eye to the floor for dropped ticket stubs:** Michael Larkin interview.

28 **When the arena lights dimmed:** Dave Damore, Kerry Ryman, and Jim Balmer interviews.

CHAPTER 3: FIRST QUARTER

PAGE

31 **Warriors in Hershey were eleven-point favorites:** *New York Herald-Tribune* (March 2, 1962).

31 **the Dipper winning the opening tip:** Sam Goldaper, "The BIG Game," *HomeCourt*, Utah Jazz magazine (March 1997): 70.

31 **The Dipper rebounded and dunked:** Ibid.

31 **"We've never beaten Minneapolis . . .":** Carl Bennett interview.

32 **oranges, crushed paper cups, a shoe:** Johnny Oldham and Boag Johnson interviews.

32 **"Let them do what they want":** Vern Mikkelsen and John Kundla interviews.

32 **"Why are you doing this?":** Boag Johnson interview.

32 **pregnant woman pulled out an umbrella:** Johnny Oldham interview.

32 **"Lakers Defeated 19-18 . . .":** *Minneapolis Tribune* (November 23, 1950).

32 **"slow motion that would shame the movies":** *St. Paul Dispatch* (November 23, 1950).

32 **"[The Pistons] gave pro basketball a great . . .":** Ibid.

33 **"I want to find out to what extent league rules . . .":** *Minneapolis Tribune* (November 24, 1950).

33 **neither team even attempted a shot:** *Chicago Tribune* (January 7, 1951).

33 **120 total shots divided by 48:** Harvey Pollack interview.

34 **Oldham decided that if the Three Stooges:** Johnny Oldham interview.

34 **silver cufflinks that read "71":** Pluto, *Tall Tales*, 175.

34 **"I'm covering you one-on-one tonight":** *Philadelphia Evening Bulletin* (December 10, 1961).

35 **"And I think he would have scored a hundred . . .":** *Philadelphia Daily News* (December 9, 1961).

35 **"Someday I could do it if I were relaxed, cool . . .":** *Philadelphia Evening Bulletin* (December 10, 1961).

35 **"The Big Fella is going to get one hundred . . .":** Pluto, *Tall Tales*, 228–29.

35 **Guerin had driven into the lane repeatedly:** *Philadelphia Daily News* and *Philadelphia Evening Bulletin* (February 26, 1962).

35 **hear him in Convention Hall's $1.25 cheap:** *Philadelphia Daily News* (February 27, 1962).

36 **He imagined the chair as Bill Russell:** "The Playmaker," *Time* (February 1, 1960): 40.

36 **"Good luck, 'Shake Hips' ":** Ron Pollack interview.

36 **Any catcall from the crowd, Guy Rodgers heard:** Hal Lear interview.

36 **McGuire once snuck a deflated basketball:** Chamberlain and Shaw, *Wilt*, 148–49.

37 **Imhoff thrust his right forearm:** Darrall Imhoff interview.

37 **Imhoff also placed his right foot between:** Ibid.

37 **NBA referees worked seventy games a year or more:** Norm Drucker interview.

38 **"The way you called the game . . .":** Pluto, *Tall Tales*, 38.

38 **Smith, earning $120:** Pete D'Ambrosio interview.

38 **He even brought his own brown paper:** Norm Drucker interview.

38 **flow of the game early, aggressively seeking the ball:** Darrall Imhoff interview.

38 *Why am I not allowed in here?:* Ibid.

38 **"why don't you just give the guy a hundred . . .":** Ibid.

38 **with a beer in hand and hoping:** Tom Gola interview.
39 **"You're a local kid so we'll have a night . . .":** Pluto, *Tall Tales*, 208.
39 **"Wilt was Philadelphia . . .":** Tom Gola interview.
39 **accidental elbow that put a small dent:** Ibid.
39 **"What are you doing?":** Rod Hundley interview.
40 **Chamberlain was thinking about a record:** *Philadelphia Evening Bulletin* (March 3, 1962).

CHAPTER 4: THE RISE OF THE DIPPER

PAGE
41 **"to be a good boy":** Cecil Mosenson interview.
41 **wearing a scarf, a beret, and dark sunglasses:** Ibid.
42 **"You're not going to pull that crap . . .":** Ibid.
42 **"I want you to come up here and play us":** Hal Lear and Wally Nowacki interviews.
42 **front doors thrown open and neighbors pouring:** Hal Lear interview.
42 **girls said, suggestively. "How *big* is he?":** Dave Shapiro interview.
43 **"Don't tell Dippy, okay?":** Ibid.
43 **the Dipper pull from his satchel a BB gun:** Ibid.
43 **"Mainly from above the rim":** Joe Goldenberg interview.
43 **Dipper, after separating the combatants, raised his arms:** Cecil Mosenson interview.
43 **Forrest "Phog" Allen had bragged that the freshman:** Pete Newell interview.
44 **"one out of ten [classes]":** Al Oerter interview.
44 **"Somehow you don't look like Wilt":** Ibid.
44 **Saperstein offer Chamberlain one-third ownership:** Ibid.
44 **heard jazz jam sessions at nightclubs:** Maurice King interview.
45 **"How'd you like that . . .":** Neil D. Isaacs, *Vintage NBA: The Pioneer Era 1946–56* (Indianapolis, IN: Masters Press, 1996), 103.
45 **He let the Dipper drive his car:** Chamberlain and Shaw, *Wilt*, 93.
45 **Lester, his mythical hound dog:** Max Falkenstien interview.
45 **"Nobody ever asked us to leave . . .":** Maurice King interview.
45 **a police car's flashing blue lights:** Ibid.
45 **"I single-handedly integrated Kansas":** Lynda Huey interview.
45 **Chamberlain's car was already packed:** Max Falkenstien as told to Doug Vance, *Max and the Jayhawks: 50 Years On and Off the Air with KU Sports* (Wichita, KS.: The Wichita Eagle & Beacon Publishing Company, 1996), 71–72.
46 **he wore Band-Aids over his nipples:** Chamberlain and Shaw, *Wilt*, 113.
46 **"You gotta shoot more . . .":** Ibid., 108.
46 ***The greatest girl hounds:*** Ibid., 99.
46 **"You're in my country now . . .":** Louis "Red" Klotz interview.
46 **"Drive me to 4700 North Broad . . .":** Mike Richman interview.
47 **blacks were *rocks*, whites were *you-alls*:** Chamberlain and Shaw, *Wilt*, 99.
47 **"with thighs that made me want to cry . . .":** Abdul-Jabbar and Knobler, *Giant Steps*, 86–88.
47 **place himself in a woman's view, make eye contact:** Lynda Huey interview.
48 **edge of not knowing what to say by being slightly rude:** Ibid.
48 **"If we lust in earnest for each other . . .":** Wilt Chamberlain, *A View from Above* (New York: Villard, 1991), 261.
48 **a young white woman waiting for Chamberlain:** Tom Gola interview.
48 **in sixteen states, mostly in the South:** *New York Times* (June 13, 1967). This story explains

the U.S. Supreme Court unanimous ruling that individual states cannot outlaw marriages between whites and nonwhites.

48 **"Guess we won't see Wilt until game time . . .":** Frank Radovich interview.

48 **grandmother because she thought him godless:** Tom Meschery interview.

49 **They called him *Wilt's boy*:** Ibid. This anecdote is drawn from Meschery.

49 **"I'm not angry with you":** Ibid.

50 **"Wilt and I became more friendly . . .":** Ibid.

50 **"We think that the President is a fine . . .":** Arnold Rampersad, *Jackie Robinson: A Biography* (New York: Alfred A. Knopf, 1997), 362–63.

50 **Selective Patronage Program to boycott:** *Reporting Civil Rights: Part One. American Journalism 1941–1963* (New York: The Library of America, 2003), 565–572. See also: Gerald L. Early, *This Is Where I Came In: Black America in the 1960s* (Lincoln: University of Nebraska Press, 2003), 91–93. Early's essay, "Cecil B. Moore and the Rise of Black Philadelphia, 1964–68," depicts racial tensions and the resultant political mobilization of the African-American community in Philadelphia during the early and mid-Sixties. Early writes, "The level of frustration and anger in the black community [in Philadelphia] in the early 1960s was high, especially because the civil rights movement had heightened the political consciousness of ordinary blacks and because slowly improving economic conditions had heightened people's expectations."

50 **"For the Northerner . . . Negroes represent . . .":** Baldwin, *Collected Essays*, 179.

50 **Wisconsin for the candidacy of Hubert Humphrey:** Rampersad, *Jackie Robinson*, 343.

51 **"Is there a medal anywhere . . .":** Ibid., 363.

51 **a supportive boss at Chock Full o'Nuts:** Ibid., 337.

51 **"titular head of the drive intended to make democracy . . .":** A. Leon Higginbotham Jr. letter to Wilton Chamberlain, March 22, 1960. NAACP, Philadelphia branch, Urban Archives, Temple University, Philadelphia Pennsylvania.

51 **privately insisted that only black contractors:** Sy Goldberg interview.

51 **"it would reflect on me and then indirectly . . .":** *New York Times* (March 28, 1960).

51 **"I never saw any evidence of racial prejudice":** *New York Times* (March 27, 1960).

52 **"Maybe if Bill Russell said it, I'd pay attention":** *Philadelphia Evening Bulletin* (March 29, 1960).

52 **"If Wilt is worrying about the effect . . .":** *New York Post* (March 28, 1960).

52 **"It would be better for me and I could do more . . .":** *New York Times* (August 11, 1960).

53 **NAACP branch in Philadelphia threatened to boycott:** *Philadelphia Daily News* (March 10, 1962).

53 **noticed five black Packers on the court:** Pete D'Ambrosio interview.

53 **"the loneliest town in the world":** Bill Russell as told to William McSweeny. *Go Up for Glory* (New York: Coward-McCann, Inc., 1965), 155.

53 **"Woody Sauldsberry's gonna be traded":** Al Attles interview.

54 **Celtics owner Walter Brown fumed:** *Boston Globe* (October 18, 1961).

54 **"I will not play any place again . . .":** *Boston Herald* (October 18, 1961).

54 **"No thinking person in Kentucky . . .":** *Boston Globe* (October 19, 1961). Also: *Lexington (KY) Herald and Lexington Leader* (October 18, 1961).

54 **Lloyd explained to the rookie the way things were:** Earl Lloyd and Ray Scott interviews.

54 **"you were black your order always was to go":** Pluto, *Tall Tales*, 76.

54 **"you felt responsible for each other":** Earl Lloyd interview.

54 **"I about wanted to cry":** Pluto, *Tall Tales*, 75–76.

54 **you must wear a suit and tie:** Earl Lloyd interview.

54 **"I'm not crusading for anyone":** *Philadelphia Evening Bulletin* (March 29, 1960).

PAGE

56 **yet another late night:** Donnie Butcher interview.

56 **"Like a swan with a broken wing":** *Philadelphia Daily News* (December 12, 1961).

56 **"Hey, Cleeve-laaaaand!":** Sam Stith interview.

56 **"He was used to seeing country food . . .":** Johnny Green interview.

57 **Jim Krebs, feigned fear, covered his head, and ran:** Rod Hundley and Tom Hawkins interviews.

57 **"backward explosion like a whale breaching . . .":** *Philadelphia Evening Bulletin* (January 13, 1961).

57 **"was the overriding factor in Wilt's whole psychology":** Paul Arizin interview.

57 **"the jolly giant's *fee-fi-fo-fum* syndrome":** Tom Hawkins interview.

58 **"Basketball is for the birds—the gooney birds":** Shirley Povich, "Basketball Is for the Birds," *Sports Illustrated* (December 8, 1958).

58 **he was less likely to be fouled, for him a good thing:** Pluto, *Tall Tales,* 233.

58 **"I tried to interview the guy standing up . . .":** *Philadelphia Evening Bulletin* (February 4, 1960).

58 **"My family's always laughed at me singing":** Ibid.

58 **saw "Jumpin' " Bill Manning dunk:** Johnny Green interview.

58 **"Betcha can't block this shot":** Ibid.

59 **"You can't let Embry do that!":** Pluto, *Tall Tales,* 226.

59 **He pinched Wilt's leg, side, or elbow:** Clyde Lovellette interview.

60 **teeth before realizing they remained in his mouth:** Clyde Lovellette and Paul Arizin interviews.

60 **"You get your ass out of that bed and sit up . . .":** Red Auerbach interview.

60 **"What's this boy doing here?":** Ibid.

60 **"How many did ya get, Red?":** Johnny "Red" Kerr interview.

61 **"H'lo, Mister Chamberlain":** Tom Gola, Norm Drucker, York Larese, and Darrall Imhoff interviews.

61 **"Mister Bellamy, please tell Walt . . .":** Norm Drucker interview.

61 **The first nine shots Walter Bellamy took:** *Philadelphia Evening Bulletin* and *Philadelphia Daily News* (November 20, 1961).

61 **"It was sad, man":** Earl Lloyd interview. Lloyd was an assistant coach for Detroit in 1961–62 and saw this game.

62 **"*Anybody* can make a free throw":** Joe Ruklick interview.

62 **"cornpone, kind of like an addled Jerry Lee Lewis":** Alan Richman interview.

62 **"It was, honestly, the most pathetic . . .":** *Philadelphia Daily News* (February 26, 1962).

62 **referees knew Kiser as "Poison Pen":** Norm Drucker interview. See also: Neil D. Isaacs, *Vintage NBA: The Pioneer Era 1946–56* (Indianapolis, IN: Masters Press, 1996), 227.

62 **Strom, smarting from Kiser's criticism, once scuffled:** Norm Drucker interview.

62 **"You're dumping, you're shaving points . . .":** Ibid.

63 **Leonard Lewin and Leonard Koppett, liked the Dipper:** Leonard Lewin and Leonard Koppett interviews.

63 **"too many writers around the league . . .":** *Philadelphia Daily News* (December 19, 1961).

63 **"Seeing as how this is a sportswriters' dinner . . .":** *Philadelphia Daily News* (March 30, 1960).

63 **"Wasn't that a lovely acceptance speech?":** Ibid.

63 **trains blew soot that speckled copy paper:** Sandy Grady interview.

64 "Bazooms! Give me more bazooms!": Ibid.

64 *Tummeling* is what he called it: Larry Merchant interview.

64 "because Jack didn't have standout writing . . .": Sandy Grady interview.

64 "Eddie Gottlieb pays $1,000 [per game] to see Wilt . . .": *Philadelphia Daily News* (December 15, 1961).

64 "With Convention Hall attendance what it is . . .": *Philadelphia Daily News* (January 11, 1962).

64 "Wouldn't it be fitting and proper . . .": *Philadelphia Daily News* (January 30, 1962).

64 "Wasn't the ignoring of Sam Jones . . .": *Philadelphia Daily News* (January 5, 1962).

65 "There was something very intense about him": Larry Merchant interview.

65 "Why didn't you take Wilt out . . .": *Philadelphia Daily News* (November 15, 1961).

65 "Why the intense attack?": Ibid.

66 THE MAN WHO WAS NEVER A BOY: *Philadelphia Daily News* (February 2, 1960). Kiser's series, "Exclusive: The Wilt Chamberlain Story," ran for five consecutive days.

66 "Even if Chamberlain was . . . bluffing . . .": *Philadelphia Daily News* (March 28, 1960).

66 "just to show Kiser that he didn't know . . .": Jim Heffernan interview.

67 "Nobody can breathe on him without getting . . .": *Philadelphia Daily News* (November 10, 1961).

67 "They've created a monster . . .": *Philadelphia Daily News* (January 19, 1962).

67 "How do you think the other [Warriors] players . . .": *Philadelphia Daily News* (January 19, 1962).

67 "Now that Wilt Chamberlain has gone cold . . .": *Philadelphia Daily News* (January 5, 1962).

67 "At last glance Wilt was hitting 49.3 percent . . .": *Philadelphia Daily News* (February 6, 1962).

67 "It could be that all of Chamberlain's dunk shots . . .": *Philadelphia Daily News* (December 15, 1961).

67 "he pads his bank account": *Boston Traveler* (January 19, 1962).

68 source of Wheelright's material was . . . Jack Kiser: Hugh Wheelright interview.

68 "Has anybody on this club been told to feed . . .": *Philadelphia Daily News* (January 20, 1962).

68 "It was a malicious, vicious article, Hugh": Hugh Wheelright interview.

69 "It's yellow journalism!": Ibid.

69 The secret remained theirs to keep: Ibid.

CHAPTER 6: GOTTY AND THE ZINK

PAGE

70 Gotty drove to Hershey: Jim Heffernan interview. Heffernan rode with Gottlieb and Zinkoff to Hershey.

70 "A mogul is a top banana": Frank Deford, "Eddie Is the Mogul," *Sports Illustrated* (January 22, 1968): 43.

70 "Get over to that corner there . . .": *Philadelphia Evening Bulletin* (December 8, 1979).

70 "He's *meshugs*": *Jewish Exponent* (Philadelphia, PA). Undated. Eddie Gottlieb file. Greater Philadelphia Jewish Sports Hall of Fame and Museum. The Gershman Y.

71 "Why the hell did you do that?": Funzi, *Greater Philadelphia* (November 1960): 52.

71 "waitresses," he called them: *Philadelphia Inquirer* (December 26, 1985).

71 "Why buy a cow when milk is so cheap?": Ibid.

71 "Now maybe the girl thought . . .": Deford, "Eddie Is the Mogul," 44.

72 "size and shape of a half-keg of beer": *New York Times* (January 13, 1980).

72 "bloodhound, a wonderful face with big John Huston jowls": Tom Meschery interview.

72 "What do you mean, what does a promoter do?": Funzi, *Greater Philadelphia* (November 1960): 20.

72 later attended the Philadelphia School of Pedagogy: *Philadelphia Evening Bulletin* (December 8, 1979).

72 "We'll do your laundry, too": *Philadelphia Inquirer* (December 10, 1979).

72 preferably in cash since that saved him three: Deford, "Eddie Is the Mogul," 43.

72 He ripped the ball from the kid's hands: Paul Arizin interview.

72 gauge a crowd, and guess its size, invariably: Jim Heffernan interview.

72 the stakes always were the same—a prune Danish: *Philadelphia Daily News* (December 7, 1979).

72 "takes a certain kind of mechanical brain": Funzi, *Greater Philadelphia* (November 1960): 20.

73 they couldn't read the denominations: Angelo Musi, Jr., interview.

73 team's players wore Hebrew letters across their chests: James Rosin, *Philly Hoops: The SPHAs and Warriors, A Look at the First Two Professional Basketball Teams in the City of Philadelphia* (Philadelphia: Autumn Road Publishers, 2003), 3.

73 "Half [the fans] would come to see the Jews killed . . .": *Jewish Exponent*. Undated. Eddie Gottlieb file. Greater Philadelphia Jewish Sports Hall of Fame and Museum. The Gershman Y.

73 Gotty drove his eight-seat Ford touring car: Rosin, *Philly Hoops*, 9.

73 Gil Fitch, rushed into the locker room: Gil Fitch interview.

73 "Many a fella met his wife there": Funzi, *Greater Philadelphia* (November 1960): 50.

73 "And what's *your* problem?": Angelo Musi, Jr., interview.

74 Gotty instructed the Zink to drive around the parking: Jim Heffernan interview.

74 *Listen, I've got news for you:* Joe Ruklick interview.

74 "Just bring your own chair": Marty Blake interview.

75 "seventy-five percent black in five years": Carl Bennett interview. See also: Ron Thomas, *They Cleared the Lane: The NBA's Black Pioneers* (Lincoln: University of Nebraska Press, 2002), 24–25.

76 "This was my blood; this wasn't a tax gimmick": Deford, "Eddie Is the Mogul," 45.

76 "You dumb S.O.B.": Carl Bennett interview.

77 "Wait until the people in Convention Hall . . .": *Philadelphia Evening Bulletin* (October 20, 1959).

77 With ratings and sponsor interest: *Philadelphia Daily News* (January 18, 1962).

77 "And they were here as guests": *Philadelphia Daily News* (December 15, 1961).

77 "Would we draw better without Wilt?": *Philadelphia Daily News* (January 26, 1962).

CHAPTER 7: MCGUIRE AND HIS WARRIORS

PAGE

78 "to see that Wilt made the plane on time": Dean Smith with John Kilgo, and Sally Jenkins, *A Coach's Life* (New York: Random House, 1999), 73.

78 named by the Barbers of America: Ray Cave, "McGuire Raises a Standard," *Sports Illustrated* (October 30, 1961): 36.

79 McGuire had walked the New York waterfront: Carol Ann Morgan interview. Ms. Morgan is the daughter of Frank McGuire.

79 "It's a bum rap": Joe Ruklick interview.

79 On one side he'd put the cops he knew: Smith with Kilgo, and Jenkins, *A Coach's Life*, 47.

79 greasing palms, a ten-spot to the hatcheck lady: Jack Curran interview.

79 **"as dissimilar as a bagel and a steak":** Cave, "McGuire Raises a Standard," 33.

79 **drank J & B Scotch Mist:** Tom Gola interview.

79 *Wilt's making all this money:* Pluto, *Tall Tales*, 229.

79 **$10,000 in expense:** Ibid., 230.

79 **"I don't want you to worry about . . .":** Carol Ann Morgan interview.

80 **"You lost your coach last night":** Al Attles interview.

80 **"It costs twenty-five cents more . . .":** Smith with Kilgo, and Jenkins, *A Coach's Life*, 46.

80 **ball to Chamberlain "two-thirds of the time":** Pluto, *Tall Tales*, 227.

80 **"We should win the pennant . . .":** Paul Arizin interview.

80 **"We're ahead 50-0 at the start . . .":** Tom Gola interview.

80 **"Coach, whatever you say is fine . . .":** Pluto, *Tall Tales*, 227.

80 **"I'll go get him when I want to":** *Philadelphia Daily News* (February 5, 1960). Also: Joe Ruklick interview.

81 **"Wilt responds to leadership by someone . . .":** Cave, "McGuire Raises a Standard," 33.

81 **"Chamberlain will score about a hundred thirty . . .":** Jimmy Breslin, "Can Basketball Survive Chamberlain?" *The Saturday Evening Post* (December 1, 1956): 106.

81 **Naturally, Wilt won the tap, but:** Tommy Kearns interview.

81 **"How long do you want to play?":** Pluto, *Tall Tales*, 226.

81 **Chamberlain let Frankie tug on his mustache:** Carol Ann Morgan interview.

82 **football's Roosevelt Grier, smoking a cigarette:** Tom Gola interview.

82 **"I got a room twice this size . . .":** Pluto, *Tall Tales*, 334–335.

82 **"[McGuire's] challenge is to develop further . . .":** Cave, "McGuire Raises a Standard," 30.

82 **The driver kept turning over his right shoulder:** Joe Ruklick and Ken Berman interviews.

83 *"White bread, rye bread . . .":* Philip Roth, *Portnoy's Complaint* (New York: Vintage, 1994), 56.

83 **nickname, The Destroyer, grew from a collision:** Al Attles interview.

83 **"We're passing over Toledo, Ohio":** Ibid.

84 **"I've got a phone in my ass":** Ted Luckenbill interview.

84 **Dipper guzzled a bottle of 7-Up:** Jeff Millman and Larry Jacobs interviews.

85 **"Two-Hand, Underhand Loop Shot":** John Christgau, *The Origins of the Jump Shot: Eight Men Who Shook The World Of Basketball* (Lincoln: University of Nebraska Press, 1999), 12–13.

85 **still looking at his open palm:** Joe Ruklick interview.

85 **"Don't pay attention to his breathing":** Red Auerbach interview.

86 **they never had a meaningful discussion:** Paul Arizin interview.

86 **a lifelong aversion to flowers:** Ibid.

86 **"Meschery was a guy who looked slightly . . .":** Stan Hochman interview.

86 **"Tired of his guff":** *Philadelphia Evening Bulletin* (March 8, 1962).

86 **lived in the old home of the mad monk Rasputin:** Tom Meschery interview.

87 **"You must be joking, Vladimir Nikolaevich":** Alexander Kerensky, *Russia and History's Turning Point* (New York: Duell, Sloan and Pearce, 1965), 345.

87 **Lvov bribed his way out:** Tom Meschery interview.

87 **young Tom on his mother's back:** Ibid.

87 **a loaded pistol, two swords, and a photograph:** Ibid.

88 **"There are the real drinkers . . .":** Paul Arizin interview.

88 **He might even sing Bobby Darin's version:** Joe Ruklick interview.

88 **"Wilt did everything in grandiose proportions":** *Los Angeles Times* (March 2, 1987).

89 **"You ever stop to take a leak?":** Joe Ruklick interview.

89 **"he had a lot more money . . .":** Tom Meschery interview.

89 *"they could beat the New York Yankees!":* Joe Ruklick interview.

89 *"Nobody leaves until only one man . . ."*: Ibid. Also see: Chamberlain and Shaw, *Wilt*, 134–38.

90 **Gola, blushing, insisted it was a venial sin:** Joe Ruklick interview.

90 **"This is not a book in the ordinary sense . . .":** Henry Miller, *Tropic of Cancer* (New York: Grove Press, Inc., 1961), 2.

90 **"Perhaps it wasn't so pleasant to smell . . .":** Ibid., 48.

90 **"Your mother would *kill you* . . .":** Joe Ruklick interview.

91 **"Joe, you sit at the end of the bench . . .":** Ibid.

91 **"Yeah. We screw your wife!":** Frank Radovich interview.

91 **"He is the best that has ever been":** "The 7-Foot Man," *Newsweek* (December 17, 1956): 96.

91 **"Chamberlain's great performance came under . . .":** Ibid.

91 **"It's just ridiculous":** Ibid.

91 **his white Warrior teammates speaking more freely:** Joe Ruklick interview.

91 **"A bonus check, Mogul?":** Ibid.

92 **"to vote your honest opinion":** Ibid.

92 **He strung their leashes:** Ibid.

93 **"Yeah, I saw that movie":** Ibid.

93 **"You're not in college anymore":** Ted Luckenbill interview.

94 **"Why did you do that?":** York Larese interview.

94 **"Frank's boy":** Ibid.

94 **people didn't think he had an education, or any intelligence:** York Larese interview.

94 **many whites thought he couldn't write or even *talk*:** Wilt Chamberlain and Bob Ottum, "I'm Punchy from Basketball, Baby, and Tired of Being a Villain," *Sports Illustrated* (April 12, 1965): 32–33.

94 **"What's he sayin', Dip?":** Joe Ruklick interview.

94 **Dutch country inn that was a favorite of Gotty's:** Ken Berman interview.

CHAPTER 8: HALFTIME

PAGE

95 **"the only p.a. announcer I've ever known . . .":** *Philadelphia Inquirer* (December 26, 1985).

95 **a box of New Phillies Cheroots cigars:** Dave Zinkoff, "Zink at the Mike," *The Wigwam: Philadelphia Warriors vs. New York Knicks; Philadelphia Eagles vs. Baltimore Colts, Game Program* (Hershey, PA, March 2, 1962. Published by the Philadelphia Warriors): 14. (Personal files of Ron Pollack.)

95 **"I won!":** Arnie Skaar interview.

95 **certified on the page in blue ink by the Zink's handwritten:** George Dirkes interview.

96 **"You asked to *look* at it":** Jim Johnston, Paul Wice, and George Dirkes interviews.

96 **"You two guys figure it out":** George Dirkes interview.

96 **The Zink offered Dirkes and Skaar:** Ibid.

96 **"Let's keep getting the ball to Dip":** Joe Ruklick interview.

96 **"I'm glad you didn't back down from . . .":** Ibid.

97 **teammates a look of quiet resignation:** Willie Naulls interview.

97 *Sweetcakes.* **That's what Bill Russell called:** Bill Russell as told to William McSweeny, *Go Up for Glory* (New York: Coward-McCann, Inc., 1965), 100–01.

97 **"Willie Naulls was a guy I wanted to be like":** Ray "Chink" Scott interview.

97 **"suave, smooth, experienced and well under control":** Leonard Koppett, "Great Future Awaits Walt Bellamy," *Knickerbockers vs. Chicago, Game Program* (Madison Square Garden, January 23, 1962): 3. (Personal collection of Dave Budd.)

97 "Willie, if you ever get traded, can I have . . .": Sam Stith interview.

97 inviting Naulls to his home: Willie Naulls interview.

98 took Naulls to hear the Temptations and other Motown: Ibid.

98 Dipper had invited him to drive back to New York: Ibid.

98 "looked at what your parents gave you versus . . .": Ibid.

99 referred to as Willie the Black Whale: Ibid.

99 *Shooters always think they are about to make ten:* Ibid.

100 his heart set on popcorn and pinball: Kerry Ryman interview.

CHAPTER 9: IMHOFF, GUERIN, AND THE KNICKS

PAGE

101 "You're all I've got tonight": *New York Times* (March 2, 1987).

101 surfing in southern California, wearing white duck pants: Darrall Imhoff interview.

102 at $12,500 per: Ibid.

103 "If you want the ball . . .": Ibid.

103 "Get that sucker away from me!": Rod Hundley interview.

103 "Hey, Richie, I don't want any part . . .": Ibid.

103 "C'mon, Richie! I'll give you whatever . . .": Bob Cousy interview.

104 Richie will get you front row seats: Donnie Butcher interview.

104 Richie could throw down a few at Clete Boyer's: Ibid.

104 He spent nearly two hours a day: Sid Gray, "Richie Guerin—Always Trying to Improve," *Knickerbockers vs. Syracuse, Game Program* (Madison Square Garden, December 1, 1961) 3. (Personal collection of Dave Budd.)

104 "I'll punch your head off": Pete D'Ambrosio interview.

105 "Gimme twenty, rook": Johnny Green and Darrall Imhoff interviews.

105 gamblers were upset the Knicks: Darrall Imhoff interview.

105 "Darrall, there's something we need to talk . . .": Ibid.

106 "I never yet have had a player . . .": Ibid.

106 "is throw a *rock* at you": Pete Newell interview.

106 introduced him to the jazz music of Dave Brubeck: Willie Naulls and Darrall Imhoff interviews.

106 Budd mistakenly used the tightly bristled hairbrush: Dave Budd interview.

107 "His potential is such that every team . . .": Leonard Koppett, "Knicks' Future Bound to Be Better," *Knickerbockers vs. Syracuse, Game Program* (Madison Square Garden, February 27, 1962): 3. (Personal collection of Dave Budd.)

107 "Nothing indicates sufficient strengthening . . .": *New York Post* (October 17, 1961).

108 real value for their money: three hours of entertainment: Leonard Koppett interview.

108 gathered at an Eighth Avenue tavern called the Everglades: Pluto, *Tall Tales,* 51.

108 couldn't secure a sponsor: Les Keiter interview.

108 "No, but a lot of people set records against us": Sam Stith interview.

108 "freakish" or "praying mantis types": *New York Daily News* (March 4, 1962).

108 "I have strong reservations . . .": Jerry Izenberg interview.

109 *The Post* had a liberal Jewish readership: Leonard Koppett interview.

109 "Yeah, Johnny Green is only six-foot-five . . .": Jerry Izenberg interview.

109 "You've been around longer than I have": Sam Stith interview.

109 Green so enraged, pulled him from Guerin: Johnny Green, Darrall Imhoff, and Sam Stith interviews.

110 **"You're not playing cards with us tonight?":** Ibid.

110 **Maris sought a raise from $29,000:** *Philadelphia Evening Bulletin* (February 26, 1962) and *Los Angeles Times* (February 27, 1962).

110 **"What's doin', Rog?":** Leonard Koppett interview.

110 **Imhoff saw the crash site where workers searched:** Darrall Imhoff interview.

110 **more than $60,000 floated:** *Philadelphia Evening Bulletin* (March 2, 1962).

111 **Phil Jordon had been thrown out of that game:** *Philadelphia Daily News* and *Philadelphia Evening Bulletin* (February 26, 1962).

112 **local Spokane Kiwanis Club had granted his widowed:** Jim McGregor interview. See also: Jim McGregor, and Ron Rapoport, *Called for Travelling: The Incredible Life Story of One of the Best-Known Basketball Personalities in the World* (New York: Macmillan Publishing, Co, Inc., 1978), 5.

112 **his teammates wouldn't see him again until:** Ken Sears, Donnie Butcher interviews.

112 **"If I don't play, I don't care":** Donnie Butcher interview.

112 **"The last two months of the National Basketball . . .":** Bob Cousy with John Underwood, "Cousy Asks: Basketball—Or Vaudeville?" *Sports Illustrated* (March 19, 1962): 20–21.

113 **He brought a case of beer with him:** Sam Stith interview.

113 **"Richie, how ya doin'?":** Ibid.

113 **He asked Butcher to get Pepto-Bismol:** Donnie Butcher interview.

113 **"Butch, tell them I can't go":** Ibid.

CHAPTER 10: THIRD QUARTER

PAGE

114 **"Run, jump, beat the ball down . . .":** Willie Naulls interview.

115 **Chamberlain's refusal to whip the ball down:** Red Auerbach interview.

115 **They met him in force above the free-throw line:** Dave Budd, Johnny Green, Donnie Butcher, and Darrall Imhoff interviews.

115 **Donovan bit his lip, a nervous tic:** Sam Stith interview.

116 **repeatedly slid pieces of paper to him, game facts:** Toby Deluca interview.

116 **Chamberlain's points, written in black ink, crossed:** Ibid.

116 **one of the Lakers had broken through it:** Tom Gola interview.

117 **clowns used red, varnished springboards:** Kerry Ryman interview.

117 **needed to hang from the rim after each dunk:** Ibid.

118 **cranking out news releases each time a new park:** Harvey Pollack interview.

118 **his trusted Olivetti, a ditto machine:** Ibid.

118 **"Wilt fade-away, 14 feet . . .":** Ron Pollack interview.

118 **"Please detail for us every field goal . . .":** Harvey Pollack interview.

118 **"Wilt, whose number do you want . . .":** Vince Miller and Harvey Pollack interviews.

119 *The Harrisburg Patriot* **would dictate:** Harry Goff interview.

120 **"Mr. Strom informed me that Chamberlain . . .":** Norman Drucker telegram to Maurice Podoloff, January 3, 1962. (Personal files of Norm Drucker.)

120 **Ted Husing broadcast the remarkable five-set Davis:** Bill Campbell interview.

120 **details about the curtains, the chair, and the table:** Ibid.

120 **"This is Bill Campbell speaking . . .":** This quote is from the official archives of the Broadcast Pioneers of Philadelphia. It can be heard online at www.angelfire.com/tv2/philapioneers/campbell.html.

121 **"What did you have to say that for?":** Ibid.

121   "You'll never know what it looked like . . .": Tom Callahan interview.

121   "You better get out of his way otherwise": Al Attles interview.

122   "It was as if he were an enlarged version . . .": Joe Ruklick interview.

122   "My own feeling for basketball had faded . . .": John McPhee, *A Sense of Where You Are: Bill Bradley at Princeton* (New York: Farrar, Straus & Giroux, 1978), 6–7.

123   big men had been called *pituitary freaks:* Bob Kurland interview.

123   "Baseball's time is seamless and invisible . . .": Nicholas Dawidoff, ed., *Baseball: A Literary Anthology* (New York: The Library of America, 2002), 1.

124   "Well, who put the half-dollar up there?": Cal Ramsey interview.

124   slammed with such force the ball bounced over: Bob McCollough, Fred Crawford, and Cal Ramsey interviews.

124   "To the anti-basketball skeptic, Chamberlain's massive . . .": *Philadelphia Evening Bulletin* (January 16, 1962).

124   "some goon stands under the basket and taps . . .": *Philadelphia Inquirer* (March 2, 1962).

125   "I respect Russell and he's my friend": *Philadelphia Evening Bulletin* (December 9, 1961).

126   his most confident shooters suffered nightmares: Pete Newell interview.

126   "Tell Wilt when he shoots that fall-away . . .": Ibid.

127   for fear he'd get hit by eggs or coins: Norm Drucker interview.

127   "I assume you're not paying any attention . . .": Bill Russell and Taylor Branch, *Second Wind: The Memoirs of an Opinionated Man* (New York: Random House, 1979), 158–59.

127   "The best way to help integration is to live . . .": "How Do You Stop Him?" *Time* (January 25, 1963): 40–41.

127   "Is this the way you build up basketball?": *Philadelphia Daily News* (January 26, 1962).

128   "I'd like to see Russell play Wilt all alone": *Philadelphia Evening Bulletin* (January 16, 1962).

128   "You stay right here": Paul Vathis interview.

CHAPTER 11: RYMAN OF CHOCOLATE TOWN

PAGE

129   as a young girl often saw Mr. Hershey: Lucille Poorman Ryman interview.

130   "His ambition, generosity and success . . .": Lucille Poorman (Ryman), "Our Founder," poem written in 1945. Lucille Poorman Ryman's personal files.

130   a proposed split of the corporation stock: *Hershey News* (February 15, 1962).

130   women's bowling team, the Chocolettes, bound: *Hershey News* (March 15, 1962).

130   set up by his mother in a chaise longue: Lucille Poorman Ryman interview.

130   "We Like Ike, We Love Mamie!": Hershey Community Archives. "Eisenhower Birthday Party, October 13, 1953." Microfilm 85M54, No. 81-A57. This includes event coverage from the following newspapers: *Harrisburg Sunday Patriot-News, Philadelphia Inquirer, Columbia* (PA) *News, York* (PA) *Dispatch, Pottsville* (PA) *Republican, Reading* (PA) *Eagle, Lebanon* (PA) *Daily News.* Hershey Community Archives, Hershey, PA.

130   "You're growing up like a rich kid . . .": Kerry Ryman and Reuel Ryman interviews.

131   membership cost his parents three dollars: Ibid.

131   lifted little Larry Wagner, a boy known as the Flea: Larry Wagner interview.

132   for brands of cocoa beans: Java, Granada: Joel Glenn Brenner, *The Emperors of Chocolate: Inside the Secret World of Hershey and Mars* (New York: Broadway Books, 2000), 105.

132   "I am trying to build here . . .": Carter Nicholson, "Hershey—The Friend of Orphan Boys," *Success* (October 1927): 118.

132   he found, and fired, the supervisor: Oral History interview with Austin C. Geiling Jr.

1991. Accession: 910H30. Hershey Community Archives Oral History Collection, Hershey, PA, Tape 1, Side 1, transcript pp. 2–3 and 15.

132 **He was known to hire private detectives:** Brenner, *The Emperors of Chocolate,* 116.

132 **"If this turns out to be a hangout . . .":** Ernie Accorsi Jr. interview.

132 **sold his caramel business for $1 million:** Brenner, *The Emperors of Chocolate,* 105.

132 **the first spade dug into the valley's:** Ibid., 105.

133 **followed in 1907 by Hershey's Kisses:** Ibid., 113.

133 **complained of *"da chockle shtink"*:** Roy Bongartz, "The Chocolate Camelot," *American Heritage* (June 1973): 5.

133 **handshake from Hershey and $100:** Dan Sieverling interview.

133 **Henry A. Wallace dedicated its ornate theater:** Brent Hancock interview.

133 **afterwards fans unknowingly jostled him:** Ibid.

134 **mixed onions and carrots into his chocolate:** Ibid.

134 **"Listen, you dumb Wop . . .":** Ernie Accorsi Jr. interview. Accorsi, Joseph Nardi's grandson, related this entire anecdote, oft told within his family.

135 **"Hey, fellas, it sounds really good!":** Reuel Ryman interview.

135 **"Yoo-hoo, Loo-seal?":** Lucille Poorman Ryman and Kerry Ryman interviews.

136 **"We raised a little hell, but . . .":** Kerry Ryman interview.

136 **a tourist saw this, screeched his car:** Kerry Ryman, Dave Damore, and Michael Larkin interviews.

137 **earlier had chauffeured for Ryman's maternal grandfather:** Kerry Ryman interview.

137 **he saw *El Cid* in the Hershey Theater eleven:** Tim Brown interview.

137 **"You supposed to be the indestructible . . .":** Ibid.

137 **"kind of an unwritten rule":** Clarence Peaks interview.

138 **"Star performer for the Warriors, Wilt 'the Stilt' . . .":** *Hershey News* (March 1, 1962).

138 **they played "Kick Hockey" near the concession:** Kerry Ryman interview.

138 **Bugs Damore had jumped and landed:** Michael Larkin interview.

CHAPTER 12: STIRRINGS

PAGE

141 **Lucille Ryman had watched the president:** Lucille Poorman Ryman interview.

142 **"Were we to stand still while the Soviets . . .":** *Philadelphia Inquirer* (March 3, 1962).

142 **Hammond organ with the Charlie Morrison Trio:** Reuel Ryman interview.

142 **"Hey, where are the Knicks tonight?":** Jerry Izenberg interview.

143 **amounted to *rubbing it in,* an honor code broken:** *The Sporting Life,* ESPN Radio, March 2, 2002. Host Chuck Wilson, on the fortieth anniversary of the hundred-point game, interviewed Richie Guerin. "It was what was considered to be unprofessional," Guerin said. "You know there is a certain code in sports where you don't rub it in."

143 **Jurgensen, in near awe, marveled at Chamberlain's:** Sonny Jurgensen interview.

143 ***Wilt was a dominant force and he was in his own zone:*** Tim Brown interview.

143 **"Usually tall guys are sort of clumsy":** Gino Marchetti interview.

143 **thinking about beer, Marchetti and Pellington left:** Ibid.

144 **the Sandman sat on a bench at courtside:** Dave Damore interview.

144 **"If I had your money, Wilton . . .":** Pete D'Ambrosio interview.

144 **sometimes muttered sarcastic jibes:** Ibid.

144 **"This is the big fourth quarter . . .":** *Philadelphia Warriors vs. New York Knicks,* WCAU Radio, Philadelphia, March 2, 1962. (Copies of this audiotape were obtained from the Hershey Community Archives, Hershey, PA, and from Al Attles's personal collection.) The quo-

tations from Bill Campbell's play-by-play call during the fourth quarter are drawn from this tape recording. Many of the game details from the fourth quarter also are drawn from this tape and from coverage in the Philadelphia newspapers.

CHAPTER 13: MESCHERY

PAGE
145 *Frank clearly is absolutely awed by Wilt:* Tom Meschery interview.
146 **he willingly submitted to his teammate's chase:** Ibid.
146 **"The Warriors are keeping the defense honest":** *Philadelphia Warriors vs. New York Knicks,* WCAU Radio, Philadelphia, March 2, 1962.
146 **a dance with Ted Luckenbill at a Polish-American:** Tom Meschery interview.
146 **they'd bought a used TV for thirty bucks:** Frank Radovich interview.
146 **His intensity on the court was, to Attles, scary:** Al Attles interview.
146 **"like a cock-eyed wild man":** Darrall Imhoff interview.
146 **"That Meschery is going to be a real terrific player . . .":** "People on Their Way Up," *Saturday Evening Post* (December 3, 1961); cited in *Philadelphia Daily News* (December 7, 1961).
147 **get the ball to the Dipper and then . . . watch:** Tom Meschery interview.

CHAPTER 14: GUERIN

PAGE
148 *I cannot wait to get out of here!:* The Sporting Life, ESPN Radio. In this interview, Guerin told host Chuck Wilson, "My honest recollection was, I couldn't wait for the game to get over with."
148 **Meschery would see him in a New York bar late:** Tom Meschery interview.
149 **"Anatomy of Basketball," had described the game's:** Christgau, *The Origins of the Jump Shot: Eight Men Who Shook the World of Basketball,* 13.
149 **"The flexing pronators are attached . . .":** Ibid.
149 **Budd stood in front of Chamberlain, Buckner behind:** Dave Budd interview.
149 **"There's no way you can stop him . . .":** Jim Heffernan, "Warriors Riding High on Wilt the Stilt," *Sporting News* (March 14, 1962): secton 2, 2, 4.
150 **"Wait until he learns his way around . . .":** Ibid.
150 *If Wilt wants to stand in my spot:* Dave Budd interview.
150 *There's a code of honor in sports:* The Sporting Life, ESPN Radio.
150 **This was not** *earning it:* Ibid.
150 **"I'm just trying to get a job!":** Cal Ramsey interview.

CHAPTER 15: ATTLES

PAGE
151 *It's like the nose on my face: right there . . . :* Al Attles interview.
151 **he even took possession of the keys:** Ibid.
151 **"We're going to Dutch it":** Pluto, *Tall Tales,* 326.
152 **Guerin play years before on Channel 9 in Newark:** Al Attles interview.
152 *These baskets are like sewers:* Ibid.
153 **Red playing another head game, reverse psychology:** Ibid.
153 **"It's the best shot in basketball!":** Ibid.
153 **"Imagine a guy getting seventy-five points . . .":** *Philadelphia Warriors vs. New York Knicks,* WCAU Radio, Philadelphia, March 2, 1962.

CHAPTER 16: IMHOFF

PAGE

155 *Stay with him. Pin him in:* Darrall Imhoff interview.

155 **passing a ball between his own legs** *and Imhoff's:* Ibid.

155 **He slathered Firm Grip, a sticky:** Johnny "Red" Kerr interview.

156 *Lovellette will pat you on the ass and say:* Darrall Imhoff interview.

156 **knee in the Dipper's upper thigh or buttock:** Ibid.

157 **"He's broke the all-time . . .":** *Philadelphia Warriors vs. New York Knicks,* WCAU Radio, Philadelphia, March 2, 1962.

157 **Harvey Pollack notified Zinkoff that Chamberlain:** Harvey Pollack interview.

157 **"Ladies and gentlemen, a new scoring record . . .":** *Philadelphia Warriors vs. New York Knicks,* WCAU Radio, Philadelphia, March 2, 1962.

CHAPTER 17: THE DIPPER

PAGE

158 **"Luck plays a big part in scoring streaks . . .":** *Philadelphia Daily News* (December 22, 1961).

158 **"I believe I've just about reached my limit":** Ibid.

158 **"The only way to stop Wilt . . .":** "Unstoppable," *Newsweek* (February 5, 1962).

159 **"We couldn't put our hands around that spot . . .":** Johnny Green interview.

159 **he might be perceived as a** *gunner:* *Warriors Weekly Round Table: The Night Wilt Scored 100,* KNBR-Radio, San Francisco, March 2, 1993. On the game's thirty-first anniversary, a one-hour retrospective, hosted by Greg Papa, featured an in-studio interview with Al Attles and telephone interviews with Wilt Chamberlain, Darrall Imhoff, Joe Ruklick, Bill Campbell, and Harvey Pollack.

159 **"We want one hundred!":** *Philadelphia Inquirer* (February 18, 1955). Also: Vince Miller and Dave Shapiro interviews.

159 **"Okay, Wilt, we're going for the record":** Cecil Mosenson interview.

160 **"Don't shoot anymore":** Dave Shapiro interview.

160 **"We could run up the scores":** Cecil Mosenson interview.

160 **"Chamberlain might have hit 100 . . .":** *Philadelphia Inquirer* (February 18, 1955).

160 **"We were disappointed . . .":** Dave Shapiro interview.

161 **Mosenson waited to hear how Frank McGuire:** Cecil Mosenson interview.

161 **"See there, Wilt doesn't know where to go":** *Philadelphia Daily News* (January 18, 1962).

161 **"I start a play in the pivot, end up . . .":** Wilt Chamberlain as told to Tim Cohane, "Pro Basketball Has Ganged Up on Me," *Look* (March 1, 1960): 52.

161 **"I would have to set such a record . . .":** Ibid., 54.

CHAPTER 18: RUKLICK

PAGE

162 **"Joe Ruklick's beautiful hook shot apparently . . .":** *Philadelphia Daily News* (October 18, 1961).

162 **"Whatever happened to the Joe Ruklick fan club?":** *Philadelphia Daily News* (November 28, 1961).

162 **a mighty and swollen example of what the Dipper:** Joe Ruklick interview.

163 **plucking bird eggs from a tree limb:** Ibid.

163 **visceral thrill of a Mickey Mantle homer:** Ibid.

163 *would look like a marionette out there*: Ibid.

164 "When I feel like I'm doggin' it, I snap them . . .": Ibid.

CHAPTER 19: ONE HUNDRED

PAGE

165 **Donovan biting his lower lip:** Sam Stith interview.

166 **"You won't care if I hop over this . . .":** Earl Whitmore interview.

166 *This might be the best chance anyone*: Jim Heffernan interview.

166 **"You're a bum, Richie!":** Ted Russ and Jim Hayney interviews.

167 **moving the ball slowly in a Z-pattern:** Donnie Butcher interview.

167 **"Will somebody hit him! Hit him in the nuts!":** Sam Stith interview.

167 **"But I've got five fouls . . .":** Ibid.

168 **Nothing strategic, no screens:** Tom Meschery interview.

168 **performed the constables' nightly check out at the farms:** Gabe Basti and Bud Miller interviews.

168 **calling them "cows":** Larry Wagner, Kerry Ryman, Reul Ryman interviews.

168 **There had been more than a few Friday night fights:** Gabe Basti interview.

168 **frightened and hiding in the bushes:** Bud Miller interview.

169 *Don't put up any more crazy numbers*: Johnny Green interview.

169 *This is going to take forever*: Pete D'Ambrosio interview.

169 *If someone walked into the arena*: Paul Arizin interview.

170 **he now had the shooter's can't-miss feeling:** York Larese interview.

170 **Butcher grabbed him around his waist:** Donnie Butcher interview.

171 **He had twenty photos to a roll:** Paul Vathis interview.

171 **Jacobs, perspiring, removed his jacket:** Larry Jacobs interview.

172 *Every last one he's earned*: Paul Arizin interview.

172 **"When are you going to stop him, Richie?":** Ibid.

172 **Guerin called out to Frank McGuire:** *Philadelphia Warriors vs. New York Knicks,* WCAU Radio, Philadelphia, March 2, 1962.

172 **Donovan, a gentleman, never would embarrass:** Darrall Imhoff interview.

173 **"YOU'RE A BUM, GUERIN!!!!!":** Ted Russ interview.

173 **"What . . . did . . . you . . . say?":** Ted Russ and James Hayney interviews.

173 **He didn't see him, but he felt his presence:** York Larese interview.

174 **as if to say, "Let's get this over . . .":** Ted Luckenbill interview.

175 **Ruklick saw Guerin bearing down on him:** Joe Ruklick interview.

175 **heard the Dipper call out, "Woo!":** Ibid.

CHAPTER 20: CELEBRATION

PAGE

176 **Kids poured onto the court:** *Philadelphia Daily News* (March 3, 1962) and Kerry Ryman, Jim Balmer, Dave Damore, and Michael Larkin interviews.

176 *ass-whupping time*: Sam Stith interview.

176 **He made a beeline to the scorer's:** Joe Ruklick interview.

177 **"And why are you even wearing . . .":** Ibid.

177 **He wanted it duly recorded:** Ibid.

177 **"I aint' done nuthin' ":** Jerome Holtzman, *No Cheering in the Press Box* (New York: Holt, Rinehart and Winston, 1973), 103.

178 **The Dipper shook it:** Kerry Ryman interview.

178 **casually stepped in front of that man, blocking:** Jim Balmer interview.

178 **figured he would simply take a shot:** Dave Damore interview.

178 **"They'll never catch him":** Earl Whitmore interview.

178 **passed the carousel, The Comet roller coaster:** Kerry Ryman interview.

179 **He would talk to the chief constable:** Gabe Basti interview.

179 **"Wouldn't it be something if . . .":** Earl Whitmore interview.

179 **"Wilt, I'm dumping":** Joe Ruklick interview.

179 **"you're trying to influence the outcome . . .":** Ibid.

180 **"Ruh-da-lick, after the game you take . . .":** Ibid.

180 **typed "Pick-up X copy":** Harvey Pollack interview.

180 *What if Wilt only scored ninety-eight points?:* Ibid.

180 **"makes your teammates enemies":** Sam Stith interview.

181 **"We tried everything we could":** *Harrisburg Sunday Patriot-News* (March 4, 1962).

181 **ball passed around the room was being signed:** Jeff Millman and Larry Jacobs interviews.

181 **"How about if we write '100' . . .":** Harvey Pollack and Paul Vathis interviews.

181 *It's always this way:* Tom Meschery interview.

181 **"It was a wonderful tribute to the team":** *Philadelphia Evening Bulletin* (March 3, 1962).

182 **"I never thought I would ever see it happen . . .":** Ibid.

182 **called for defensive goaltending twice:** *Philadelphia Inquirer* (March 3, 1962).

182 **"It wouldn't even have been close . . .":** *Philadelphia Evening Bulletin* (March 3, 1962).

182 **"Big Fella, what's the matter?":** Al Attles interview.

182 **Gola only wished the game had been televised:** Tom Gola interview.

182 **Mosenson always knew that Wilt Chamberlain:** Cecil Mosenson interview.

183 **"I found the Knicks":** Jerry Izenberg interview.

183 **Not one head turned:** Ibid.

183 **Chamberlain climbing into the driver's seat:** Bill Campbell interview.

183 **"The Blue '52 That Runs Like New":** Ernie Accorsi, Jr., interview.

184 **"I'll let you talk to him":** Ibid.

184 **"Wasn't that amazing and unbelievable . . .":** Eliot Goldstein interview.

184 **He only heard Guerin make a passing remark:** Ibid.

185 **alone, in the midnight darkness, driving through:** Willie Naulls interview.

185 **It raced past eighty-five toward ninety:** Ibid.

185 **Knicks would have *beaten the Warriors' butts:*** Rev. Willie Naulls, "Still Water Runs Deep," *Common Ground Broker* (August 1999). Newsletter of Willie Naulls Ministries, Laguna Niguel, CA and Gainesville, FL. (The Rev. Naulls's personal collection.)

185 **Dipper counted receipts at halftime with the promoter:** Ibid.

185 **Chamberlain talked freely about tax shelters:** Willie Naulls interview.

186 **talked about the nicknames they loathed:** Ibid.

186 **he would win his NBA championships:** Ibid.

186 **"You've got to give it back":** This scene is drawn from interviews with Kerry Ryman and Lucille Poorman Ryman.

187 **"The ball goes back where it belongs":** Reuel Ryman interview.

187 **The Dipper would finally fall asleep at 8:00 A.M.:** *New York Post* (March 5, 1962).

187 *"Did you hear about Wilt?":* *New York Post* (March 4, 1962).

188 **"Basketball is not prospering because . . .":** *New York Daily News* (March 4, 1962).

188 **"plays the guitar and bass fiddle, sings folk . . .":** *New York Times* (March 4, 1962).

188 **source of the information was Wilt Chamberlain:** Ralph Bernstein interview. As Associ-

ated Press sports bureau chief in Philadelphia, Bernstein, on the day after Hershey, wrote the AP story about Chamberlain that appeared in *The New York Times* and other papers.

188   **"Impossible? Sure it was impossible"**: *Philadelphia Daily News* (March 3, 1962).

188   **"Not one of them was tainted"**: Ibid.

189   **"Yeah, Pops, but look at the competition . . ."**: Tom Hawkins interview.

189   **"How about this: He's the world's worst . . ."**: Johnny "Red" Kerr and Dolph Schayes interviews.

189   **dismissed it as a game that must have raged**: Bob Cousy interview.

189   **"He's playing against nobody"**: Red Auerbach interview.

189   **"The Big Fella finally did it"**: Tom "Satch" Sanders interview.

CHAPTER 21: THE LEGEND GROWS

PAGE

193   **living in Nevada and writing about stamp collecting**: *Philadelphia Daily News* (January 16, 1993). Also see: *Philadelphia Inquirer* (January 22, 1993).

194   **"way beyond the call of duty"**: Associated Press, February 28, 1987.

194   *Must be Wilt Chamberlain time*: Darrall Imhoff interview.

194   **"In all honesty I was annoyed . . ."**: *The Sporting Life*, ESPN Radio, March 2, 2002.

194   **"They passed Wilt Chamberlain the ball . . ."**: Marge Donovan interview.

194   **"The game was not a fluke . . ."**: Willie Naulls interview.

194   **"I break out into a rash"**: Darrall Imhoff interview.

194   **"spend twelve years in Wilt's armpits"**: *Los Angeles Times* (March 2, 1987).

195   **"the man who held Wilt Chamberlain . . ."**: Rod Hundley interview.

195   **"Wilt only got eighty-five off me"**: Sonny Jurgensen and Rod Hundley interviews. Jurgensen attended the celebrity golf tournament in Lake Tahoe.

195   **"I wasn't a great player, and feel privileged . . ."**: Darrall Imhoff interview.

195   **"The game was a farce"**: Ibid.

195   **A telegram for Darrall Imhoff arrived two days**: Ibid.

196   **he was slow and lacked stamina**: Chamberlain and Shaw, *Wilt*, 152–53.

196   **"Let's run 'em tonight, Wilt"**: Ibid.

196   **"As the time goes by, I feel more . . ."**: *Warriors Weekly Round Table: The Night Wilt Scored 100*, KNBR-Radio, San Francisco, March 2, 1993.

197   **"How many of you would want to play . . ."**: Al Attles interview.

197   **his estate would bequeath more than $6 million**: Seymour (Sy) Goldberg interview.

197   **A chauffeur driving Chamberlain's new Bentley**: Cal Ramsey interview. Ramsey joined Chamberlain at the March on Washington.

198   **"Wilt wasn't a guy that existed . . ."**: Harry Edwards interview.

198   **would later say that Nixon cynically exploited him**: Chamberlain and Shaw, *Wilt*, 242.

198   **"I'm just as aware of the injustices done to the black . . ."**: Ibid., 64.

198   **"Wilt would vacillate between feeling exempt . . ."**: Lynda Huey interview.

198   **keeps folded in his wallet a yellowed newspaper**: Ted Luckenbill interview.

199   **so often he had it laminated**: York Larese interview.

199   **heard for a while on NBA Commissioner David Stern's office**: Bill Campbell interview.

199   **"It's like Babe Ruth leading the league . . ."**: Pluto, *Tall Tales*, 326.

199   **movie business; his parents and several siblings lived**: Chamberlain and Shaw, *Wilt*, 232.

200   **"The West Coast was more Wilt's style . . ."**: Nate Thurmond interview.

200   **Dipper and Russell met 142 times**: Jan Hubbard, ed., *The Official NBA Encyclopedia*. 3d ed. (New York: Doubleday, 2000), 32–33.

200 **"We might've won one with Wilt":** Bob Cousy interview.

200 **"I mean I had the big ego, too":** Red Auerbach interview.

201 **picking up a photographer's wooden stool:** *Philadelphia Inquirer* (April 2, 1962).

201 **"Mendy threw the game":** Tom Gola interview.

201 **telling his friends at home he was "going to S.F.":** Deford, "Eddie Is the Mogul," 43.

201 **the Mogul charged him $25:** Joe Ruklick interview.

202 **Ruklick wore his "Phila 17" jersey:** Ibid.

202 **drowned in the swollen night waters:** *The Tacoma News Tribune* (June 8, 1965).

202 **"You're asking 'How close is close?' ":** *Philadelphia Evening Bulletin* (December 8, 1979).

203 **"What's the single greatest historical sports . . .":** Jim Trelease interview.

203 **five-story drainpipe that made a splendid antenna:** Ibid.

203 **merged this tape with the earlier Dictaphone tape:** Todd Caso interview.

203 **"You can hear Dave Zinkoff's voice . . .":** Ibid.

204 **"Remember, if I can . . .":** Tom Meschery, "Mourning Wilt The Day After His Death." This poem was written in October 1999. Tom Meschery personal files.

204 **"Wilt had rung the bell of freedom . . .":** Rev. Willie Naulls, "Still Water Runs Deep," *Common Ground Broker* (August 1999). Newsletter of Willie Naulls Ministries, Laguna Niguel, CA and Gainesville, FL.

204 **"The ride and the fellowship on the night . . .":** Ibid.

204 **in Portland, where he went to buy waders:** Darrall Imhoff interview.

205 **"Always glad to see you, Ruh-da-lick . . .":** Joe Ruklick interview.

205 **"Eddie put on a circus . . .":** Ibid.

205 **"Gola would have gone to Gottlieb . . .":** Ibid.

206 **"As we got older, the more we liked . . .":** Videotape of Wilt Chamberlain memorial service. Joe Ruklick personal files.

206 **"People would never be happy . . .":** Frank Deford, "Doing Just Fine, My Man: At 50, Wilt Chamberlain Has Finally Mellowed," *Sports Illustrated* (August 18, 1986): 62.

206 *To Al: Who Did All the Right Things* . . . : Al Attles interview.

207 **Gola spoke of his enduring appreciation:** Tom Gola interview.

207 **The Dipper embraced her and pushed her wheelchair:** Paul Arizin interview.

207 **"Wilt, I'm in your debt":** Ibid.

CHAPTER 22: THE BALL

PAGE

208 **Ryman worked a fifteen-ton remote control:** Kerry Ryman interview.

209 *Wow, what a treasure:* Mike Blouch interview.

209 **"Mike, that ball's not worth a damn . . .":** Kerry Ryman interview.

209 **"upper-lower class":** Mike Blouch interview.

210 **never mind, the Dipper doesn't want:** Kerry Ryman interview.

210 **"Don't say the ball was 'stolen' ":** Mike Blouch interview.

210 **Blouch would get three-eighths:** Ibid.

210 **"put that thing in a burn barrel":** Reuel Ryman interview.

211 *It doesn't matter what this ball looks like:* Mike Heffner interview.

211 **a piece of Joe DiMaggio's wedding cake:** *Leland's Auctions Catalogue,* April 27–28, 2000 (New York: Dartmouth Printing Company, 2000), 160. Mike Blouch personal files.

211 **" 'What the hell is that?' ":** Mike Heffner interview.

211 **"the most important piece of basketball memorabilia . . .":** *Leland's Auctions Catalogue,* April 27–28, 2000, 44.

211 **Blouch rented a big car:** Kerry Ryman interview.

211 **"Can we use this?":** Mike Blouch interview.

211 **"He's obviously no longer a teenager":** *The Today Show,* National Broadcasting Company, April 26, 2000, NBC News Transcripts.

212 **"I scored a couple hundred thousand . . .":** Ibid.

212 **"Union property":** Mike Blouch interview.

212 **"Blouch plugged in the blow dryer":** Ibid.

212 **Willie Smith took the historic ball out of play:** Harvey Pollack interview.

212 **placed it in the Dipper's bag, and covered it:** Jeff Millman interview.

212 **giddy Guy Rodgers joyfully heaving basketballs:** Ibid.

213 **Ryman must've grabbed a replacement ball:** Harvey Pollack interview.

213 **he had only six of the twelve balls:** Jeff Millman interview.

213 **Zink had used liquid white-out:** Harvey Pollack interview.

213 **given his hundred-point game ball to Al Attles:** Pluto, *Tall Tales,* 223. In this book, Attles is also quoted saying, "Wilt gave me the ball that he scored the 100th point with, even though some kid claimed to have run off with it." However, Attles insisted in interviews with me that Chamberlain gave him a different ball.

213 **"I don't want people climbing into my . . .":** Joe Ruklick interview.

213 **"You're on the front page":** Kerry Ryman interview.

214 ***"building a hot dog stand . . .":*** Joe Ruklick interview.

214 **demanded that Ryman take a lie detector test:** Joe Ruklick and Kerry Ryman interviews.

214 **gathering signed affidavits from locals:** Mike Blouch, Marty Appel, Earl Whitmore, Jim Balmer, and Kerry Ryman interviews.

214 **"If anything, the conflicting tales create . . .":** *Leland's Auctions Catalogue, October 5–6, 2000* (New York: Dartmouth Printing Company, 2000), 60–61. Also: Marty Appel interview. Appel worked as Leland's publicist for the auction.

214 **bidder who won the ball in the first auction hadn't bid:** Mike Heffner interview.

214 **a used Dodge Arrow to replace:** Kerry Ryman interview.

215 **$10,000 in video company stock:** Ibid.

EPILOGUE

PAGE

217 **"Yes, that's correct, twenty thousand different ladies":** Wilt Chamberlain, *A View from Above: Sports. Sex. And Controversy* (New York: Villard, 1991), 258–62.

217 **"That's what an athlete did":** Peter Gethers interview.

217 **Gethers created a list of one hundred questions:** Ibid.

218 **"That's nine in one night":** Ibid.

218 **"He obviously was a little pathological . . .":** Ibid.

218 **"As soon as a female has a kibosh position . . .":** Seymour (Sy) Goldberg interview.

218 **self-described environmentalists:** George Meyer and Maria Semple interviews.

218 **"the funniest man behind the funniest . . .":** David Owen, "Taking Humor Seriously— George Meyer, the Funniest Man Behind the Funniest Show on TV," *New Yorker* (March 13, 2000): 64.

219 **"If you're woman enough to live in Wilt . . .":** George Meyer interview.

219 **"beating the system, like Hugh Hefner or Robert Evans . . .":** Ibid.

219 ***God, I know you're famous:*** Ibid.

219 **"That is so *not* what this is about":** Ibid.

219 **"You respect Wilt's individuality and his nerve":** George Meyer interview.

220 "There was just one bookshelf . . .": Maria Semple interview.
220 "Do you think Wilt was happy . . .": Ibid.
220 "What's a zero between friends?": Lynda Huey interview.
220 "I believe the 2,000 number": Ibid.
221 "ended up with each other at the end—by default": Ibid.
221 "far too much nothingness": Chamberlain. *A View from Above*, 66.
221 "Why did I ever think that I could fool myself . . .": Ibid.
221 told fond stories about "us" and "we": Lynda Huey interview.
222 "He refused to be loved or to love": Ibid.
222 "Why do they tell me that they came . . .": Ibid.

BIBLIOGRAPHY

Abdul-Jabbar, Kareem, and Peter Knobler. *Giant Steps.* New York: Bantam Books, 1983.

Baldwin, James. *Collected Essays.* New York: The Library of America, 1998.

Bradley, Bill. *Values of the Game.* New York: Broadway Books, 2000.

Branch, Taylor. *Pillar of Fire: America in the King Years, 1963–65.* New York: Simon & Schuster, 1998.

Brenner, Joel Glenn. *The Emperors of Chocolate: Inside the Secret World of Hershey and Mars.* New York: Broadway Books, 2000.

Castner, Charles Schuyler. *One of a Kind: Milton Snavely Hershey, 1857–1945.* Hershey, PA: The Derry Literary Guild, 1983.

Chamberlain, Wilt. *A View from Above: Sports. Sex. And Controversy.* New York: Villard, 1991.

Chamberlain, Wilt, and David Shaw. *Wilt: Just Like Any Other 7-Foot Black Millionaire Who Lives Next Door.* New York: Warner, 1975.

Cohen, Stanley. *The Game They Played.* New York: Carroll & Graf, 2001.

Cramer, Richard Ben. *Joe Dimaggio: The Hero's Life.* New York: Simon & Schuster, 2000.

Creamer, Robert W. *Babe: The Legend Comes to Life.* New York: Fireside, 1992.

Dallek, Robert. *An Unfinished Life: John Kennedy, 1917–1963.* Boston: Little, Brown and Company, 2003.

Dawidoff, Nicholas, ed. *Baseball: A Literary Anthology.* New York: The Library of America, 2002.

Derks, Scott, ed. *The Value of a Dollar, 1860–1999.* Millennium Edition. Millerton, NY: Grey House Publishing, 1999.

Du Bois, W. E. B. *The Philadelphia Negro.* Millwood, NY: Kraus-Thomson Organization Limited, 1973.

———. *The Souls of Black Folks.* New York: Avon Books, 1965.

Early, Gerald L. *This Is Where I Came In: Black America in the 1960s.* Lincoln, NE: University of Nebraska Press, 2003.

Einstein, Charles. *Willie's Time: A Memoir.* New York: J.B. Lippincott Company, 1979.

Falkenstien, Max, as told to Doug Vance. *Max and the Jayhawks: 50 Years On and Off the Air with KU Sports.* Wichita, KN: The Wichita Eagle & Beacon Publishing Company, 1996.

George, Nelson. *Elevating the Game: Black Men and Basketball.* New York: HarperCollins Publishers, 1992.

Gitlin, Todd. *The Sixties: Years of Hope, Days of Rage*. New York: Bantam Books, 1987.

Halberstam, David. *The Fifties*. New York: Villard Books, 1993.

———. *October 1964*. New York: Villard Books, 1994.

———. *The Powers that Be*. New York: Alfred A. Knopf, 1979.

Halberstam, David J. *Sports on New York Radio: A Play-By-Play History*. Lincolnwood, IL: Masters Press, 1999.

Hillenbrand, Laura. *Seabiscuit: An American Legend*. New York: Random House, 2001.

Holtzman, Jerome. *No Cheering in the Press Box*. New York: Holt, Rinehart and Winston, 1973.

Houts, Mary Davidoff, and Pamela Cassidy Whitenack. *Hershey*. Charleston, SC: Arcadia Publishing, 2000.

Hubbard, Jan, ed. *The Official NBA Encyclopedia*. 3rd ed. New York: Doubleday, 2000.

Huey, Lynda. *A Running Start: An Athlete, A Woman*. New York: Quadrangle / The New York Times Book Co., 1976.

Isaacs, Neil D. *Vintage NBA: The Pioneer Era 1946–56*. Indianapolis: Masters Press, 1996.

Johnson, James Weldon. *Black Manhattan*. New York: Da Capo Press, 1991.

Kahn, Roger. *The Boys of Summer*. New York: Harper & Row, Publishers, 1972.

Kashatus, Bill. *Connie Mack's '29 Triumph*. Jefferson, NC: MacFarland & Company, 1999.

Kerensky, Alexander. *Russia and History's Turning Point*. New York: Duell, Sloan and Pearce, 1965.

Koppett, Leonard. *24 Seconds to Shoot: The Birth and Improbable Rise of the NBA*. Kingston, NY: Total/Sports Illustrated, 1999.

Leavy, Jane. *Sandy Koufax: A Lefty's Legacy*. New York: HarperCollins Publishers, 2002.

Lewis, David Levering. *W.E.B. DuBois: Biography of a Race*. New York: A John MacRae Book, Henry Holt and Company, 1993.

———. *When Harlem Was in Vogue*. New York: Alfred A. Knopf, 1981.

Malcolm X, as told to Alex Haley. *The Autobiography of Malcolm X*. New York: Grove Press, 1964.

McGregor, Jim, and Ron Rapoport. *Called for Travelling: The Incredible Life Story of One of the Best-Known Basketball Personalities in the World*. New York: Macmillan Publishing, 1978.

McPhee, John. *Levels of the Game*. New York: Farrar, Straus & Giroux, 1969.

———. *A Sense of Where You Are: Bill Bradley at Princeton*. New York: Farrar, Straus & Giroux, 1978.

Meschery, Tom. *Nothing We Lose Can Be Replaced*. Reno: The Black Rock Press, 1999.

Miller, Henry. *Tropic of Cancer*. New York: Grove Press, Inc., 1961.

Neft, David S., ed., Richard M. Cohen, and Michael L. Neft. *The Sports Encyclopedia: Baseball, 2002*. New York: St. Martin's Griffin, 2002.

Nelson, Rodger. *The Zollner Piston Story*. Fort Wayne, IN: Allen County Public Library Foundation, 1995.

Pluto, Terry. *Tall Tales: The Glory Years of the NBA, in the Words of the Men Who Played, Coached, and Built Pro Basketball*. New York: Simon & Schuster, 1992.

Rampersad, Arnold. *Jackie Robinson: A Biography*. New York: Alfred A. Knopf, 1997.

Rand, Ayn. *The Fountainhead*. New York: Plume/Penguin Books, 1994.

Reporting Civil Rights: Part One. American Journalism 1941–1963. New York: The Library of America, 2003.

Ritter, Lawrence S. *The Glory of Their Times: The Story of the Early Days of Baseball Told by the Men Who Played It*. New York: Quill, William Morrow, 1984.

Robertson, Oscar. *The Big O: My Life, My Times, My Game*. Emmaus, PA: Rodale, 2003.

Rosin, James. *Philly Hoops: The SPHAs and Warriors, a Look at the First Two Professional Basketball Teams in the City of Philadelphia.* Philadelphia: Autumn Road Publishers, 2003.

Roth, Philip. *Portnoy's Complaint.* New York: Vintage, 1994.

Russell, Bill, as told to William McSweeny. *Go Up for Glory.* New York: Coward-McCann, Inc., 1965.

Russell, Bill, and Taylor Branch. *Second Wind: The Memoirs of an Opinionated Man.* New York: Random House, 1979.

Shaara, Michael. *The Killer Angels.* New York: Ballantine Books, 1996.

Smith, Dean, with John Kilgo, and Sally Jenkins. *A Coach's Life.* New York: Random House, 1999.

Stump, Al. *Cobb.* Chapel Hill, NC: Algonquin Books, 1996.

Thomas, Ron. *They Cleared the Lane: The NBA's Black Pioneers.* Lincoln, NE: University of Nebraska Press, 2002.

Weigley, Russell F., ed., et al. *Philadelphia: A 300-Year History.* New York: W.W. Norton & Company, 1982.

Catalogs and Programs

Leland's Auctions, April 27–28, 2000. New York: Dartmouth Printing Company, 2000.

Leland's Auctions, October 5–6, 2000. New York: Dartmouth Printing Company, 2000.

HersheyPark Arena: 50-Year Birthday Celebration, 1936/1937–1986/1987. Hershey Community Archives.

Warriors 2002–03 Media Guide. Sacramento: Blue Moon Printing and Graphics, 2002.

2002–2003 New York Knicks Media Guide. New York: Citation Graphics, 2002.

New York Knickerbockers game programs, Madison Square Garden, 1961–1962 season.

Zinkoff, Dave, ed. *The Wigwam: Philadelphia Warriors vs. New York Knicks; Philadelphia Eagles vs. Baltimore Colts.* Game program. March 2, 1962, Hershey, PA. Published by Philadelphia Warriors.

Television and Radio

WCAU Radio, Philadelphia, PA, *Philadelphia Warriors vs. New York Knicks,* fourth quarter play-by-play and postgame show, March 2, 1962.

ESPN Radio, *The Sporting Life,* Chuck Wilson, program host. March 2, 2002. An interview with Richie Guerin on the fortieth anniversary of the hundred-point game.

Philly Hoops: The SPHAs and Warriors, WHYY-TV, Channel 12, Philadelphia Public Television, April 12, 2003. A documentary produced and directed by James Rosin.

Warriors Weekly Round Table: The Night Wilt Scored 100, KNBR-Radio, San Francisco. March 2, 1993. On the game's thirty-first anniversary, a one-hour retrospective hosted by Greg Papa and featured an in-studio interview with Al Attles and telephone interviews with Wilt Chamberlain, Darrall Imhoff, Joe Ruklick, Bill Campbell, and Harvey Pollack.

List of Interviews

More than 250 interviews were conducted for this book between November 2002 and May 2004. A number of subjects graciously agreed to multiple interviews.

Players from the 100-Point Game Rosters

Paul Arizin, Tom Gola, Darrall Imhoff, Al Attles, Frank Radovich, Donnie Butcher, Ted Luckenbill, Dave Budd, Johnny Green, Tom Meschery, York Larese, Joe Ruklick, Willie Naulls, Sam Stith, Whitey Martin

The New York Press
Sam Goldaper, Leonard Lewin, Leonard Koppett, Les Keiter, Murray Janoff

The Philadelphia Press
Larry Merchant, Stan Hochman, Sandy Grady, Bill Campbell, Jim Heffernan, Bob Vetrone, Ralph Bernstein, Alan Richman, Mike Rathet

Hershey, Pennsylvania, and Environs
Paul Serff, Brent Hancock, Pam Whitenack, Earl Whitmore, Lucille Ryman, Gabe Basti, Irvin "Bud" Miller, Reuel Ryman, Kerry Ryman, Mike Blouch, Evo Ionni, Bern Sharfman, John Bolan, Ernie Accorsi, Paul Vathis, James Neill Flaherty, Harry Goff, Sanford Krevsky, George Krevsky, Todd Thompson, John Rowan, Jeff Adams, Larry Wagner, Ted Russ, Jim Balmer, Bob Seiverling, Dan Seiverling, Jack Snavely, Woody Slaybaugh, Dave Damore, Michael Larkin, Bill Pavone, Eliot Goldstein, James Hayney

Philadelphia
Cecil Mosenson, Larry Jacobs, Gerald Early, Vince Miller, Angelo Musi Jr., Harvey Pollack, Ron Pollack, Ken Berman, Hal Lear, Gil Fitch, Jeff Millman, Mike Richman, Charles Blockson, Simcha Gersh, Wally Nowacki, Marv Bachrad, Dave Shapiro, Ray Scott, Joe Goldenberg, Irv Cross, Tommy McDonald, Tim Brown, Sonny Jurgensen, Clarence Peaks, A. Toby Deluca

The NBA
Bob Cousy, Pete Newell, Red Auerbach, Earl Lloyd, Pete D'Ambrosio, Nate Thurmond, Bill Sharman, Tom "Satch" Sanders, Marty Blake, Rod Hundley, Clyde Lovellette, K.C. Jones, Norm Drucker, Carl Bennett, Boag Johnson, Vern Mikkelsen, Johnny "Red" Kerr, Dolph Schayes, John Kundla, Ken Sears, John Oldham, Pat Williams, Todd Caso, Al Cervi, Cal Ramsey, Tom Hawkins, Fred Schaus, Louis "Red" Klotz, Frank Selvy, Tom Heinsohn, Fred Crawford, Tom Stith, Bob McCollough, Brian McIntyre

Others
Tom Kearns, Clarence "Bevo" Francis, Newt Oliver, Ron Thomas, Bob Kurland, Carol Ann Morgan, Marge Donovan, Elsie Richter, Dr. Robyn Fivush, Tom Callahan, Al Oerter, Jack Curran, Marty Appel, Maria Semple, George Meyer, Max Falkenstien, Jerry Waugh, Lynda Huey, Maurice King, Jim McGregor, Mike Heffner, Harry Edwards, Dorothy DaCosta, Joe Goldstein, Ed Schuyler Jr., Bert Rosenthal, Peter Gethers, Hugh Wheelright, George Sullivan, Jim Trelease, Bob Boyd, Jim Mutscheller, Gino Marchetti, Andy Nelson, Lloyd Williams

Magazines Consulted
American Heritage; Ebony; Fortune; Greater Philadelphia; Jet; Life; Look; McClure's Magazine; Newsweek; Saturday Evening Post; Senior Scholastic; Sport; Sporting News; Sports Illustrated; Success; Time

Newspapers Consulted

Amsterdam News; Boston Globe; Boston Herald; Boston Traveler; Chicago Defender; Chicago Tribune; Harrisburg (PA) News; Harrisburg (PA) Patriot; Hershey News; Lebanon (PA) Daily News; Lexington (KY) Herald; Lexington (KY) Leader; Jewish Exponent (Philadelphia, PA); Long Island (NY) Daily Press; Los Angeles Times; Minneapolis Tribune; Newsday; New York Daily News; New York Herald-Tribune; New York Journal-American; New York Mirror; New York Post; New York Times; New York World Telegram; Philadelphia Daily News; Philadelphia Evening Bulletin; Philadelphia Inquirer; Philadelphia Tribune; Pittsburgh (PA) Courier; Pottsville (PA) Republican; St. Louis Post-Dispatch; St. Paul (MN) Dispatch; Tacoma (WA) News Tribune; Washington Post; York (PA) Dispatch

Libraries and Archives Consulted

Doe Library, University of California, Berkeley; Woodruff Library, Emory University; New York Public Library; Paley Library, Urban Archives, Temple University; Greater Philadelphia Jewish Sports Hall of Fame and Museum; Hershey Community Archives; Derry Township Historical Society

ACKNOWLEDGMENTS

AT THE HERSHEY HIGH MEADOWS CAMPGROUND, in a barn's second-story loft, I found the hardwood floor from the hundred-point game. It had been brought there years before. Decayed around the edges, warped in places and loaded down with various campground materials, the famous floor, nearly seven decades old, had been clicked together haphazardly, out of sequence as if by a drunken or dyslexic carpenter—a piece of the lane (where the Dipper held sway over Imhoff) set here, another piece of the lane set over there. I walked to the free-throw line—or at least a portion of it—near the far wall. Standing there, striving to connect to March 2, 1962, and then acting silly perhaps, I bent low and pretended to shoot an underhanded free throw. (I only did it once, not thirty-two times.) I walked across the floor slowly, taking time to imagine Rodgers and Attles leading the break, Imhoff and Buckner and Naulls and Budd building a human wall around the Dipper. Then, I left. As I neared my car, a young worker shouted from behind, "Hey!" I turned. He said, "I got this for you." In his hand he held a small piece of wood, perhaps three inches by fifteen inches. He'd just ripped it from the edge of the famous floor. "I can't take that," I said. "Go ahead," he replied, adding, "It isn't doing much in here. I'll just throw it out if you don't take it." Reluctantly, I took it. Its surface had darkened from age and wear, covered over by time. Scratching at that surface, though, revealed a lighter wood beneath, closer to its color on that long-ago night. In trying to recover the lost game, I sought to find that light wood, that moment when the game lived.

For this book, a reconstructive period piece that is a hybrid of history and journalism, that was no small challenge. The hundred-point game was not televised; the print media coverage was limited. I turned necessarily to the people who were there. I conducted more than 250 interviews, many lasting two hours and more. As I probed deeper, I often returned to an interview subject multiple times, trying not to be intrusive. In that regard, I wasn't always successful. Once, broadcaster Bill Campbell, hearing my voice on the phone line, said, wearily, "Not again . . ."

From the two teams' rosters in Hershey, I interviewed fifteen players (besides Chamberlain and Jordon, two other players died before I started this project: the Warriors' Guy Rodgers from a heart attack and the Knicks' Al Butler from cancer, both in 2001). For the most part, players from the hundred-point game were overwhelmingly kind and generous with their time and reflections. I sat in the living rooms of Paul Arizin and Tom Gola in Philadelphia and Tom Meschery in Truckee, California. The poet is married to a novelist, Joanne Meschery, and their home is brimming with books and warmth. The Rev. Willie Naulls and his wife, Anne, served me lunch in their home in north Florida. Dave Budd gave me a tour of his produce packaging plant in New Jersey. At the U.S. Basketball Academy near Eugene, Oregon, I shared time on a basketball court with Darrall Imhoff, who demonstrated his defensive tactics against the Dipper and even put his well-placed elbow between my shoulder blades. (All these years later, Imhoff still knows how to inflict momentary discomfort.) At the Golden State Warriors offices in Oakland, California, Al Attles gave me a copy of Campbell's WCAU play-by-play call. Sam Stith walked me along Seventh Avenue in Harlem, regaling me with stories about the Knicks and Harlem. (On another occasion, former NBA players Fred Crawford, Tom Stith, and Cal Ramsey joined us over lunch in Harlem and shared their favorite Wilt stories.) After an interview in San Francisco, Joe Ruklick fired off lengthy email responses to my legions of follow-up questions. Ruklick's emails from Chicago were full of fire, full of deep thought, and often lengthy. "*Longueurs,*" Ruklick called his dispatches. ("It's amazing," Ruklick wrote once, "how time has transformed the players from that game into historical figures.") Only two players from the hundred-point game declined to be interviewed: Richie Guerin and Cleveland Buckner. "That part of my life is over. I've moved on," is how Guerin explained himself over the phone.

Members of Buckner's family urged him to add his voice—his story—but for whatever reasons, he did not. An interview with the Warriors' Ed Conlin, suffering from illness, could not be arranged.

The majesty of oral history is that it fills the spaces beyond the reach of written documentation. It adds texture and luster to our understanding of the past. In all, I heard the stories of fifty-six people who were at the Hershey Arena on that long-ago night; a handful of others claimed to have been there, though I could not discern whether truly they had.

With memory, Emory University psychologist Robyn Fivush says, "There is always a self-serving or self-defining function. We want to place ourselves closer to moments of great historical import or joy and further away from [the negative]. . . . We remember in ways to be consistent with our present goals." At the time of my interviews for this book, players of the hundred-point game ranged in age from sixty-three to seventy-four years old. Fivush says there is a memory phenomenon known as the "reminiscence bump." "There is a bump [in recalled memory of events] between the age of fifteen to the middle twenties; it's when we are defining ourselves," she says. "They are important markers for who we are." I attempted to corroborate, when possible, every fact and anecdote in this book. With several players from the hundred-point game I listened to the fourth quarter play-by-play; the audiotape jarred their memories and prompted revealing observations about the game.

Of course, some memories proved imperfect. For years, Knicks players had talked of their bus ride from New York to Hershey—a bus ride that did *not* happen for the March 2 game. In his attic in New Jersey, Dave Budd found an old box of materials from his Knicks career. He phoned me: "It's mostly programs, stat sheets, and some team itineraries, a lot from that 1961–62 season," Budd said. "You interested in seeing them?" Days later, I opened the box and found the Knicks itinerary from the week of the hundred-point game; the team had flown from Chicago to Hershey and stayed at the Hotel Penn Harris. The only bus ride was from the Hotel Penn Harris to the game. I'm indebted to Budd for sharing that material.

The basketball community in Philadelphia is tightly knit and so once tapped it quickly produced the Dipper's coach at Overbrook, Cecil Mosenson, Chamberlain's boyhood friend Vince Miller, and the hundred-point game referee, Pete D'Ambrosio. ("You probably thought I was already dead, didn't you?" said D'Ambrosio, still spry at eighty-three.) During my trips to Hershey, Pam Whitenack of the Hershey Community Archives and her staff showed me kindness, professionalism, and transcripts—such wonderful transcripts—of interviews conducted down through the years with prominent and not so prominent Hershey townsfolk. These oral histories offer fascinating insights into the people and pacing of community life in the chocolate factory town. I'm also grateful that Kerry Ryman offered his time and candor. Together we walked through Hershey Arena while a youth hockey game was being played. He walked me along the path of his escape with the basketball. We strolled along Chocolate Avenue, through the old neighborhood, past the back alley where Kenny Snyder's basket once hung on the detached garage, though no more.

For a day-to-day understanding of the Warriors' 1961–62 season, I turned to microfilm to read Jack Kiser's work in *The Philadelphia Daily News* (available in Philadelphia at the Free Library and the Van Pelt Library at the University of Pennsylvania) and Jim Heffernan's coverage in *The Philadelphia Evening Bulletin* (available at Temple University's Paley Library). Two excellent books about the NBA also provided wonderful context of the league's formative years: Ron Thomas's *They Cleared the Lane: The NBA's Black Pioneers;* and Terry Pluto's *Tall Tales: The Glory Years of the NBA, in the Words of the Men Who Played, Coached, and Built Pro Basketball.*

Many claimed to have been in Hershey on the night the Dipper scored one hundred points. With the help of Jim Carlson, assistant sports editor of *The Harrisburg Patriot-News,* I placed a brief story in the sports section of that newspaper, seeking to identify and interview fans that attended the famous game in Hershey. In all, that story prompted ten responses, by phone, letter, and email. Whether or not each respondent had actually been in the Hershey Sports Arena that night I could not be certain; some reminiscences offered little. But several other respondents provided revealing details that convinced me they had attended the game. These details, which either corroborated stories I'd already learned or told small new ones, resonated in ways small and large. They had the power of truth.

I'm also indebted to a panel of readers who read parts or all of this manuscript in its earlier forms and helped me to eradicate errors of fact and/or interpretation: Professor Gerald Early, Director of African and Afro-American Studies at Washington University in St. Louis, a Philadelphia native, and author of *This Is Where I Came In: Black America in the 1960s;* Sandy Grady, retired sports columnist and political columnist for *The Philadelphia Daily News,* who knew or covered most of the characters in this book for *The Daily News* and earlier for *The Philadelphia Evening Bulletin;* Neil D. Isaacs, Emeritus Professor of English at the University of Maryland and author of *Vintage NBA: The Pioneer Era, 1946–56,* a wonderful oral history of the NBA's earliest years; and Dick Weiss, *The New York Daily News* sportswriter and basketball griot in his native Philadelphia, known affectionately as "Hoops." Other readers offered helpful suggestions: Andy Mathieson, Ben Lefkowitz, Eric Segall, and Greg Pomerantz. In Philadelphia, I received some timely research assistance from April White (www.knowmoreresearch.com) and in Atlanta from Randy Gue. I'm indebted, too, to the longtime NBA referee Norm Drucker and to my uncle, Robert Katz (a longtime basketball referee in Westchester County, New York), for their wisdom about the game, its history, and its ever-evolving rules.

My editor at Crown, Chris Jackson, is smart and insightful, and a tenacious reader. Plus, he's got a splendid bedside manner for overstressed writers. His colleague, Genoveva Llosa, was a model of efficiency and kindness. Steve Ross, Crown's publisher, remains a fabulous ally and advocate. My literary agent, David Black, is nearly two feet shorter than Wilt Chamberlain. (He's even shorter than Gotty.) But he's got Richie Guerin's spit and fire and will to win, and as the Zink might say with affection, *"He's meshugs."* His colleagues at the David Black Literary Agency—Joy Tutela, Gary Morris, Susan Raihofer, Leigh Ann Eliseo, and Jason Sacher—make a great starting five.

A family bears the burden of living with a grumpy author. By *family,* I include my buddy Dave Kindred, who, on the other end of my phone line, remains an incorrigible voice of reason and my life raft from the doldrums. My wife, Carrie, and our sons, Ross and Win, and daughter, Leigh, have noticed me occasionally wearing a rubber band on my wrist. ("What's that for, Daddy?" asks Leigh. Answers big brother Win, proving he listens to the tales I spin: "To hold up Dad's socks, in case one breaks. It's a spare.") Watching NBA games on television together at home, I'll say to the kids, "Betcha nobody catches Wilt's one hundred tonight." My son Ross (a big fan of Peja Stojakovic) has heard me say this so often he only rolls his eyes. Without Carrie and the kids, I am lost. Writing a book is an obsessive process of immersion. I'd like to say that one day they'll understand. More than likely, they never will.

INDEX

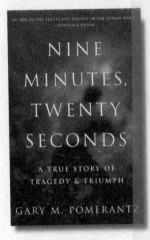

3 1143 00732 6656